ELECTRIFYING INDONESIA

New Perspectives in Southeast Asian Studies

ELECTRIFYING INDONESIA

*Technology and Social Justice in
National Development*

Anto Mohsin

THE UNIVERSITY OF WISCONSIN PRESS

Publication of this book was supported by a grant from
the Association for Asian Studies (AAS; http://www.asianstudies.org)
through its First Book Subvention Program.

The University of Wisconsin Press
728 State Street, Suite 443
Madison, Wisconsin 53706
uwpress.wisc.edu

Gray's Inn House, 127 Clerkenwell Road
London EC1R 5DB, United Kingdom
eurospanbookstore.com

Printed in the United States of America
This book may be available in a digital edition.

Library of Congress Cataloging-in-Publication Data

Names: Mohsin, Anto, author.
Title: Electrifying Indonesia : technology and social justice
in national development / Anto Mohsin.
Other titles: New perspectives in Southeast Asian studies.
Description: Madison, Wisconsin : The University of Wisconsin Press, 2023. |
Series: New perspectives in Southeast Asian studies |
Includes bibliographical references and index.
Identifiers: LCCN 2023014987 | ISBN 9780299345402 (hardcover)
Subjects: LCSH: Electrification—Indonesia—History.
Classification: LCC HD9685.I52 M64 2023 |
DDC 333.793/209598—dc23/eng/20230719
LC record available at https://lccn.loc.gov/2023014987

For my loved ones

Contents

Illustrations

TABLES

Acknowledgments

The journey that led to this book began when I decided to embark on a new adventure enrolling in a graduate program in science and technology studies at Cornell University. At the time my wife, Titin, and I just had our first child, and even though I was at first uncertain and intimidated about the sojourn we were about to take, Titin supported me wholeheartedly. For the support, confidence, and love she's given me throughout the years, I thank her very much.

I owe a debt of gratitude to many individuals at Cornell University where I did my graduate training in science and technology studies. I especially thank Ronald R. Kline, Sara B. Pritchard, the late Trevor Pinch, Stephen Hilgartner, Bruce V. Lewenstein, Tamara Loos, Tom Pepinsky, and Eric Tagliacozzo, who have taught me so much on how to be a good scholar and teacher. I am also thankful to my fellow graduate students and friends for their support and camaraderie.

Following the completion of my graduate training and a postdoctoral fellowship, I landed a position as new faculty member at Northwestern University in Qatar (NUQ). NUQ has been a nice place to grow personally and professionally. I'm blessed to be working in a supportive environment and surrounded by many wonderful colleagues, helpful staff, and engaging students. For encouraging and supporting me to undertake this book project, I thank Everette E. Dennis, Hariclea Zengos, and Scott Curtis. I am also indebted to the support and leadership of Marwan Kraidy and Kathleen Hewett-Smith. Dean Kraidy initiated a series of professional development workshops that I found very useful. Senior Associate Dean Hewett-Smith gave me helpful advice as I was completing the book manuscript. I thank Liz Lance from the NUQ Research Office, who supported this project from the start. My sincere gratitude also goes to Sami Hermez, Joe Khalil, and Zachary Wright for their friendship and mentorship. I'm grateful to many of my wonderful NUQ colleagues for their collegiality and camaraderie. I thank Ibrahim N. Abusharif, Jocelyn Mitchell, Kirsten Pike, and Torsten Menge for inviting me to be part of various faculty groups discussing our research projects and writing, and Hasan Mahmud, Ilhem Allagui, Rana Kazkaz, Susan Dun, Jairo Lugo-Ocando, Spencer Striker, Venus Jin, and Gregory F. Lowe for productive conversations and collaborations. For their help with my library needs, I thank NUQ librarians Mark T. Paul, Iman Khamis, Ryza Odencio-Tenorio, Jocelyn Casambros, Victoria Ng'eno, and Mel Aquino. I thank all my undergraduate research assistants and teaching assistants for their invaluable help with many projects and courses. Their names are too many to list them here (I recruited and hired close to three dozen students over the years), but I'd like them to know that I am very appreciative.

I am indebted to several people who have helped me think about and complete the book in various ways. I thank Laurie Ross, Lisa Yoshikawa, Jonathan Coopersmith, Sulfikar Amir, Suzanne Moon, Julie Cohn, Jenni Lieberman, and Janet Browne who gave helpful input and guidance as I was formulating the book in its beginning stages. Michael Fisher, Jörg Matthias Determann, Upik Djalins, and Joe Khalil read drafts of earlier versions and provided useful comments and feedback. I thank Petra Shenk for her invaluable editorial input and her helpful, incisive, and sometimes lighthearted comments on my drafts. Daysi Ramirez lends her skills to the maps in the book. Wah Guan Lim, Jack Chia, and Taomo Zhou have always been there to give moral support and cheer me along the way, and I am thankful for their counsel and friendship. I attended professional development workshops given by Jessica Winegar and Pablo J. Boczkowski and I am grateful for their insights and tips and for sharing career development strategies. I thank Jessica especially for her advice in navigating the academic publication process.

The research and writing of this book have taken me to several different places since 2010. I would like to reiterate my sincere thanks to those who have helped me during my research in Indonesia. In Jakarta, Aswinny Sudhiani, Bu Srikalbarini, Pak Christiana Samekta, and Pak Hartono PA. I also thank Pak Agung Mastika, Pak Maman Suriarsa, Pak I.B.M. Padangrata, Bu Estie Paripurnadinie, Pak Wayan Widia, and Eko Subagyo in Bali; Bu Wiratni Budhijanto and Pak Agus Prasetyo in Yogyakarta; Pak Fahmi, Pak Andi Tenriangka, and Pak Andi Muhammad Nur in Palopo; Pak Susma in Lombok; and Anas Ari Wibowo in Lampung. I thank Pratama Yudha Pradeksa for his assistance in locating and copying much-needed materials from a university library in Surabaya. In the U.S. I thank Rosita Rahim for believing in me and what I was doing in graduate school. For their invaluable help, I thank Cornell librarians Jeff Petersen, Suzanne M. Schwartz, Carole E. Atkinson, and Sharon Elizabeth

Powers. Bu Kaja McGowan and her husband, Pak Ketut, welcomed me and my family to their home and helped us in times of need. I thank them for their generosity and kindness. In the Netherlands I'm grateful to Bu Lita and Pak Santo as well as Wiek and her husband, Peter, for hosting me while I was looking for research materials at the libraries in Leiden. When I needed additional sources from the University of Leiden libraries, Alodie Prihutama and Erick Paulus came to my aid. I thank them both.

I'm grateful for the opportunities to present earlier versions of some chapters at several symposia. I thank Sang-Hyun Kim for inviting me to the International Workshop "Science, Technology, and Modern Dictatorship in Asia" in Seoul in 2017 and the attendees for their feedback. I thank fellow panelists, chairs, and organizers of the following meetings I attended where I presented my work. At the Society for the History of Technology (SHOT) meeting in 2018: Leo Coleman and Fredrik Meiton. In the 2019 SHOT annual conference: George Wilkenfield, Ute Hasenöhrl, Jonas van der Straeten, and Damilola Adebayo. Finally, at the 2022 Association of the Asian Studies meeting (when we had to switch to online at the last minute): Ying Jia Tan, Elizabeth Chatterjee, Zhaojin Zeng, Yeonsil Kang. Portions of an earlier version of chapter 2 were published in *Sojourn: Journal of Social Issues in Southeast Asia*. I thank the then managing editor of *Sojourn*, Michael J. Montesano, for granting permission to reprint and for helpful comments on earlier version of that article.

My deepest thanks go to my family members who supported me in many ways as I was conducting fieldwork, collecting data, and drafting the manuscript: my dad and my mom, my brother, Kemal, and his family, my sister, Diana, and her family, my father-in-law and my mother-in-law, my sisters-in-law Femmy and Yana and their families. My mom inspired me to study engineering and my dad the social sciences and humanities. My dad inspired me further when at the age of seventy-two he completed and defended his PhD dissertation in political science at the National University in Jakarta.

At the University of Wisconsin Press, I thank Nathan MacBrien, Jackie Teoh, Janie Chan, Holly McArthur, and Jessica Smith for their help throughout the process. My thanks and appreciation also go to Laura Poole for her copyediting service and the two anonymous reviewers for their critical reading and helpful suggestions. Their extensive and detailed comments have helped me revise the book to make it more accessible to nonspecialists.

Research for this book was made possible from generous funding from Cornell University Sage Fellowship, Cornell Graduate Research Travel Grant, Mario Einaudi Center Travel Grant for Summer Research, and the American-Indonesian Cultural and Educational Foundation Grant. I appreciate financial support from the NUQ Professional Development Funds and the NUQ Internal Scholarly Research Grant in 2019. Funding from NUQ enabled me to visit the three different sites of the rural electric cooperatives in Indonesia and to conduct archival research in libraries and archives in Indonesia and the Netherlands.

I have thanked my wife, Titin, in the beginning, but I'd like to thank her again, this time along with our daughters, Sophia and Dela. They have accompanied me to many of the places I visited to conduct research and present my work. Other times they have patiently given me the space and time to think and write. Without them, completing this book would have been a much lonelier process. Perhaps more than anything, they remind me that there is life outside academia. Out of curiosity and as a kind of encouragement, Sophia and Dela often asked me, "When are you going to finish your book, Daddy?" Well girls, I've finally completed it. *Alhamdulillah*, we did it!

Abbreviations

ANIEM	N.V. Algemeene Nederlandsch Indische Electriciteits Maatschappij (General Netherlands Indies Electricity Company)
ANRI	Arsip Nasional Republik Indonesia (Indonesian National Archive)
BAPPENAS	Badan Perencanaan Pembangunan Nasional (National Development Planning Agency)
BATAN	Badan Tenaga Nuklir Nasional (National Agency for Nuclear Power)
Bimas	Bimbingan Massal (Mass Guidance)
BPUPLN	Badan Pimpinan Umum Perusahaan Listrik Negara (General Management Board of the State Electricity Company)
BPUPKI	Badan Penyelidik Usaha-usaha Persiapan Kemerdekaan Indonesia (Body to Investigate the Preparation of Indonesian Independence)
CIDA	Canadian International Agency for Development
Depernas	Dewan Perantjang Nasional (National Planning Council)
DGC	Directorate General of Cooperative (Direktorat Jenderal Koperasi)
DGP	Directorate General of Power (Direktorat Jenderal Ketenagaan)
DIP	Daftar Isian Proyek (Project Content List)
Disjaya	Distribusi Jakarta Raya and Tangerang (Jakarta and Tangerang Distribution)
DME	Department of Mining and Energy
DMTC	Department of Manpower, Transmigration, and Cooperative
DPP	diesel-fueled power plant

DPR	Dewan Perwakilan Rakyat (People's Representative Council)
DPWEP	Department of Public Works and Electric Power
EHV	extra high voltage
Gatrik	Direktorat Djenderal Tenaga dan Listrik (Directorate General of Power and Electricity)
GBHN	Garis-Garis Besar Haluan Negara (Broad Guidelines of State Policy)
GEBEO	N.V. Gemeenschappelijk Electriciteitsbedrijf Bandoeng en Omstreken (Joint Electricity Company Bandung and Surroundings)
GFDC	German Foundation for Developing Countries
Golkar	Golongan Karya (Functional Groups)
GPP	geothermal power plant
HPP	hydroelectric power plant
ICA	US International Cooperation Administration
IPP	independent power producer
ITB	Institut Teknologi Bandung (Institute of Technology in Bandung)
Jamali	Java-Madura-Bali
KLP	Koperasi Listrik Pedesaan (Rural Electric Cooperative)
KNIWEC	Komite Nasional Indonesia—World Energy Conference (Indonesian National Committee-World Energy Conference)
Kopkamtib	Komando Operasi Pemulihan Keamanan dan Ketertiban (Operational Command for the Restoration of Security and Order)
Korpri	Korps Pegawai Republik Indonesia (Indonesian Civil Servants Corps)
KUD	Koperasi Unit Desa (Village Unit Cooperative)
LMD	Listrik Masuk Desa (Electricity Entering Villages)
LMK	Lembaga Masalah Ketenagaan (Power Research Institute)
LWB	Landswaterkrachtbedrijf (State Hydropower Company)
MHPP	micro or mini hydroelectric power plant
MPR	Majelis Permusyarawatan Rakyat (People's Consultative Assembly)
MPRS	Majelis Permusyawaratan Rakyat Sementara (Provisional People's Consultative Assembly)
NIEM	N.V. Nederlandsch Indische Electriciteits Maatschappij (Netherlands Indies Electricity Company)
NIGM	N.V. Nederlandsch Indische Gas Maatschappij (Netherlands Indies Gas Company)

NRECA	National Rural Electric Cooperative Association
OGEM	N.V. Overzeesche Gas en Electriciteits Maatschappij (Overseas Gas and Electricity Company)
P3LG	Penguasa Perusahaan Peralihan Listrik dan Gas (Central Administering Board for Electricity and Gas Enterprises)
P4	Pedoman Penghayatan dan Pengamalan Pancasila (Guidelines for Internalizing and Practicing Pancasila)
PDI	Partai Demokrasi Indonesia (Indonesian Democratic Party)
PDO	Project Development Office
PEC	PT Paiton Energy Company (PEC),
PELITA	Pembangunan Lima Tahun (Five-Year Development)
Pertamina	Perusahaan Pertambangan Minyak Bumi dan Gas Negara (State Oil and Gas Company)
PGN	Perusahaan Gas Negara (State Gas Company)
PKI	Partai Komunis Indonesia (Communist Party of Indonesia)
PKD	Paket Kelistrikan Desa (Village Electrification Package)
PLN	Perusahaan Umum Listrik Negara (State Electricity Company)
PLTD	Pembangkit Listrik Tenaga Diesel (Diesel-fueled Power Plant)
PPKI	Panitia Persiapan Kemerdekaan Indonesia (Committee for the Preparation of Indonesian Independence)
PPP	Partai Persatuan Pembangunan (United Development Party)
PT	Perseroan Terbatas (Limited Liability Company)
RE	rural electrification
REC	rural electric cooperative
REPELITA	Rencana Pembangunan Lima Tahun (Five-Year Development Plan)
SPLN	Standar Perusahaan Listrik Negara (PLN Standards)
SPP	steam power plant
STS	science and technology studies
TVRI	Televisi Republik Indonesia (Republic of Indonesia Television)
UI	Universitas Indonesia (University of Indonesia)
USAID	United States Agency for International Development

ELECTRIFYING INDONESIA

Introduction

ON A CLOUDY AFTERNOON on Saturday January 17, 1987, in the Marunda neighborhood (*kelurahan*) in the subdistrict of Cilincing in North Jakarta, many people gathered to attend a village electrification inauguration ceremony (*peresmian listrik masuk desa*). Before the official ceremony began, the Indonesian State Electricity Company (Perusahaan Umum Listrik Negara, PLN) Kebayoran Branch's Dangdut Orchestra and comedians Benyamin Sueb and the Tom Tam Group entertained the spectators. The gray sky soon gave way to a heavy downpour and soaked the unsheltered attendees. Although shivering in the cold, they stayed patiently through the ceremony listening to a string of speeches made by government officials. At the end of the ceremony, Mr. Sudharmono, the State Secretary and chair of the Functional Groups (Golongan Karya, Golkar)'s Central Leadership Council, pushed a button that let out a loud siren marking the beginning of an electrified era for Marunda and the other forty-nine neighborhoods recently connected to the grid. Upon hearing the signal, the audience clapped thunderously.[1] At the time, Indonesia's capital city of Jakarta was surrounded by and dotted with *kampong*s (urban villages) inhabited by poorer residents. Each village made up a neighborhood unit under the administration of the Province of the Special Capital District of Jakarta (Provinsi Daerah Khusus Ibukota Jakarta). Fifty neighborhoods in North, Central, and East Jakarta had just been electrified, and the ceremony celebrated this milestone.

In his speech, Sudharmono said, "This electrification inauguration ceremony is an indicator that [our national] development is ongoing in all fields. . . . If we want to advance, then we need to continue our electric infrastructure development. Thus, those of us who have enjoyed electricity must be grateful and thank God. This development is for us, from us, and by us."[2] Connecting electricity to the national development agenda of the New Order regime (1966–98) and to the divine was a strategic rhetorical move to project the idea of a caring government.[3] Sudharmono congratulated the residents of the fifty neighborhoods and thanked the PLN, the Jakarta provincial government, and the central government for this achievement on Golkar's behalf. After Sudharmono, other high-ranking officials took turns speaking. The governor of Jakarta, R. Suprapto, said, "The New Order government is the Development Order," further underscoring the regime's development agenda as an important source of its legitimacy.[4] Ir. Soejanto Soejitno, the leader of PLN Jakarta Raya and Tangerang Distribution Division (Disjaya), detailed the technical components of the constructed electric infrastructure by listing the length of transmission and distribution lines built, the transformers installed, and the funds used (Rp 9,644,470,500).[5] This information is always provided in speeches delivered by PLN officials in such ceremonies: electric infrastructure must be quantified in terms of the number of material things built and how much they cost to remind people of the government's investment to deliver electricity to their homes.

After the ceremony, Sudharmono delivered a letter containing a Presidential Decree regarding an assistance to build a mosque and a religious school in the Tugu neighborhood.[6] He also gave a color TV set to PLN Disjaya's millionth customer. A photo accompanying the article recounting this event, which was published in PLN's internal magazine *Berita PLN* (PLN News), shows the lucky person grinning widely as he shook hands with Sudharmono, alongside two government officials smiling and clapping. The fortunate gentleman and many others who joined the ceremony that day left the event satisfied.[7]

In the same month, Dr. Subroto, minister of Mining and Energy, was busy touring several provinces to officiate other inauguration ceremonies. He inaugurated eight diesel-fueled power plants (DPPs) with a total capacity of 800 kW and sixty-eight electrified villages in West Nusa Tenggara Province on January 15, 1987.[8] Then Subroto traveled to East Nusa Tenggara, and on January 16, 1987, he inaugurated eleven DPPs and twenty electrified villages in the province.[9] Two days later, Subroto was in Dili, the capital of East Timor, to inaugurate the energization of twelve DPPs and five recently electrified villages in several districts in the province.[10] Subroto concluded his four-province working visits (*kunjungan kerja*) in West Java. On January 20, 1987, he inaugurated the Ungaran Area Control Centre and the start of the 150 kV Yogyakarta–Rawalo transmission line.[11] As if those were not enough, on January 23, 1987, he was in the village of Sidogiri to preside over the ceremony of 126 electrified villages in three East Java districts.[12] In April, Subroto visited the city of Kediri in East Java to officiate the operation of the Java–Madura underwater cable that linked the island of Madura to Java's sophisticated ultrahigh-voltage transmission system and thirty-seven recently lit villages in the Kediri District.[13] On April 6, 1987, Minister of Youth and Sports Abdul Gafur inaugurated 112 electrified villages in the Maluku Province.[14] Earlier on March 5, 1987, Transportation Minister Roesmin Nurjadin inaugurated 109 electrified villages in South Sumatra.[15]

On April 23, 1987, the New Order held its fourth general election, by which time, thousands of people had seen or heard government and PLN officials deliver speeches about the virtues of the New Order's national development and the material benefits it delivered to the people. Many citizens, like the lucky millionth customer in Jakarta, had received various gifts from the government, which used electricity and other development programs as campaign materials. This strategy complemented another proven tactic from the provincial to the subdistrict levels: pressuring village heads to generate votes for the ruling political party.[16] Unsurprisingly, given the resources at its disposal, Golkar garnered 73 percent of the vote in 1987, up 9 percent from the election in 1982.[17] The New Order government was doing well politically. Golkar's win ensured Soeharto would stay in power, and he was reelected by the People's Consultative Assembly (Majelis Permusywaratan Rakyat, MPR) in 1988.

Although the New Order government had been electrifying villages since the early 1970s, it was not until the start of the third Five-Year Development Plan (Rencana Pembangunan Lima Tahun, REPELITA) in April 1979 that rural electrification was prioritized as the leading village improvement program and efforts to connect electrification to electoral politics increased. For example, in the months leading up to the 1982 general election, President Soeharto sent his cabinet ministers to inaugurate thousands of recently illuminated villages in many places. The strategy was fruitful and helped Golkar win the election that year. Soeharto repeated the practice again five years later in 1987 with better results for Golkar.

Indonesia's economy in 1987 was also doing well despite a drop in oil and gas revenue (the government's main source of income) the year before. The New Order government instituted several reform measures, "including hiring a foreign company to replace its corruption-ridden customs service, liberalizing its banking system, improving its domestic tax-collecting apparatus, devaluing the [Indonesian currency] rupiah, and seeking additional foreign loans and aid."[18] Good political economic indicators in 1987 led political scientist William Liddle to pen an analysis and claim that year was "the New Order at the height of its power."[19]

The year 1987 was also a special year in terms of the country's electric infrastructure. Besides having built several largescale power plants and hundreds of DPPs and electrified thousands of villages, the Soeharto government operated the country's first interisland electric interconnection transmission system and issued a permit for a rural electric cooperative in Lampung, one of three established in the country.[20] In the same year, to expedite the construction of rural electrification facilities, PLN issued Village Electrification Standards (Standar Listrik Pedesaan) and the Indonesian Standards Council published the General Electrical Installation Requirements (Persyaratan Umum Instalasi Listrik) to standardize and expedite home wiring installations. The publication of these two standards indicates the government's confidence in its electrification program. So optimistic was the mood and outlook of the electrification endeavors among energy professionals, the Indonesian National Committee–World Energy Conference (KNIWEC), an energy professionals' organization that had been organizing energy seminars on various topics since 1974, held the Third National Energy seminar in July 1987. The theme of the seminar captures the hopeful expectations of the Indonesian electrification program: "Developing a National Energy System to Support Take-Off Toward the Twenty-First Century."[21] Thus, electrically, the New Order state can also be regarded to be at the peak of its infrastructural development in 1987. The New Order government's drive for political power was entangled with the development of the country's electrical power. It is this entanglement that will be explored in the book.

I discuss the electrification processes and outcomes from the 1890s, when the Dutch introduced electricity in the Netherlands East Indies, until the end of the 1990s, when the New Order regime fell, but the focus of the book is on the Soeharto era (1966–98). This book argues that the Soeharto government deemed electricity a public good and delivered it as a social service to the people in exchange for political support and approval of the government's visions for Indonesian society. During Soeharto's New Order, electrification was made a national agenda with the Listrik Masuk Desa (Electricity Entering Villages) program, a leading village improvement scheme used to improve rural people's welfare and deliver material benefits in exchange for votes in the general elections. To this end, the Indonesian state established the state-owned electricity company that would function as a technical and a social organization. It generated and delivered electricity, as well as channeled other social services, such as donations, scholarships, and loans to the population. Electricity became a new energy technology for the masses and was used to serve the political economic objectives of the Soeharto regime. The Soeharto government linked electricity rhetorically and materially to the country's goals of enriching the life of the nation (*mencerdaskan kehidupan bangsa*) and achieving a just and prosperous society (*mencapai masyarakat yang adil dan makmur*). The regime believed electricity would propel Indonesia toward industrialization and modernization and play a crucial role in achieving their version of idealized Indonesian society.

Historian Thomas P. Hughes once wrote, "Electric power systems embody the physical, intellectual, and symbolic resources of the society that constructs them."[22] In other words, even though electric power systems require the same fundamental technical components and knowledge, different societies in different times require different resources and function in different political economic systems. These variations result in different historical trajectories. Each society shapes and is shaped by the electric power system it develops. Indonesia was not the only country trying to build its nation using electricity. After World War II, many newly emerging Asian and African countries endeavored to develop their fledgling nations using various scientific and technological projects.[23] Electrification received a lot of attention from these governments because it was deemed vital for industrialization and modernization. These nation-states carried out their electrification projects by marshaling state resources and securing substantial funds from international donors. The World Bank noted that in 1975, its member countries had invested $10 billion by 1971 and planned to invest $10 to $15 billion more in the following decade to connect 300 million people to the grid.[24] The different pathways each country took to electrify their territories form a crucial technological story of the second half of the twentieth century. The story of how and why Indonesia carried out its electrification efforts is part of this larger historical narrative of the historiography of electrification in the Global South to which this book contributes.[25]

Sociotechnical System and Patrimonial Technopolitics

To examine the historical trajectory of Indonesia's electrification, I use the sociotechnical system approach developed by Hughes, who argued that to understand the development of large technological systems, historians need a more holistic analytical framework than just investigating the technical components of the built infrastructure.[26] Organizations, economic conditions, political order, available resources, key people, decision makers, and laborers all play important roles in shaping and building that infrastructure. Hughes put forth an analytic tool he called the sociotechnical system.[27] In this approach, analysts view technology not just as a standalone artifact but as part of a seamless web of objects, people, regulations, organizations, scientific knowledge, technical knowhow (codified and tacit), work practices, and ideology. The system builders are not only the engineers, technicians, and construction workers but others involved in the development of the system, including, in this case, government bureaucrats, energy professionals, PLN employees, rural electric cooperative managers and workers, and foreign consultants.

Hughes paid particular attention to the political dimension of technological development, a key theme that interests many historians of technology and science and technology studies (STS) scholars. In his account of the development of electric power systems in Berlin, Chicago, and London, he concluded, "[in] Chicago, technology dominated politics; in London, the reverse was true; and in pre–World War I Berlin there was coordination of political and technological power."[28] Although perhaps this seems too tidy a summary of his detailed and lengthy study, Hughes highlights the interconnectedness of politics and technology. Increased interest in examining the political dimension of technology follows the publication of Langdon Winner's influential essay, "Do Artifacts Have Politics?"[29] Further refinement of the idea and analysis of the entwinement of politics and technology led Gabrielle Hecht to coin the term "technopolitics," which she defines as "the strategic practice of designing or using technology to constitute, embody or enact political goals."[30] Hecht clarifies that her notion of technopolitics is not simply technology in and of itself, which she understands "broadly to include artifacts as well as nonphysical, systematic methods of making and doing things," but how technology is "used in political processes and/or toward political aims."[31] In other words, the sociotechnical system interlaced with political practices and goals forms technopolitics.[32]

In my examination of the connection between technology and politics in New Order Indonesia, I found another useful term: patrimonialism. Patrimonialism is a political science concept that has its origin in Weber's analysis of "various forms of *Herrschaft* (authority, domination, or perhaps better, in Roth's term, 'rulership,')" in his book *Economy and Society*.[33] Scholars have categorized patrimonialism into two types: one "based primarily upon traditional grounds" and the more common of the two called "'personal rulership' [that] does not require any belief in the ruler/leader's personal qualifications, but is based mainly on material incentives and rewards."[34] One big factor that enabled the second type to exist in emerging countries "is the cultural and political heterogeneity of the new states—a heterogeneity that confronts their governments with the task of welding diverse social units into a nation."[35] Robin Theobald suggests that "there are vital links between the phenomenon of patrimonialism and broader socioeconomic factors," for example, the function of bureaucracy in a patrimonial state depends less on state revenue from taxes than on the distribution of benefices to key members of the ruling elite and income from other means (usually exporting natural resources).[36]

In the field of Indonesian political science studies, Soeharto's New Order regime and its politics of development have been characterized variously as, for example, a "bureaucratic polity" by Karl D. Jackson, a modernizing nation that retains patrimonial characteristics by Harold Crouch, an extension of Dutch colonial state by Benedict Anderson, a form of "bureaucratic pluralism" by

Donald K. Emmerson, and "a steeply-ascending pyramid" with Soeharto at its apex who controlled the military by R. William Liddle.[37] Jamie Mackie and Andrew MacIntyre persuasively argue that patrimonialism represented an enduring feature of the New Order.[38] They write, "[the term] highlights the extent to which control over key financial resources, licenses and essential facilities needed by business enterprises derive from the president and his immediate circle of lieutenants at the apex of the power structure."[39] But more than just controlling and distributing government largesse to the ruling elite and entrepreneurial classes, the New Order regime used its control over financial and technical resources to create a patron–client relationship with the populace. In short, the New Order state was patrimonial.

By combining the terms "technopolitics" and "patrimonialism," I offer the conceptual tool of "patrimonial technopolitics" to examine the entanglement of politics and technology of a patrimonial regime.[40] Since Theobald contends that personal rulership "is by no means absent from modern industrial societies," there could be cases of patrimonial technopolitics in industrialized and industrializing nations.[41] For the patrimonial New Order state, the concept examines how the regime designed and used technology to enact its political goals. The New Order government channeled its munificence to large swaths of the population, with promises of more in the form of electricity and other benefits that PLN employees and customers enjoyed. The regime exercised power over the ruled population through their acquiescence in exchange for modern amenities.

Throughout this book, I argue that the New Order regime electrified Indonesia not only to illuminate and energize the country but in exchange for electoral and political support. The founding of PLN and schemes to light up the countryside revolved around the idea of using electricity to establish political economic patronage between the rulers and the general population. In an increasingly technological world, a patrimonial state like the New Order needed to function as a technopolitical state to maintain its legitimacy to rule and ensure its longevity. In an electrified era, channeling government patronage in exchange for securing political support demanded that it distributes electricity to the people as an affordable and reliable commodity. In other words, Indonesia's electric infrastructure was designed and developed mainly as a patrimonial technopolitical project. My examination of the technopolitical nature of the electrification program underscores that technological development is not apolitical. Knowing that politics is entwined with technoscience means not only realizing and investigating "technology as a site and object of politics" but also understanding that society and technology shape one another, science and social order are coproduced.[42] The patrimonial New Order government shaped how Indonesia was electrified, and its electrification program, in turn, fashioned the regime's envisioned sociopolitical order.

Social Justice, Development, and Nation-Building

Three key themes figured in Indonesia's New Order electrification endeavors: social justice, national development, and nation-building. Electrification influenced how social justice was understood by different groups, energized Soeharto's national development agenda, and helped realize the imagined Indonesian nation.[43] A constructed, ideal version of social justice known as Pancasila (Sanskrit for "five principles") was made into the Indonesian state ideology. The principles are mentioned in preamble of the country's 1945 Constitution and taught in schools so that children can recite them by heart. The fifth principle explicitly states the country's aim to achieve "social justice for all Indonesians." Such an ideal was borne out of Indonesia's colonial experiences and forcefully expressed by the country's first two nationalist and independence leaders: Sukarno and Mohammad Hatta. They saw that electricity was enjoyed by many resident Europeans but was out of reach to most local inhabitants of the Dutch colony.[44] Noticing this unequal distribution of electricity and other inequalities resulting from the Dutch colonial regime's exploitative capitalist practices, these leaders sought to correct the imbalance when they proclaimed Indonesia's independence on August 17, 1945. Sukarno's Pancasila proposal as the state ideology was quickly adopted by other nationalists. Hatta's vision of the country's socialist economy influenced the social welfare clause (Article 33) of the 1945 Constitution, which mandated that the state control the country's natural resources and its vital means of production for the people's maximum prosperity.

National development was carried out by both the Sukarno (1945–66) and Soeharto (1966–98) regimes, although it found its strongest expression in the Soeharto era. In 1959, a year after all Dutch private electric companies were nationalized, Sukarno created the National Planning Council to formulate a comprehensive development plan. The council produced what came to be known as the Planned Universal National Development (Pembangunan Nasional Semesta Berencana), the first stage of which was slated to cover the period 1961–69. Although there were some development projects conducted before then, systematic national development planning did not begin until 1961, after which many electricity projects across the country were carried out by the PLN.[45] Sukarno's development agenda was cut short when in 1965, the September 30th Movement paved the way for the rise of the New Order regime with Soeharto seizing power from Sukarno.

To maintain its legitimacy to rule the population, the New Order government emphasized "development," a modernizing project in which many other emerging economies participated. On this, Itty Abraham writes:

> Development was the name given to a wide range of practices that took as their object the "third" world of newly independent nations. These practices sought especially to improve economic growth as measure through GDP statistics; saw economic change as something that could be induced from without, relying on strengthening the state and using Keynesian fiscal policy; and were based on a selective and partial reading of Western experiences in the eighteenth and nineteenth centuries to reify *a normalised trajectory of historical change*. This was a modernist project, deeply influenced by the Enlightenment's values of secularism, faith in science, exploitation of nature, and above all, optimism for the future that transmutes into hubris about what is possible through the application of these values. These ideas and practices were institutionalized as the ideology of modernisation, its "house name" being development studies.[46]

One aspect of this "normalised trajectory of historical change" is the notion of unproblematic technological (and implied social) progress moving along a linear path. STS scholars have unpacked and problematized this so-called master narrative of history of technology, that is, the belief that the historical trajectory of technology in the West could or should be a model or even a standard for the development of technology elsewhere. This thinking spurred activities known as technological and scientific transfers that are often thought of as one-way transfer of knowledge and knowhow from one country to another. The realities are more complex.[47] The introduction of technology from one society to another often involved, as Suzanne Moon has shown, a "technological dialogue" between the "transferring and receiving agents" (even though this "dialogue" was usually asymmetrical).[48] Even when a new technology is introduced in a society, there could have been modes of "transformative resistance" that shaped how it would be eventually used and given meanings by its users.[49]

The New Order government not only believed in the idea of linear developmentalism, it also institutionalized and practiced it using its REPELITA framework. Soeharto explained this step-by-step development framework in his autobiography:

> People must be made to understand, that a just and prosperous society based on Pancasila, which is our national goal, cannot be achieved all at once, cannot

come down from the sky just like that. We must achieve it through development, in stages and according to our abilities. . . . The general pattern of long-
term development spelled out in GBHN [Garis-Garis Besar Haluan Negara,
Broad Guidelines of State Policy], which is the strategy of long-term development, spells out that *the foundation of a just and prosperous society* can be achieved
after doing five to six times *Repelita* . . . This way, in Repelita VI (1994–1999) a
just and prosperous society based on Pancasila can be realized with our strengths
[and this period] is known as *tinggal landas* [take off].[50]

In this quote, Soeharto sets the objective of reaching the "takeoff" stage within
Indonesia's first twenty-five years of development (1969–94), after which he
planned to launch the country into the next stage to achieve its national goals.

Soeharto's thinking was undoubtedly influenced by modernization theorist
W. W. Rostow, given that he was surrounded by technocrats familiar with
Rostow's ideas. In his book, *The Stages of Economic Growth: A Non-Communist
Manifesto* (1960), Rostow argued that nations go through five stages of growth
from a traditional society to a mass consumptive nation passing through a
middle stage called "take off."[51] Although many scholars now criticize his theory as Western-biased, naively linear, and having an environmentally destruc-
tive end goal, it was quite influential at the time.[52] Following the end of World
War II, many newly independent nations in Asia and Africa, as well as liber-
ated nations in Latin America, engaged in national development informed by
the discourses of modernization theory.[53] Michael Adas shows that modernization theory was born out of a historically specific moment during the Cold
War when the United States wanted to exert and maintain influence in many
newly created nation-states as it was fighting an ideological war with the Soviet
Union.[54] The subtitle of Rostow's book is a clear indication that he was
advancing an alternative to Soviet communist–style development.

For the Sukarno and Soeharto regimes, Indonesia's nation-building goals of
creating a unified nation and achieving a "just and prosperous society" were
part and parcel with having a fully electrified nation. That is, electrification was
viewed as a prerequisite without which Indonesia would not fulfill its objectives. In a 1960 speech, Sukarno explicitly urged Indonesians to become an
"electricity minded" nation,[55] a goal Soeharto also pushed when he launched
the Cirata Dam project in 1986, saying, "Without sufficient electrical provision,
it would be difficult to realize our development goal of creating an advanced,
prosperous, and just society based on Pancasila."[56]

Constructing a sense of national unity was one of Indonesia's primary concerns. This emerging and vast archipelagic nation, advancing from colonialism and forged in purported shared experiences (and supposed future des-

tiny), needed to be continually shored up lest it disintegrate into its smaller constituents. Indonesia's answer to the challenges of unifying its diverse regions and peoples was the state ideology Pancasila.[57] PLN, the primary bureaucracy tasked with bringing electricity to the country, played a central role in making the Pancasila principles plain to citizens. Through a series of mandatory training courses in the 1980s, PLN employees were taught to internalize and embody Pancasila principles and invoked them every chance they had to talk excitedly about their duties in electrifying the country.

Other groups understood electrification and electricity in connection to the three themes (social justice, development, and nation-building) differently, which influenced their actions and decisions. Government technocrats, for example (mainly cabinet ministers and other high-ranking bureaucrats), believed in state-led electrification because they thought that private companies would be less inclined to electrify rural areas. As a result, they invested heavily in PLN and gave fewer incentives and assistance to other entities, including rural electric cooperatives (RECs). PLN managers and employees (part of the state's Civil Servant Corps) considered bringing electricity to the countryside their sacred duty to realize the Pancasila principle of social justice. Although they received financial and political support from the government, they needed to balance this unprofitable endeavor with the goal of turning the company into a profitable utility business.

In addition, four social scientists from the University of Indonesia, who analyzed Soeharto's rural electrification (RE) program in 1980, noted that although RE was an important program and social justice a noble goal, in practice, some villages would inevitably be prioritized over others based on the villages' development stage (see chapter 2). To them this policy was not in line with social justice and equalization.[58] Instead they advocated to make electricity prices affordable for average villagers. Other researchers who examined rural electrification noted how electrification brought some benefits but worsened some existing inequalities. All the while, most villagers just wanted cheap and reliable electricity in their homes regardless of who provided it and deemed it an injustice when they could not access it or had to wait a long time to receive it.

The Visibility of Electric Infrastructure

One salient feature of electricity is that it needs to be transmitted and distributed using wires. Electric current has not been successfully transmitted wirelessly long distance despite it being more than a century-old development. Electricity has been and will continue to be a wired technology. Cables and wires are needed to transmit and distribute electricity, a requirement that made electrifying groups of islands such as Indonesia particularly challenging. Building a physical, integrated electric infrastructure that would span the entire country would be impossible. Even with underwater cables, Indonesia could only string a few islands together because of the vast number of islands and smaller archipelagos in its territorial waters. The topographies of the big islands of Java, Sumatra, Kalimantan, Sulawesi, and Papua presented challenges. For example, Java is home to many dormant and active volcanoes; Sumatra's western and eastern coastlines are divided by a mountain range spanning the length of the island; Kalimantan is covered by large swaths of tropical jungles where some of the biggest rivers in the country can be found; Sulawesi is covered by mountain ranges of different elevations with flatter lands found only in the southern part and along the coastlines. Similar conditions are found on Papua in addition to thick forests enveloping much of the island. These challenging physical constraints prevented Indonesia from having a countrywide power grid.

Outside the three most populated islands of Java, Madura, and Bali, PLN mainly constructed standalone power systems, some of which became part of a limited regional electric network. Although there are local primary energy sources that might be harnessed (such as water, wind, and geothermal), practical considerations like the availability of cheap oil (in the beginning), standardized construction methods, ease of operation, and maintenance narrowed PLN's choices. Instead of relying on largescale power plants and a single power grid, Indonesia ended up developing hybrid power systems: big power plants that became part of a few regional grids and standalone small to medium electric generators with limited distribution networks. The big power plants were built in Java and near urban centers elsewhere and run mostly on coal, geothermal, and falling water. In contrast, the small to medium plants were constructed across the islands and mostly use diesel fuel. Even though the diesel-fueled power stations are not all connected physically, they are integrated organizationally because they are run by PLN employees. In this sense, they form a separate power grid. Thus, Indonesia's electric landscapes are made up of these two distinct power grids.

The wired nature of electricity also means that an electric infrastructure is materially visible, especially in the countryside, contrary to the assertion of some infrastructure studies scholars who claim it has an "invisible quality."[59] Richer countries, regions, municipalities, or cities can afford to bury electrical cables underground for aesthetic reasons. But in many parts of the world, electric infrastructure is visible (poles and wires) and does not always function effortlessly, which led Paul N. Edwards to argue the idea that smoothly operating invisible infrastructure is a "western bias."[60] Even in cities where the electric cables were placed underground, people could still see the transmission towers and cables that bring electric current long distances from outside the cities.

In the countryside, many people have come to accept electric poles and cables as part of the landscape. Usually, the poles are erected alongside paved roads, which function as an "installed base."[61] But what if there are no such roads? This was another challenge to electrifying Indonesia's rural areas, where roads used as the installed base for electric infrastructure often did not exist. As a result, electric poles could be seen erected along dirt roads or paddy fields in many places, sometimes on private lands. But the visibility of Indonesia's electric infrastructure is not confined to the towers, poles, wires, and electric lightbulbs in houses. The presence of PLN could be felt in some of the remotest places in the archipelago. As the primary electric bureaucracy, PLN successfully developed its organizational reach to encompass the whole country. It created divisions and branches down to the subdistrict level and built thousands of offices and power stations emblazoned with its visible and readily identifiable logo. Almost every citizen has come to associate electricity with PLN, even in areas where independent power producers (IPPs) supply part of the electric power. Electricity remains a very visible material affair in the country, the absence of which raises questions of imbalance, injustice, uneven development, and exclusion among the communities yet to be served by PLN.

As I have written elsewhere, one of villagers' strongest motivations for electricity in the 1970s and 1980s was to power a television set, an exciting new technology that many desired.[62] The desire for television facilitated the Soeharto government using electricity and the television tubes it powered to spread its development messages and propaganda. In 1962 the Sukarno government built a national broadcasting station called the Republic of Indonesia Television (Televisi Republik Indonesia, TVRI), which it followed up in 1976 by launching a communication satellite (Palapa) and constructing a national network of ground stations to receive and relay satellite signals, making Indonesia the first country in the Global South to own this wireless communication technology.[63] Before Palapa, Indonesia was constructing a microwave transmission system linking the islands of Sumatra, Java, and Bali to relay TV signal broadcasts from TVRI stations in Jakarta. Indonesia's geography, however, made the effort difficult and expensive. The Soeharto government decided to stop building additional link stations on the other islands and purchased a communication satellite instead.[64]

The satellite enabled the government to broadcast its programs to the farthest reaches of the country, though people still needed television sets to receive and watch them. Following the launch of Palapa, "the Department of Information distributed thousands of public access receivers (*televisi umum*) in rural areas now within the satellite footprint."[65] The idea was to have the television placed in the village square, but many sets ended up in *Bupati's* [district head's] houses.[66] As the number of television sets increased, so did the demand for electricity to power them. Some villagers used car batteries to power their electronics before the arrival of electricity. Often the government delivered a free TV receiver for a newly electrified village to signal that both *televisi* and *listrik* have come to the village. Thus, television sets became a visible material manifestation of the presence of electricity in Indonesia's rural areas. In addition, the New Order government used TV sets as a communication medium to broadcast its development projects, which served as a political message to further anchor its patrimonial technopolitics.

Reorienting STS

I situate my book at the intersection of two main bodies of scholarship: STS and Southeast Asian studies. I focus on a geographic region (Indonesia and Southeast Asia broadly) largely left out of STS scholarship and study a less examined topic in Southeast Asian studies (history and sociology of technology). Although there is abundant scholarship produced on Indonesia, it is mainly generated by scholars of more established disciplines, such as anthropology, linguistics, ethnomusicology, history, political science, art history, development sociology, and economics, which largely relegate science and technology to the background or touch on only one aspect of a broader assemblage of a sociotechnical system. Drawing on these two bodies of scholarship, I bring technology to the forefront of my narrative and examine it in its broader social, cultural, and political contexts. Fortunately, there has been a growing body of STS scholarship on Indonesia produced by anthropologists and historians and scholars trained in STS.[67] Building on this burgeoning scholarship, this book adds materiality to Indonesia's sociocultural and political history by showing how electricity figured prominently in the discourses and practices of social justice, national development, and nation-building.

Studying technoscientific projects in Indonesia or another Southeast Asian country matters because it can help us get a better understanding of technological development and meaning making in our increasingly global and interdependent technological culture. Technoscientific artifacts were not merely conceived, invented, developed, and transferred from one place to another, they were also used, reconfigured, given (different) meanings, shaped (individually and communally), and employed by different regimes to achieve various ends. For this reason, STS scholar Warwick Anderson has called for reorienting STS toward Southeast Asia to explore the possible synthesis of science and technology studies with area studies and postcolonial studies.[68]

That said, as scholar Gregory Clancey points out, although there has not been a strong research agenda about "technology" and "Asia," greater interest in this subject has recently emerged.[69] In this regard, my work contributes to the snowball effect of producing critical humanistic and social scientific studies of technology in Asia. My work shows that in narrating technology stories, technology storytellers need not always focus on the origins or future orientations of technology but that the historical processes by which the technology was creatively adapted and used in the context of changing social, cultural, and political factors is also crucial to advance the field. This narrative is in line with the important and vibrant conversations among STS scholars to decenter innovation as a focus of technology studies.[70]

Chapter Summaries

I start in chapter 1 by providing the historical context of electrification before the New Order era. I discuss electrification in the late colonial period (1890–1942), the Japanese occupation (1942–45), and the Sukarno era (1945–66). Dutch private companies along with the Batavia-based colonial regime introduced electricity to the Dutch East Indies in the late nineteenth century. Electricity was used to power extractive industries in the colony and illuminate houses, stores, buildings, markets, and entertainment centers for the convenience of European inhabitants. The Dutch made electricity available in small towns and urban areas and sold electrified modernity to the white European residents through a popular Dutch-language periodical. Java's electric infrastructure became the most developed, and when the Japanese invaded and occupied the archipelago, the Japanese army controlled Java's electric infrastructure while the Japanese navy controlled the infrastructure on the other islands. During the occupation, an opportunity opened up for more Indonesians to work in the electric industry and learn the knowledge and skills needed for operating and managing electrical facilities. Following Indonesian independence in 1945, the Sukarno government took over Dutch utility companies and completed their nationalization in 1958. It used electricity to unify Indonesian territories and articulate a vision of a socialist state that would lead to industrialization and modernization. It energized the new nation and Jakarta for the hosting of the Fourth Asian Games in 1962.

Chapter 2 describes the emergence and rise of the New Order regime and the rationale and motivation for its national development ideology. One aspect of the New Order government's national development project was to improve the villages by coming up with and imposing three different linear typologies. The government's goal was to make all of Indonesia's villages self-sufficient (*swasembada*) by the end of the twentieth century. According to the

New Order, a crucial component in this effort was bringing electricity to rural areas. Although the stated objective was to reduce the gap between electrified urban areas and unelectrified rural areas, bringing electricity to the villages was also tied to the regime's electoral politics. It provided the Soeharto government a way to channel material benefits such as electricity, a new technology that many villagers wanted, in exchange for their votes for Golkar during the general elections. Consequently, the New Order government mandated PLN to electrify hundreds of villages in the runup to the general elections and distribute other government handouts. President Soeharto sent his aides and Golkar officials to preside over village electrification inauguration ceremonies to link the provision of electricity with the New Order development agenda.

Chapter 3 discusses the founding and historical trajectory of the New Order's main electric bureaucracy, the state-owned electricity corporation (PLN). Created as a vertically integrated utility company, PLN was tasked with generating, transmitting, distributing, and selling electricity. PLN received huge financial and political support from the government, which constrained its role as an electricity company because it needed to conform to government's demands and directives. It fashioned itself "an agent of development" with the dual mission of being a profitable utility company and delivering electricity to the countryside, an endeavor that did not generate profit. The latter was called its "social mission," and in fact, PLN evolved to become both a technical and social organization, disseminating government largesse in the form of highly subsidized electricity, educational scholarships, and donations of many kinds to PLN employees and people in the villages. PLN also served as a vector of the state ideology Pancasila. PLN employees were mandated to take indoctrination courses and, on many occasions, invoked Pancasila to talk about electrification policies and projects. In this way, PLN helped transmit the state ideology to the citizenry who were told that electricity and the national electrification programs would help achieve the Pancasila social justice ideals.

Chapter 4 highlights the Soeharto government's Java-centrism in national governance and development and how this approach shaped the resulting imbalance of electrification coverage, continuing the colonial legacy that made Java a central place for electrical illumination. In the process, PLN created two power grids. The first was a sophisticated electrical backbone connecting regional grids in Java, Madura, and Bali, three of the most populated islands. The transmission system was managed by a load dispatching center based in Java to deliver electricity to consumers from several new largescale power plants on the island. The second power grid is an ensemble of limited regional networks and standalone power systems generated by thousands of DPPs on the other islands. Although not all of them were physically interlinked, they were all operated and maintained by an army of technically skilled PLN employees, making them a separate power grid. I also discuss PLN's rationale to select DPPs as the main power generator technology outside Java and the resulting intended and unintended consequences, including the underdevelopment of alternative power generation technologies and the creation of Java as a destination for many Indonesian citizens seeking opportunities for upward mobility.

Chapter 5 discusses Indonesia's energy challenges in the 1970s and the attempts by government officials, energy professionals, PLN employees, and Indonesian social scientists to produce social knowledge of rural life and energy use. They realized that to provide reliable, sustainable, and affordable energy alternatives (including electricity) in rural areas to replace the high consumption of firewood and kerosene, knowledge of what the villagers were using and how much they were using was warranted. They discussed these issues in a series of seminars, invited US consultants to train PLN employees to produce rural electrification feasibility studies and energy use surveys, and collaborated with four University of Indonesia social scientists to produce a report on the conditions of recently electrified villages. These activities resulted in a formulation of Indonesia's national energy policy, the Village Master Archive, feasibility studies manuals and reports, energy use survey results, and a *Listrik Masuk Desa* report by the university academics. Combined, this knowledge of the social made Indonesian villages more visible to the government and further solidified the rural electrification program. Other Indonesian social scientists who examined the New Order's village electrification critically challenged the government's positive outlook and effect on village electrification. Their studies revealed that PLN's categorization of "productive versus consumptive" uses of electricity was too limiting and that electricity without other supporting facilities could not improve the lot of the villagers as much as the government hoped.

In chapter 6, I recount the rise and fall of three independent RECs in Indonesia. Founded with the technical and financial assistance of the United States Agency for International Development and the National Rural Electric Cooperative Association, the Luwu, Lombok, and Lampung RECs grew to serve tens of thousands of customers by the early 1990s. Each managed to create a power system complex and distribution network that delivered electricity to areas previously untouched by the PLN grid. However, all three RECs finally collapsed, and their customers were transferred to PLN. The experiences of the RECs are similar, although the details and timelines differ. All three faced challenges setting up their sociotechnical systems at the beginning but managed to take off and functioned as independent electric business entities starting in 1987. They expanded their operations and enrolled thousands of new customers in the respective area of operations but faced mounting challenges to meet increasing electric power demands. Load shedding and sustained poor services followed, which sparked anger among their customer bases, who demanded the cooperatives be dissolved and PLN take over their operations. The government stepped in and, through prolonged processes and negotiations, allowed PLN to deliver its electricity to the former members of the cooperatives.

Late Colonial and Early Postcolonial Electrification

E
LECTRICITY ARRIVED EARLY in the Dutch East Indies, Holland's biggest and most profitable colony in Southeast Asia. Batavia (now Jakarta), then the seat of the colonial government, received electricity in 1897, a mere fifteen years after the Pearl Street Station in New York City began operation in 1882. Dutch private electric companies played a crucial role in introducing and spreading the novel technology and over four decades helped expand electricity coverage in the islands. By the early 1940s, many urban areas in Java, the most populated island, and several towns on other islands had been electrified. Whether in the city or the countryside, the colonial residents who enjoyed electricity were mostly Europeans. Electricity was hardly extended to the villages, so the rural areas were largely left in the dark and, for much of the population, electricity was a luxury item unattainable, undesirable, or "part of an inaccessible dream world."[1]

The introduction of electricity in the Dutch East Indies was intended to replace gas lighting and fuel the colonial government's extractive enterprises, which was largely successful. Alongside this, Dutch companies that marketed and sold the new energy technology and electrical appliances traded in stories, images, and ideas about a modern life facilitated by electricity. They published articles about the new wonders of the electric world and promoted electrical products in popular periodicals that largely targeted European readers. At the same time, as the technologies became more widely available and native people were exposed to and used them, the introduction of electricity and its concomitant modern technologies to colonial society had unintended effects. Ideas of modernity and nationalism began to manifest in the desire to liberate the colony and create the new nation-state of Indonesia. Spearheading the endeavor were nationalist leaders who were educated in the colony and the Netherlands. The two most influential were Sukarno and Mohammad Hatta.

The two men, born a year apart at the beginning of the 1900s, came from different regions and were brought up in separate cultures (Hatta from Sumatra and Sukarno from Java). They received different formal educations (Sukarno in engineering and Hatta in economics) and had distinctly opposite personalities. They endured the hardship of being arrested and tried, and their defense speeches in Dutch courts were printed and disseminated widely in the East Indies. When their paths eventually crossed, at first they did not see eye to eye. In the end, Sukarno and Hatta managed to put their differences aside and become the most prominent nationalist leaders, known later as Indonesia's duumvirate (*dwi tunggal*). In their memoirs, they observe how their experiences with Dutch technologies shaped how they thought electricity should be provided in postcolonial Indonesia.

In this chapter, I describe the introduction of electricity in the Dutch East Indies and its intended and unintended consequences. I argue that electricity was initially made available mainly for the benefit and enjoyment of Dutch colonists and enterprises. Later it played an increasingly important role in engendering nationalism and formed the centerpiece of Sukarno's vision of national unification, independence, and internationalization that linked social justice to modernization in the postcolonial period.

Electrifying the Dutch East Indies

Electricity was introduced in the East Indies in the last decade of the nineteenth century. Dutch private companies spearheaded the efforts after the regulation for electricity provision was passed in 1890.[2] The regulation stipulated that an enterprise could sell electricity to the public by applying for a permit to electrify a certain area. Licenses to supply electricity to the public were given for a maximum of forty years, but private uses were "terminable at notice."[3] Although initially many electric enterprises appeared on the scene, economic considerations led many of them to merge, and by the late 1930s three private businesses dominated the electricity market: ANIEM (N.V. Algemeene Nederlandsch Indische Electriciteits Maatschappij), OGEM (N.V. Overzeesche Gas en Electriciteits Maatschappij), and GEBEO (N.V. Gemeenschappelijk Electriciteitsbedrijf Bandoeng en Omstreken, a continuation of the N.V. Bandoengsche Electriciteit Maatschappij).

Besides private companies, the colonial regime, municipal governments, and several people participated in the electricity business. The colonial government constructed hydropower plants and distribution networks and collaborated with private companies to manage power plants and deliver electricity. Local governments established municipal electricity companies (*gemeentelijk electriciteitsbedrijf*) that either purchased electricity from government-owned power plants or generated their own power and distributed it in their respective towns, such as in Madiun, Pematang Siantar, Tanjung Balai, and Padang.[4] In smaller cities such as Jambi, Kuala Tungkal, Rengat, Tanjung Pinang, Mempawah, and Manokwari, private citizens funded small businesses that produced electric power that ranged from 20 to 400 horsepower (about 15–300 kW).[5]

The availability of electricity benefited many businesses in the Dutch East Indies. Paper mills in Padalarang and Letjes, a Malabar radio station near Bandung, and a Goodyear tire and rubber factory in Buitenzorg (present-day Bogor) are some examples.[6] Electricity was used by extractive enterprises such as coal, gold, and silver mines; sugar factories; and tea companies. The Dutch colonial regime, for example, constructed the Ombilin Coal Mining Company in West Sumatra to extract, process, and transport coal from mines. Electricity from the Sawahlunto power station (figure 1) powered the machines, underground trolley locomotives, screening houses, and other electric devices at the Ombilin collieries.[7]

Staatsspoorwegen ter Sumatra's Westkust, a colonial government–owned train company, operated the railway that carry coal from the Ombilin mines to the Emmahaven (Teluk Bayur) port in Padang. It built a steam-powered electrical generator in Kampung Durian, on the bank of the Batang Arau river to

Figure 1. Power plant of the Ombilin coal mine in Sawahlunto ca. 1890.
Source: Photo by C. Nieuwenhuis, courtesy of Leiden University Digital Collections.

light the Emmahaven port.[8] Another electric power plant, built at Tais in southern Sumatra, supplied electricity to the Tambang Sawah and Redjang Lebong silver mines.[9] Many power plants at these extraction sites used coal, but a few used other types of fuel. Power stations at the sugar factories, for instance, used hydropower and sugarcane waste products (*ampas*).[10]

Selling electricity proved to be profitable business for Dutch private enterprises and by 1930, several urban areas in Java had been well illuminated. Some towns and regions outside Java also had electricity, but the focus of the electricity business was on Java, the center of Dutch colonial rule. The pattern of unequal electrical development between Java and elsewhere, or what the Dutch called de Buitengewesten (the Outer Regions), as we shall see, continued in postcolonial Indonesia. Even within illuminated areas, there was an imbalance of electricity coverage and uses. Overall, in Java and other places, electricity was enjoyed mainly by European homes and businesses and the privileged few. Only very wealthy or high-status locals could afford to electrify their homes. It was reported, for example, that the Sultan of Kutai electrified his palace in the kingdom's capital of Tenggarong in East Kalimantan in 1896 after attending an electrical exhibition in Singapore.[11] Likewise, in 1903, the Sultan of Langkat installed an electric generator in Tanjung Pura in northern Sumatra to light up his palace plus some other houses, buildings, and streetlights.[12]

Before electric lamps, households in the Netherlands East Indies used candles or oil lamps as a lighting source.[13] Biofuels such as coconut oil were used before 1864, when kerosene became available.[14] When gas lighting was introduced in the second half of the nineteenth century, J. J. Rochussen, the Dutch Minister of the Colonies, granted a twenty-year business license to L. J. Enthoven & Co. in the Hague on November 19, 1859, to install a public gas lighting system in Batavia and surrounding areas.[15] The company began operating its gas factory in 1862, but after the death of the firm's head, it transferred its business license to the newly founded company N.V. Nederlandsch Indische Gas Maatschappij (NIGM) in 1863.[16] In later years, NIGM obtained additional concessions to supply gas to three other cities: Surabaya, Semarang, and Buitenzorg.[17] Over the next few decades, NIGM's gas lighting business thrived as consumers steadily increased (table 1).[18]

While NIGM was supplying gas to Batavia, a private company called N.V. Nederlandsch Indische Electriciteits Maatschappij (NIEM) started an electricity business in the early 1890s. NIEM's electricity permit was issued on January 13, 1893, and initially lasted for ten years, but was later extended to thirty years from the first date of issuance.[19] With its permit, NIEM constructed a steam-powered electric power station and began supplying electricity to Bata-

Table 1. Total number of gas meters in five cities
of NIGM's operation

	Total Gas Meters Installed				
	1884	1891	1898	1905	1912
Batavia	1,270	1,048	1,759	3,096	5,064
Soerabaia	304	371	1,021	2,571	3,944
Semarang	—	—	253	1,137	2,375
Buitenzorg	—	—	—	430	840

via in 1897.[20] In 1905, NIGM acquired NIEM.[21] The company's director's house (*Directeurswoning*) in Batavia is one of the best-preserved colonial buildings; on October 27, 2011, it was declared a cultural heritage site. It is now located inside the compound of PLN Disjaya (figure 2).[22]

The arrival of electricity in the city did not replace the existing gas lighting system overnight. Typically, a newly introduced technology is used alongside the older one. In some cases, older technologies do not disappear altogether but are preserved by those who still find some benefits in the seemingly out-dated technology.[23] In Batavia, electric lighting coexisted with gas lighting for a few decades until the former eventually replaced the latter.[24] When Moham-mad Hatta relocated to Batavia in June 1919 to continue his secondary school-ing, he wrote the following observation in his memoirs:

> In my room, besides the iron bed frame, there was a closet and a small table, a
> desk for me to work that is about 75 cm long and 60 cm wide, along with a chair.
> Parallel to my bedroom, there was a veranda with a "zitje" and above it hung a
> kerosene lamp. There was no electric lamp at the time. The big houses of the
> Dutch government officials usually used gas lamps. This type of lighting was
> called "druklicht." The gasoline was poured [into a tank and from the tank it was
> pumped] into the gas lamps inside the house.[25]

As Hatta noted, gas lighting was still used in houses of well-to-do Dutch fami-lies in Batavia even two decades after electricity was introduced.

After Batavia, several other cities began to receive electricity. Medan fol-lowed in 1899,[26] but Surabaya had to wait until 1911 despite its status as the busiest port and the colony's biggest city in the early 1900s.[27] The availability of gas lighting might have been a factor in the delayed arrival of electricity to the city. In addition, ANIEM, the private company that eventually supplied

Figure 2. Former NIGM director's house inside the PLN Disjaya complex.
Source: Photo by Anto Mohsin, July 2019.

electricity to Surabaya, was only founded in 1909.[28] Once electricity was available, electric lighting illuminated Surabaya's buildings and streets. Streetlights hung above a busy street (figure 3) using cables in a similar fashion to the streetlights in the Netherlands.[29] This streetlight design and other technologies, such as the canals and canal bridges in Batavia, support the notion that the colonial masters built their settlements in the East Indies in the image of their mother country.[30] Some adjustments were made for the colony's different conditions, but in many cases the Dutch colonial masters copied what they did in the metropoles in the colony.[31] In other words, the Dutch imported their country's technological style to the East Indies, trying to claim its colonial possession not just politically but also technologically.[32]

Just as Hatta noted the electricity conditions where he lived, Sukarno made similar observations in his autobiography. When the young Sukarno was attending secondary school in 1916, he observed, "Surabaya already boasted electricity. Each room had an outlet and each boarder paid extra for his lamp. Only my room didn't have one. I had no money for the bulb. I would study late into the night by [a] candle."[33] In 1923–24, when an electric tramway was completed, Surabaya extolled the existence of a modern public transportation system, which served thousands of commuters for more than four decades.[34] Unfortunately, as the city population swelled, the electric tramway did not expand to keep pace, and by the mid-1960s it was considered old-fashioned.[35] The Indonesian state company that managed it since 1949 did not have the funds to rehabilitate it. After the closure of Jakarta's electric tramway in the early 1960s, Surabaya decided to do the same and replaced the tram with public buses.[36] Not every technology that the Dutch introduced was kept and maintained after independence. The closure of Dutch electric tramways is one example of technological erasures in the postcolonial period.

The Great Depression of the 1930s forced Dutch electric companies to merge. In the end, ANIEM, NIGM (which later changed its name to OGEM), and GEBEO controlled the largest share of the electricity business. By 1938, they "accounted for 75 percent of sales in Java, and 72 percent throughout the whole

Figure 3. Hanging streetlights above Jalan Gemblongan Surabaya, ca. 1935.
Source: Photo courtesy of Leiden University Digital Collections.

of the Netherlands East Indies."[37] ANIEM was managed by the well-known trading company Maintz & Co. and operated its business mostly in Central and East Java.[38] OGEM, formerly known as NIGM, started in the gas lighting business and entered the electricity market in 1905 when it bought NIEM. In 1950, NIGM changed its name to OGEM to reflect its expanded business portfolios, although its "electricity business had outstripped the gas business as far back as 1920."[39] OGEM mainly served West Java and other cities in "the Outer Possessions."[40] GEBEO was a special venture, "capitalized jointly by the local and central governments and by a firm of managing agents also responsible for the management of ANIEM [Maintz & Co.]."[41] It served the city of Bandung and surrounding areas.

The colonial government's interests in electricity were mainly on the supply side. It recognized the huge potential for hydropower in the whole Netherlands East Indies, estimated at around 6.6 million horsepower (about 4.9 million kW) in 1930.[42] Initially, it planned to use hydroelectricity to power the state railways, but it decided to expand electricity usage for other purposes to facilitate "industrial development."[43] In 1917, the hydropower bureau of the state railways and the electrical engineering branch of Department of Government Companies combined to form the Dienst Voor Waterkracht en Electriciteit or the Hydropower and Electricity Service (a.k.a. the Service) headquartered in Bandung.[44]

Once founded, the Service began constructing hydropower plants that supplied electric power to several Javanese cities. In West Java it completed the Ubrug, Kracak, Plengan, Lamajan, and Bengkok plants. It also built the Giringan (near Madiun, East Java) and the Tes (in Bengkulu, Sumatra) hydropower plants. To manage the plants, the colonial government founded four state-owned hydropower companies (Landswaterkrachtbedrijf, LWB): (1) LWB West Java, (2) LWB Bandung Plateau, (3) LWB Madioen, and (4) LWB Benkoelen. Each was headed by an engineer and all except the last was managed from Bandung.[45] GEBEO and NIGM were two significant customers of LWB West Java.[46] It was reported that the four LWBs sold a total of 134.5 million kWh electric energy in 1938.[47]

In addition, the Dutch government in Batavia constructed a network to transmit and distribute electricity from the hydropower stations. It erected two transmission networks in the 1920s in West Java: one supplied electricity to Batavia and the other to Bandung and surrounding areas.[48] By 1924, the West Java grid began operation and the Ubrug hydropower plant supplied electricity to a suburb of Batavia called Meester Cornelis (a district in eastern Jakarta now called Jatinegara) using a 70 kV transmission line 110 km long. By

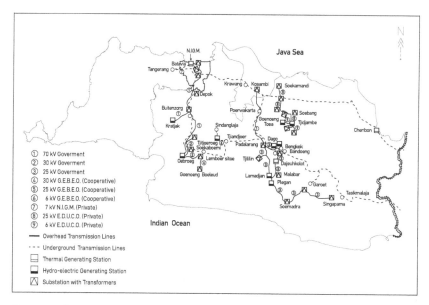

Figure 4. Electric power and transmission systems in West Java, ca. 1930.
Source: Map drawn from the Division of Commerce, *1930 Handbook of the Netherlands East-Indies.*

1930, these investments made the West Java grid to be the most developed system in the whole colony (figure 4).

Ethical Policy and Electrification

In 1901, Dutch Queen Wilhelmina made a speech in which she espoused a new approach to governing the colonies overseas. Stating that the Dutch owed their colonies a "debt of honor" for many years of Dutch prosperity, her "ethical policy" called for a renewed sense of responsibility in establishing a relationship with the local population.[49] The Dutch ethical policy, a program that mirrored the "civilizing mission" of other European colonial powers in their respective colonies, provided the sociopolitical backdrop for colonial policies that were intended to benefit the locals more, including rural electrification. Although there were some attempts to bring electricity to the rural areas, they generally fell short because the endeavors were not profitable for the Dutch companies. The government noted that there were not many electricity permits granted to businesses that wanted to electrify the villages.[50] There was evidence that one company tried to make rural electrification more affordable. ANIEM installed a transformer on a pole of an electric distribution line instead of building a costly transformer house.[51] But successful examples like this are very few and they lend support to historian Merle Ricklefs's assertion that "there was more promise than performance in Ethical policies."[52]

Still, when a remote town or area was successfully electrified, the chief electricity consumers were typically the minority European settlers. We know, for example, about the electrification of Barabai in southern Kalimantan from the written and visual account of Gerard Louwrens Tichelman, a low-ranking Binnenlandsch Bestuur (Interior Administration) official posted in Borneo (Kalimantan). He documented the progress of electrification in Barabai in his daily logbook (*dagboek*) from the day he arrived when the construction of new substation had just begun until its completion three years later. He took many photos of the substation, of the electric generators, and of the Juliana theater (named after the daughter of Queen Wilhelmina), a local cinema that received electricity from the substation.[53] Tichelman's texts and photographs, Susie Protschky writes, "reveal that electricity was being established in Barabai in the same pattern that it had followed on Java: at the convenience of a privileged few, mostly Europeans and the urban dwellers among whom they lived. The rest of the region remained immersed in darkness."[54]

The imbalance between urban and rural electricity coverage also elicited self-criticism by one of the practitioners of the electrical industry. Ing. D. W. Sparnaay, the Dutch director of a state-owned electric company, complained in 1938 about the approach of building electrical infrastructure using an expensive network construction that prevented a more even distribution of electricity. He blamed the skewed Dutch colonial energy policy, its "cardinal fault," by saying, "here, in the Indies, amidst purely an Eastern society, [we] build up an electric technology on an exclusively Western basis."[55] He pointed to the simpler and cheaper electric construction methods employed in Japan, China, Australia, and the United States and wondered, "Why we, the Dutch in the Indies . . . do not follow the example of so many . . . why do we remain so stubbornly attached to the perfectionist system of network construction? Why did the Indies have the stiffest electricity regulations imaginable?"[56]

It wasn't only technologies that were built unevenly in the Dutch East Indies. The technical education was also distributed to serve the colonial project. Sukarno recounted his experience studying at the Bandung's Technische Hogeschool (the precursor of the Institute of Technology in Bandung, ITB):

Our curriculum was geared toward a society of Dutch rule. The science I learned was [the] science of a capitalist technique; for instance, the knowledge about irrigation systems. It was not how to irrigate rice fields in the best manner. It was only about the water supply systems for sugar cane and tobacco. This was irrigation in the interest of imperialism and capitalism, irrigation not to feed the starving masses, but to fatten the plantation owners. Our instruction in road building could never benefit the population. Roads weren't engineered to be cross-jungle or interisland so our people could ride or walk better. We were taught only to plan byways along the seacoast from harbor to harbor so factories might have maximum transportation of goods and proper communication between sailing vessels. Take mathematics. No universities anywhere else taught the measure chain. Here it was taught. This is a tape 20 meters long used solely by overseers of slave labor on plantations. In sketching class, when we drafted a model town we also had to indicate the residence of the *Kabupaten*, the District Chief who watches over the slaving peasants.[57]

Even though Sukarno realized the main aim of his colonial education was to perpetuate colonial rule, he admitted, "And so it seemed that although I was to devote my entire life to crushing the colonialists' rule, I had them to thank for my education."[58] Sukarno's experience shaped his desires to use technologies, including electricity, to promote his vision of what independent Indonesia should be.

Selling Electrical Modernity in the Dutch East Indies

Dutch electric companies did not merely sell electricity in the East Indies. They also promoted electrical appliances in popular periodicals and marketed the ideas, images, lifestyles, and machines of modernity. In 1931, a monthly Dutch magazine called *Alles Electrisch in Huis en Bedrijf* (Everything Electric at Home and Business) began publication and ran until 1941.[59] *Alles Electrisch* became a popular periodical with 25,000 copies sold monthly the first year, 30,000 in the second, and even more in later years.[60] The magazine later changed its name to *Alles Electrisch in het Indische Huis en Bedrijf* (Everything Electric in the Indies House and Business) and the number of copies in circulation for each printed edition in 1936 and 1937 was 32,000.[61] ANIEM was a major sponsor of the magazine. Its logo appeared on the cover of the first six editions in 1936.[62] ANIEM's well-lit pavilion in Surabaya's annual fair graced the cover of the magazine's November 1936 issue.[63] The cover of the February 1937 issue featured ANIEM's first-prize float called "The Victory of the Light" (*De overwinning van het licht*) in Surabaya's Light Parade.[64]

Browsing the covers of the magazine, one can see that the target audience of *Alles Electrisch* was the female inhabitants of the colony, particularly white Dutch homemakers. Women models in fashionable dresses and hairstyles (even while sleeping) adorned many covers, showing them in different poses alongside household electrical appliances or with meals supposedly made using electric cooking machines.[65] Native women also appeared on covers, but usually in the role of a domestic servant (hair in a bun, head down, dressed in *kebaya* while busy ironing clothes).[66] Only when in the kitchen cooking, it seems, does the native woman wear European-style dress with a white apron covering her body.[67] In other words, photos of European women enjoying the conveniences of electric devices are juxtaposed against how native female inhabitants are supposed to use them, which is to complete household chores.

Pages are filled with articles and advertisements for all kinds of household appliances, such as electric cookers, electric irons, electric pots, electric washers, and electric air conditioners, to name a few. In one edition, the magazine extolls the model kitchen (*model-keukentje*) that "contains a fully scaled electric refrigerator, an electric stove, an electric water heater, dish washer, etc." enjoyed by "American housewives" (*Amerikaansche huisvrouwen*), which could also now be owned by Dutch women in the Indies.[68] Virtually every single edition would have "electric recipes" (*elektro recepten*) of cakes and other delicacies to be prepared with the advertised electrical appliances.

ANIEM did not just publish electricity-related articles and advertise electrical products, it also held special electrical events. For example, in the February 1937 magazine, there is an article about a series of Christmas cooking demonstrations in ANIEM's electric kitchen organized by the Association of Housewives in Surabaya. It is reported that the fourteen-day cooking shows were well attended, and the quick and clean preparation of the dishes impressed the women who had not yet used electricity to cook at home. ANIEM held the last demonstration on December 23, 1936, in a hall tailored for this purpose, where a meal for four people was cooked in less than an hour. The attendees were served snacks baked using electricity and cold drinks from an electric refrigerator while being pampered and serenaded by a Philips device playing cheerful music, "so that not only the tongue but also the ear was caressed."[69] The article claims that these demonstrations convinced many Dutch women in attendance of the advantages and convenience of electric cooking.

An attempt to sell a Philips light bulb in *Pandji Poestaka*, a Malay-language periodical published and circulated in the East Indies, seems to be an advertisement directed toward the native middleclass population. The ad's language (Malay) and image suggest this. It shows a Javanese family of three with the caption "*Terang Sebagai Siang*" (Bright as Day) gathered around a table under the illumination of a Philips light bulb: a father reading a newspaper, a mother embroidering, and their daughter reading a book. A more critical look at the ad reveals incorrect assumptions and misunderstandings of local people. Henk Maier provides an insightful analysis of a Philips' electric light bulb advertisement in the 1940 editions of *Pandji Poestaka.*[70] Of the image, Maier writes, "The picture would have difficulty persuading, or even attracting, a Javanese public—too Western in design [the daughter in the image seems to be curiously European looking], too Western in concept."[71] He comments: "[The ad] reads like perfect propaganda of a colonial order that tries to domesticate anxiety and desire; this is how all Javanese people are supposed to live: in small and peaceful nuclear families. . . . Family values, literacy, reading, smiling, and embroidering in the rhetorical light that is created by Philips—these are elements in the set of words that could be related to the forces of modernity."[72]

Philips, the Dutch company selling the electric lightbulbs, conveniently overlooked the fact that not many Javanese or other natives of the East Indies had electricity. Rudolf Mrázek quotes a Dutch source with telling statistics. In 1930, there were "76,000 natives in Java who used electricity—less than 0.2 percent of the Javanese native population. The number even decreased, to 54,000, in the next four years as the depression set in."[73] Toward the end of the decade, in 1938, "only 9 percent of the population of Java, the best-illuminated island of the Dutch colony, lived in areas where electricity was theoretically available. Merely 5 percent used it."[74] The ad, therefore, was out of touch with local realities.

Maier recounts there were four Philips light bulb ads in *Pandji Poestaka* published in the 1940s. While Philips's intention was putatively commercial, there were unintended consequences of these advertisements. Unlike *Alles Electrisch*, which used Dutch, a language accessible only to Dutch, Eurasians, and a few native elites, *Pandji Poestaka* used Malay, the lingua franca of the Dutch East Indies. This helped elevate Malay, a more egalitarian language than the hierarchical Javanese, to be readily taken up as the unifying language of the peoples in the archipelago.[75] Maier asserts, "One of the great contributions Balai Poestaka [the publisher of *Pandji Poestaka*] made to modernity, nationalism, and the concurrent feelings of transience in the Indies was the leading role it played in propagating a standard for written Malay, to be followed by all inhabitants of the Indies alike."[76] Malay formed the basis of Bahasa Indonesia, the official language of the Republic of Indonesia.[77]

Japanese Occupation and Indonesia's Independence

In early 1942, the Japanese imperial military invaded the Dutch East Indies and by March 8 had defeated the Dutch colonial government. Their aim was to gain access and control the mineral-rich archipelago to fuel their war efforts. Using the propagandist term "Greater East Asia Co-Prosperity Sphere," the Japanese claimed that their military presence in the region was to liberate

Southeast Asia from their colonial masters to create a Japanese-led East Asian bloc. The Japanese encouraged and even facilitated Indonesian nationalists to prepare themselves for eventual Indonesian independence, although they were defeated by the Allied forces before they could grant Indonesia freedom. Instead, Sukarno and Hatta proclaimed Indonesia's independence on August 17, 1945, two days after Emperor Hirohito announced the Japanese surrender.

Shortly after they landed, the Japanese military forces took over the operation of vital facilities, including the electric infrastructure. The Japanese navy controlled areas outside Java, and the army controlled Java. They divided Java into three electrification areas: Seibu Djawa Denki Djigjo Kosha in West Java, Tyubu Denki Djigjo Kosha in Central Java, Tobu Djawa Denki Djigjo Kosha in East Java.[78] The Japanese rounded up and jailed many Dutch residents, including top administrators. McCawley writes, "ANIEM's top executive, Mr. E. van Elk, was interned soon after the Japanese occupation, but the majority of the Dutch employees remained at work until January 1943 when most of the remainder were also interned."[79] One result of Dutch workers' internment was a shortage of laborers to run and maintain the electrical facilities. While Japanese civilians took over the management positions, Indonesians were asked to fill other empty spots or complete other tasks. In Surabaya, two ANIEM employees, a Dutch man named Spanjaard and an Indonesian man named Ir. R. M. Saljo, taught Indonesians the skills needed to run the power system to ensure the continuous supply of electricity.[80] In Jakarta, Indonesian workers were tasked with finishing the installation of two generators for a diesel power station in Kebon Jeruk left incomplete by the Dutch.[81]

Although the Japanese occupation in Indonesia was short, many Indonesians remember it as a brutal subjugation.[82] The Japanese military instituted a forced labor system called *romusha*, in part to mobilize labor to build new and restore damaged electrical facilities. Countless *romusha* workers were compelled to construct an electric transmission line between Ketenger and Tegal in Central Java; to dig a two-kilometer water tunnel in Baturaden in Purwokerto, Central Java, to provide additional flow of water to the Ketenger hydropower plant; to channel water from the Cilaki River to Cileunca Lake to increase the Lamajan and Plengan hydropower plants; and to construct another tunnel for the Tulungagung hydropower plant (the locals called it the Romusha Jolusutro Project).[83] In another case, hundreds of *romusha* laborers were sent to repair the Mendalan and Siman hydropower plants, which had been bombed by the Allied forces.[84]

Hatta and Sukarno had different takes on *romusha*. Hatta criticized it as cruel and institutionalized indentured servitude, and his concerns with the conditions of *romusha* prompted him to investigate and establish a relief aid organization called the Body to Help the Worker Soldier (Badan Pembantu Prajurit Pekerja). He criticized the "Japanese authorities for their treatment of these young laborers, putting forward evidence which he had collected over the previous six months to show the extent of their maltreatment."[85] Sukarno, on the other hand, sought to take advantage of the situation. Speaking to a friend shortly after the Japanese had landed in Padang in 1942, Sukarno said, "I know all about their brutality. I know of Nipponese behavior in occupied territory—but okay. I am fully prepared for a few years of this. I must rationally consider what they can do for my people. We must be grateful to the Japanese. We can use them."[86] And use them he did. Sukarno persuaded the Japanese to give military and administrative training to Indonesians. Another time, he told Hatta, "At Japanese government expense we will teach our people to be executives. To give orders, not just take them. To prepare them to be chiefs and administrators. To put the reins of government in their hands for that someday when we take over and proclaim independence."[87] Sukarno's "collaboration" with the Japanese was encapsulated in his statement: "I did not say we were cooperating with the Rising Sun. I said we were cooperating *under* the Rising Sun."[88]

Under the auspices of the Japanese and to fulfill their earlier promise to grant Indonesia's independence, the Investigating Body to Investigate the Preparation of Indonesian Independence (Badan Penyelidik Usaha-usaha Persiapan Kemerdekaan Indonesia, BPUPKI) was established on April 29, 1945. BPUPKI held its first session May 29 to June 1, 1945. Hatta biographer Mavis Rose wrote, "During the session the issue of whether Indonesia should be an Islamic state was debated. Hatta proposed the establishment of a state which separated the affairs of government from religious affairs."[89] On June 1, Sukarno gave his famous speech on Pancasila, his proposed state ideology for an independent Indonesia. The five principles in the order he introduced them were: *kebangsaan* (nationalism), *internasionalisme* or *perikemanusian* (internationalism or humanitarianism), *mufakat* (consensus), *kesejahteraan sosial* (social welfare), and *ketuhanan* (belief in God).[90] Sukarno's Pancasila was later adopted as the country's founding ideology and the five principles, in modified order, were incorporated into the preamble of the country's 1945 Constitution.

After BPUPKI completed its work, in July 1945 the Committee for the Preparation of Indonesian Independence (Panitia Persiapan Kemerdekaan Indonesia, PPKI) was established. Unlike BPUPKI, PPKI had better representation of people from outside Java, something Hatta welcomed, knowing that their support would be valuable.[91] After the bombings of Hiroshima and Nagasaki in Japan, Hatta, Sukarno, and Radjiman Wedyodiningrat (an older and re-spected member of PPKI) were sent to meet a representative from the Japanese government in Vietnam. On August 9, the three men were flown to Saigon with a stopover in Singapore. It then took them three days to reach Dalat, where they finally met Field Marshal Hisaichi Terauchi, the top Japanese military commander in Southeast Asia. Hatta recounted in his memoirs that Terauchi gave a short speech that basically said the Japanese government decided to grant Indonesia independence. Upon hearing this, Hatta was ecstatic because Terauchi made the announcement on August 12, his birthday. He wrote: "In my most inner heart I consider Indonesian independence as a gift to me for my years of struggle for Indonesia's freedom."[92]

Upon their return to Indonesia, Sukarno and Hatta followed international events closely and worked to resist mounting pressure by Indonesian youths (*pemuda*) who were demanding they declare independence as soon as possible. Sjahrir, one youth leader, argued that if they proclaimed independence soon, they would seize the opportunity from Japan instead of the Allies, who would most likely take over the administration of the region. Even though they agreed with Sjahrir, Sukarno and Hatta proceeded cautiously and preferred to work under the auspices of PPKI.[93] *Pemudas'* impatience reached a point of zeal when, on the morning of August 16, they kidnapped Hatta and Sukarno, along with Sukarno's wife and their baby son. Sukarno recalled that when they came to his house to take him, they shouted excitedly: "The moment is now. Now. Now is when Japanese morale is low and their spirit crushed. Now they are already broken. Now is when we must take arms!"[94] Refusing the *pemudas'* call to action, Sukarno and Hatta were taken to Rengasdenklok, a military barracks on the outskirts of Jakarta. PPKI was to hold a meeting that morning to discuss a proc-lamation text but was enraged upon learning Sukarno was not in attendance.[95] The *pemudas* finally decided to take the leaders back to Jakarta later that night.

Hatta tried to rearrange the canceled PPKI meeting at the Des Indes Hotel but was unable to do so because the hotel refused to hold gatherings past 10 p.m., which had been part of its longstanding regulations. Instead, Hatta, Sukarno, several *pemuda* representatives, and PPKI delegates met at the house of Admiral Maeda, a high-ranking Japanese military officer who sympathized with the Indonesians' desire for independence.[96] After a short text of the proc-lamation was drafted, agreed to, and signed by Sukarno and Hatta, they de-cided to read it the following morning. On August 17, Sukarno and Hatta proclaimed Indonesia's independence in a small ceremony at Sukarno's home in Jakarta. The event did not mark the end of the struggle for liberation, but the beginning of a revolutionary period.

The next day, PPKI worked to elect the country's executive leaders (Sukarno and Hatta were unanimously voted as the country's first president and vice president, respectively) and draft the country's constitution. The final document, written hastily given the emergency nature of the sociopolitical conditions, included a preamble that contains the Pancasila principles and a total of thirty-seven articles outlining the structure, characteristics, and ideals of the new nation. Article 33 bears the imprint of Hatta's socioeconomic thoughts and spells out the desire to achieve social welfare. Article 33 has three clauses that influenced the conduct of Indonesia's electricity business. The first establishes the underlying structure of the nation's economy as a welfare state, and the second reads: "Branches of production that are vital to the state and govern the livelihoods of the people are controlled by the state." The third: "The earth and water and the natural resources contained therein are controlled by the state and used for the greatest prosperity of the people." This article, coupled with the fifth Pancasila principle, made up the country's social justice ideals.

Following the proclamation of independence in August 1945, Indonesia entered a revolutionary period. After the Japanese surrender, the Netherlands with the help of the Allied forces returned to reclaim their former colony. Battles to defend the newly independent republic ensued, and the fledging republican army fought two major Dutch military offensives euphemistically called "police actions" (*politionele acties*). The first occurred in mid-1947, and the second was from December 1948 to January 1949. Indonesian utility workers formed civilian and paramilitary units with names such as the Indonesian Electricity and Gas Labor Force (Barisan Boeroeh Listrik dan Gas Indonesia) and the Indonesian Electricity and Gas Worker Troops (Lasjkar Boeroeh Listrik dan Gas Indonesia) to fight alongside the republican army.[97]

Sukarno founded the Office of Gas and Electricity on October 27, 1945, to take over and manage the electric facilities vacated by the Japanese. He appointed Ir. M. A. Safwan to be in charge. The office had four regional branches in Java and two branches outside Java, one in South Sumatra and another one in Aceh. Despite the office's existence, expansion of electrical facilities slowed to a halt. In fact, there was a negative growth rate because some facilities were deliberately destroyed to prevent being taken over by the Netherlands Indies Civilian Administration, a semi-military organization set up to administer recaptured areas of the East Indies.[98] The revolutionary period finally ended with the signing of accords at the Dutch–Indonesian Round Table Conference in which the Netherlands officially recognized Indonesia's sovereignty on December 27, 1949.

Nationalizing the Dutch Utilities Companies

In 1950, with the war of independence behind them, Indonesian leaders moved to consolidate their government and take control of vital industries. Whereas in December 1949, the Round Table Conference dictated the creation of a federal government called Republik Indonesia Serikat or the United States of Indonesia, on August 17, 1950, the government dissolved it and united the states under a unitary republic. The 1950 provisional constitution relegated the president to a head of state and the government to be run by a cabinet headed by a prime minister. The hope was that a newly elected legislature would draft a new constitution. However, as we will see later, the new constitution never materialized.

On October 25, 1950, Kobarsjih, a labor activist, and six colleagues filed a motion in the Indonesian parliament to nationalize all Dutch electrical companies so they would be included in the 1951 national budget.[99] The Wilopo cabinet finally carried out Kobarsjih's motion on December 23, 1952, and nationalized (on paper) all Dutch electricity companies. Gas corporations were not nationalized until September 2, 1953, by the Ali Sastroamidjojo cabinet and then legalized by a presidential decree, retroactively starting on December 23, 1952.[100]

In September 1953, the government began implementing the nationalization of smaller Dutch electric companies such as N.V. Electriciteit Maatschappij Ambon and N.V. Electriciteit Maatschappij Balik Papan.[101] The takeover of bigger companies followed. OGEM was nationalized in 1954, and their facilities in Jakarta and Cirebon were renamed State Corporation for Electric Power Distribution (Perusahaan Negara Untuk Distribusi Tenaga Listrik) led by Ir. Soedoro.[102] On November 1, 1954, the government took over ANIEM's Central and East Java facilities and the rest of its subsidiaries when their concessions expired.[103]

By the end of 1954 most Dutch electric companies in Java had been nationalized, but others outside Java were still run by the Dutch. Kobarsjih urged the newly installed Boerhanoedin Harahap cabinet to nationalize the remaining private enterprises by the end of 1955, suggesting that nationalization could lead to lowering the deficit in the state budget.[104] Prime Minister Harahap rejected this argument, showing that the already nationalized companies "showed losses running at the rate of Rp 20 million annually" instead of turning a profit.[105] According to John O. Sutter, the debates on Kobarsjih's motion in parliament and the drawn-out process of nationalizing the Dutch companies do not indicate that the political climate was opposed to nationalization. Rather, it was against the timing of nationalization. The "radical nationalists and ultra-Marxists," Kobarsjih and his friends, wanted to nationalize immediately, but moderate members of the legislature, as well as government bureaucrats, wanted to nationalize after Indonesia had acquired more funds.[106]

In 1957, a turn of events sped up the nationalization effort. Western New Guinea (West Papua) was part of Holland's colony and thus understood to be a part of the new Republic of Indonesia. The Dutch, however, maintained control of it and insisted on keeping it during the Round Table Conference. Indonesian leaders expected the Dutch government to eventually transfer the region in the early 1950s, but the Dutch resisted, and after failed negotiations, Indonesia took matters into its own hands. In 1957, it seized all Dutch corporations and expelled Dutch nationals, and in 1960 cut diplomatic ties with the Netherlands.[107] In 1958 Sukarno issued Government Regulation No. 23 to put all Dutch companies under Indonesian control; by the end of the year, the legislature ratified this decision and passed the Nationalization Bill.[108]

Initially, the Indonesian army took charge of the seized Dutch companies but handed them over to civilian control later. In 1960, the government issued Government Regulation No. 19, which paved the way for creating the General Management Board of the State Electricity Company (Badan Pimpinan Umum Perusahaan Listrik Negara, BPUPLN). McCawley writes that the establishment of BPUPLN was an important event that marked "the end of the transition phase to full nationalization, which had in effect been taking place for almost a decade and was the first attempt to lay down a permanent set of basic ground rules and an organizational structure."[109] Because BPUPLN managed all the nationalized Dutch utility companies, it handled gas and electricity. Sukarno broke up BPUPLN in 1965, and two separate companies were formed: the State Gas Company (Perusahaan Gas Negara, PGN) and the State Electricity Company (Perusahaan Umum Listrik Negara, PLN).

Electricity and Sukarno's Vision

After nationalizing all the Dutch utility companies in 1958, Sukarno sought to consolidate his power in 1959. He used Pancasila as his rhetorical centerpiece to articulate a vision of a prosperous and planned nation, in which electrification would play a crucial role. In 1955, Indonesia held its first general elections on September 29 to elect 260 people's representatives to the People's Representative Council (Dewan Perwakilan Rakyat, DPR), and on December 15 to elect 520 members of the Constituent Assembly (Konstituante), a body created to formulate a new constitution for Indonesia.[110] The general elections were a success and considered free and fair, and elected members of the DPR were inaugurated on March 25, 1956. The Konstituante members were inaugurated on November 9 and 10, 1956.[111] After working for about two and a half years, however, the Konstituante reached a stalemate. Growing impatient of the

Konstituante's impasse, Sukarno decreed a return to the 1945 Constitution on July 5, 1959.

On July 22, 1959, the government issued four decisions to follow up the July 5 decree, one of which was the creation of the National Planning Council (Dewan Perantjang Nasional, Depernas), a new body tasked to draw up the country's development agenda.[112] In Sukarno's mind, to accomplish the objective of a "just and prosperous society, a society in which every single citizen can live prosperously, a society without oppression, and a society without human exploitation, a society that provides happiness to all of the Indonesian people from Sabang until Merauke," Indonesia needed systematic development planning.[113] Depernas was tasked with conceiving this important plan, which Sukarno dubbed the "Development of a Pancasila Society" (Pembangunan Masjarakat Pantjasila), linking national development to state ideology.[114]

On August 17, 1959, Sukarno delivered his Independence Day speech titled "The Rediscovery of Our Revolution," in which he introduced his new sociopolitical economic agenda, known widely by its Indonesian acronym Manipol USDEK.[115] Sukarno used every opportunity to promote the Manipol USDEK program, including during a commemoration of the Fifteenth National Gas and Electricity Day. In his speech on this special occasion, October 27, 1960, he urged Indonesians to transform from a "water-minded" nation, meaning an agricultural country, to an "electricity-minded" one, an industrialized state. Connecting electricity with socialism in a clear reference to Lenin's famous phrase, "Communism is Soviet power plus the electrification of the whole country,"[116] Sukarno said, "Electricity is very important to our life as a nation, and it is especially very important in our life as a nation aiming at socialism. . . . It is my wish and my desire that we should also become electricity minded, because socialism is not possible without electricity."[117] Sukarno explicitly linked his sociopolitical aspirations with electricity, essentially claiming that without the new energy technology, the new nation's dreams could not be fulfilled. He acknowledged the importance of agriculture, for "man cannot live without food and drink and for those we need water," but he continued, "next to irrigation we now need industrialization and other things also. In these other fields we more and more realize the need for electricity."[118] Before 1960 there were efforts to industrialize, but electrification provided a powerful way to articulate industrialization as a central program for state-led socialist development.[119]

To this end, the Sukarno government installed electric generators in the rural areas with technical aid from the US International Cooperation Administration or ICA (precursor to USAID) and the government of Czechoslova-

Table 2. Distribution of diesel power plants from
the United States and Czechoslovakia

Location	Number of Cities	Total Capacity (kW)
Sumatra	27	16,800
Java	9	3,640
Nusa Tenggara	8	3,640
Kalimantan	18	9,154
Sulawesi	20	4,926
West Irian	7	1,540
Total	89	39,700

kia. Early reports show the ICA was to provide diesel generators in forty-one cities and the Czechoslovakian government in forty-eight cities (table 2).[120] Later reports indicate that ICA helped install diesel power plants in forty areas in Sumatra and Kalimantan. The Czechoslovakian generators were installed in fifty-four sites, mostly in eastern Indonesia. PLN also bought small-scale German-made diesel generators ranging between 150 and 250 kW.[121] McCawley writes that these three schemes were employed to appease "increasing dissatisfaction in the Outer Islands," where a series of rebellions occurred between 1957 and 1958.[122] That may be the case, but the Indonesian government faced logistical challenges setting up these power stations. Maintaining them later was not easy either because the machines were sourced from three different countries. Procuring replacement parts proved difficult. Many of these diesel power plants, especially outside Java, could not be fixed once broken.[123]

There were several hydropower projects carried out in the 1960s. Depernas's plan included constructing three plants in West Java, eight in Central and East Java, two in Sumatra, one in Kalimantan, and one in Nusa Tenggara. Although begun before Depernas was formed, the most notable project was the Jatiluhur Multipurpose Dam, which was built for irrigation, flood control, and water and electricity supply for Jakarta. Sukarno prioritized the completion of this megaproject over other hydropower plants.[124] Later a separate state-owned company was founded to operate the dam and sell the electricity to PLN. A 150 kV transmission line delivered electricity from the Jatiluhur hydropower plant to Bandung and Jakarta.

Electrical projects energized the nation, and in the case of the Fourth Asian Games, they literally energized Indonesia's debut as a host for international sporting events. After winning a bid to organize the games in Jakarta in 1962, Sukarno, a trained engineer, ordered the construction of several new facilities: a new sports complex, a new hotel, a new press house, a new boulevard with a cloverleaf bridge, a new welcome monument in the center of the city, and a new television station. To supply electricity to these new buildings, two new power plants (the Tanjung Priok steam power plant and the Kebayoran diesel power plant), a new substation in Angke, and high-voltage transmission lines were erected. In addition, the Kemayoran airport and telecommunications system were modernized. Street lighting along Jakarta's thoroughfares were upgraded, and other buildings were touched up.

Some of the Asian Games projects introduced new construction techniques to Indonesian engineers or facilitated the invention of new ones. For example, the Semanggi cloverleaf bridge was built using the new construction method of prestressed concrete, introduced in Indonesia for the first time with this project.[125] The new fourteen-story Hotel Indonesia was one of the first skyscrapers in the city. The TVRI, which continuously broadcast the Asian Games from August 24 until September 12, 1962, was established in a mere ten months.[126]

Perhaps the most notable infrastructure breakthrough was the invention of the "chicken feet foundation" (*pondasi cakar ayam*), a stable concrete foundation for swampy lands. PLN engineers faced the challenging task of building seven transmission towers to bring electricity from the Tanjung Priok power plant in northern Jakarta to the Senayan sports complex in Central Jakarta. In 1961, Dr. Sedijatmo and his team managed to build the first two transmission towers using a conventional foundation design that was both costly and time-consuming. Sedijatmo came up with a new foundation design with flat horizontal concrete supported by vertical cylindrical concrete underneath, allowing the whole setup to "grip" the mushy soil and create a stable foundation. This design is much like the way chicken feet support the bird's body weight on marshy lands. The patented invention found wide use for laying out strong and stable foundations on boggy lands for buildings, roads, and runways.[127] Sedijatmo was honored decades later when the toll road from Indonesia's new Soekarno-Hatta International Airport in Cengkareng to the city center was named after him.

The successful completion of these significant projects boosted the confidence of the Indonesian engineering community. An editorial of a national engineering journal wrote that accomplishing the projects "had a huge psychological impact, namely: it makes us aware of the Indonesian nation's capabilities and capacities and lay a strong foundation for a sense of national pride."[128] Their pride was well earned through accomplishments both technical and managerial. Not only did Indonesian engineers manage to build all the facilities, but their supervision and management ensured the punctual completion of the projects. It helped that they worked in a conducive atmosphere. Residents of Jakarta had "Asian Games fever" and were very supportive of the projects.[129]

Conclusion

The late colonial, revolutionary, and postcolonial periods in Indonesia were progressively built on and powered by the move toward more electricity coverage. While electrification motives and players differed in each period, electricity was never simply about illuminating new areas. Sociopolitical and economic considerations shaped electrification programs, and electrification influenced the social, political, and economic conditions in each period.

The Dutch introduced electricity in the East Indies in the late nineteenth century. The resulting systems made electricity available in many urban areas in Java and other islands. Dutch government buildings, homes, businesses, and extractive enterprises benefited greatly from the new energy technology, and private companies sold electrical modernity to European inhabitants in the forms of stories, images, and appliances advertised in popular publications. The efforts of the Dutch to electrify its largest overseas colony made Netherlands East Indies towns some of most electrified areas in the archipelago. However, access to electricity and other technologies fomented nationalist sentiments among natives, especially those who studied in higher learning institutions setup in the colony and the metropole. They observed that while many Dutch and other Europeans enjoyed electricity, the technology was out of reach for many natives. The unequal distribution of the electrical system shaped their thinking about how electricity and other commodities should be provided in an independent Indonesia.

During the Japanese occupation, electrification was mainly geared toward supporting the Japanese war efforts. However, during this time many Indonesians learned technical and managerial skills in the electricity business and other enterprises, knowledge used widely once independence was proclaimed. After independence, the revolutionary period saw attempts to defend the proclamation of independence. During this time (1945–49), electrification in the country saw a negative expansion rate. It was not until the 1960s that the electrification rate picked up again, spurred by Depernas's development plan and the Fourth Asian Games.

As I have argued, electricity introduced in the Dutch East Indies became more than just a commodity enjoyed by the select few inhabitants of the colony.

In postindependence Indonesia it was transformed into an important technology in the new state's desires for unity, independence, social justice, and modernization. As we will see in the next chapter, electrification had to take a back seat during the political turmoil that led to a transfer of power to Soeharto in the second half of the 1960s until Soeharto had consolidated his power and started his own development agenda in 1969.

The New Order's Patrimonial Technopolitics

The Sukarno government was replaced by the Soeharto regime in the latter half of the 1960s. After consolidating his power and establishing a new regime, Soeharto sought to develop Indonesia's countryside, and rural electrification was a crucial component of the village development agenda. The Soeharto government's stated motivations to electrify rural areas were to achieve social welfare in the villages and social justice in the country. The regime hoped that electricity would improve villagers' socioeconomic conditions and reduce the rural–urban gap.

I argue that although it was touted to improve villagers' socioeconomic conditions, Soeharto's rural electrification program had a political dimension. Electrifying rural areas served the alternative purpose of securing votes from rural people in the general elections. Through a practice I call patrimonial technopolitics, or using technology to disburse patronage for political ends, the Soeharto regime brought electricity to the villages to win and retain political support from those who lived in the countryside. It did so by extending PLN's transmission lines to and constructing diesel-fueled power plants for the villages. In some cases, particularly on the eve of a general election, Soeharto even gave rural communities free electric generators so they could build a diesel power station. He donated several electric generators to a few West Javan villages in 1976, which the local government could use to electrify twenty villages.[1]

In addition, Soeharto dispatched his cabinet ministers to preside over village electrification inauguration ceremonies to send the important message that his government made modern amenities such as electricity possible. In return, they were asked to elect the government's political party, Golkar, in the general elections. This way, Golkar representatives could again nominate and reelect Soeharto as president. Soeharto's scheme of distributing material benefits using electricity to the populace clarifies that his rule did not rely solely on repression and fear, as some scholars have argued.[2] Rather, his rule also depended on technopolitical patronage and an implicit quid pro quo arrangement with the population: their votes in return for the government's largesse. Although PLN leaders disagreed with Soeharto's attempts to politicize village electrification, they did not oppose his attempts openly. Rather, they worked within the structural constraints and offered expertise to help electrify villages with the firm belief that electricity would improve the villagers' socioeconomic conditions.

The Rise of the New Order

Soeharto's New Order government came into power following events that came to be known as the September 30th Movement (also known as Gestapu for its Indonesian contraction, Gerakan September Tigapuluh).[3] On the evening of September 30, 1965, six army generals and a lieutenant were abducted and killed by members of the presidential guard unit Tjakrabirawa, led by Lieutenant Colonel Untung. On the morning of October 1, Untung and his men occupied Medan Merdeka Square in central Jakarta. They seized the main radio station to broadcast a message that their actions were preemptive measures taken to prevent an attempted coup by the so-called Council of Generals (consisting of the kidnapped generals) against Sukarno.

Major General Soeharto, a relatively unknown officer who was not on the hit list, later that day led his Army Strategic Reserve Command (Komando Strategis Angkatan Darat) troops to regain control of the situation. Soeharto's soldiers managed to take over Medan Merdeka Square and the radio station by the evening of October 1. Historian Merle Ricklefs wrote, "At 9 p.m. Soeharto announced over the radio that six generals had been kidnapped by counter-revolutionaries but that he was now in control of the army and would crush the 30 September Movement and safeguard Sukarno."[4] The elite army para-commando regiment were later ordered to surround the Halim Air Force Base where, the remaining movement's soldiers were concentrated and after "some skirmishes, the air force commander there ordered a ceasefire. The coup was over in Jakarta" by October 2.[5] The next day, President Sukarno, who sympathized with and had the support of the Indonesian Communist Party (Partai Komunis Indonesia, PKI), issued an emergency order authorizing Soeharto to restore order. Soeharto followed up by forming the Operational Command for the Restoration of Security and Order (Kopkamtib).[6] Soeharto ordered Kopkamtib soldiers to hunt down and capture the remnants of the movement's troops and members of PKI, whom Soeharto blamed as the mastermind of the movement.

On March 11, 1966, Soeharto received broader authority to restore order in a letter signed by Sukarno. Despite Sukarno's protest, Soeharto treated the letter as a legal document for the transfer of power.[7] Using the authority of the letter, Soeharto and his troops moved to completely crush the PKI. He decreed the political party and its mass organizations illegal on March 12, and in the months that followed, he launched an anticommunist purge. Aided by religious vigilante groups in certain areas of Indonesia, the army hunted down and killed members and alleged sympathizers of the PKI, mostly in Java and Bali, but also in a few other islands. Because of lack of reliable data, the estimates of the number of victims vary widely from "78,000 to two million" people murdered.[8]

Following the March 11 letter's issuance, Soeharto sidelined Sukarno, demoted him as a figurehead, and put him under house arrest until his death on June 21, 1970. Three years before Sukarno died, on March 12, 1967, Soeharto was named acting president by the Provisional People's Consultative Assembly (Majelis Permusyawaratan Rakyat Sementara, MPRS); the same assembly appointed him president on March 27, 1968. Soeharto finally succeeded in wresting power from Sukarno and began a regime he called the New Order (Orde Baru) to distinguish it from his predecessor's era, which he called the Old Order (Orde Lama).

The New Order's official history on the Gestapu affair has been met with skepticism by many academics who have offered different theories on the events. For example, Hermawan Sulistyo wrote, "The first problem with this 'PKI-as-mastermind' theory is that its proponents were the winning parties—military officers and government bureaucrats. Much of the supporting material appeared very late in the reconstruction of Gestapu, when the new regime started to fear the sensitivity of the issue and closed the door to open discussion."[9] Sulistyo adds that there are four other interpretations of the events. They include Sukarno as mastermind, Soeharto as mastermind, the Indonesian army intelligence aided by U.S. and Chinese intelligence agencies as actors behind the plot, and an internal conflict within the Indonesian army.[10] Sulistyo finds holes in all interpretations except the last one. Nonetheless, he admits that "no interpretation of the September 30 Movement is entirely satisfactory" and that this dark episode will continue to cast a long shadow on Indonesia's future generations.[11]

The New Order's Development Ideology

After gaining the presidency, Soeharto sought to maintain his grip on power by legitimizing his rule through a national development agenda that aimed to transform Indonesia into a "modern, just and prosperous society," a repeat of Sukarno's goals but framed and achieved differently.[12] Soeharto based his development plan rhetorically on the 1945 Constitution and Pancasila, formulated by

Sukarno in a speech delivered on June 1, 1945.[13] The five principles of Pancasila are (1) belief in one God, (2) just and civilized humanity, (3) Indonesian unity, (4) democracy guided by the wise and consensus deliberations among representatives, and (5) social justice for all Indonesians.

Under Soeharto, Pancasila became the "operational ideology" of the state, and the New Order regime proclaimed Indonesia "a *Pancasila State*, in which every aspect of daily life would be interpreted and conducted on the principles of Pancasila and the 1945 Constitution."[14] To achieve this objective, the New Order regime rolled out massive indoctrination efforts to inculcate Pancasila principles to the masses starting in 1978. It did so through two-week long courses widely known as P4 (Pedoman Penghayatan dan Pengamalan Pancasila, Guidelines for Internalizing and Practicing Pancasila). The scope of Pancasila inculcation in Indonesian society during the New Order was extensive. Initially, Soeharto mandated state employees and military personnel to take the course.[15] The program slowly expanded to require college students, academics, teachers, professionals, farmers, fishermen, and laborers to complete the course. In September 1982, Hari Suharto, head of the agency created to institutionalize P4 courses called Badan Pembinaan Pendidikan Pelaksanaan Pedoman Penghayatan dan Pengamalan Pancasila or better known as BP-7 (Education Development Agency for the Implementation of Guidelines for Internalizing and Practicing Pancasila), tried out the course materials on some prisoners in the Lowokwaru Penitentiary in Malang.[16] Later, prisoners incarcerated elsewhere also received training in the P4 courses.[17] Finally, the Soeharto regime passed Law No. 3 of 1985 mandating all organizations, including the three political parties in general elections between 1977 and 1997, to hold Pancasila as their sole ideology.

Pancasila became pervasive in the New Order modernizing project and functioned as an adjective for the kind of politics, labor relations, economy, and morality the New Order claimed to be operating. Hence, the New Order promoted Pancasila democracy, Pancasila industrial relationship, Pancasila economy, and Pancasila morality. Although these terms weren't always clearly defined, they were supposed to embody the Pancasila ideals. Seung-Won Song writes that the New Order's ideal of a Pancasila democracy seems to be about instilling "civic values" in the masses "as the antithesis of primordial ties," which was essentially to recondition the diverse populations and the political parties representing them into a more homogeneous people and political parties, respectively.[18] In other words, Pancasila democracy was to serve the New Order's agenda of national unity and political stability. Likewise, the New Order's understanding of the Pancasila industrial relationship (formerly called Pancasila labor relations) centered around tamed and controlled organized labor to create harmony and order in industrial relationships.[19] A Pancasila economy expressed that the "three pillars of economy [government-owned enterprises, private businesses, and cooperatives] should work at the same level (*sejajar, setaraf, setingkat*)."[20] Pancasila morality was taught in schools across the country through a newly invented subject known as Pendidikan Moral Pancasila or Pancasila moral education. The government-issued textbooks taught school children about Pancasila-based morality values, which were an elaboration of the five principles translated into forty-five moral codes, with the number forty-five signifying the year Indonesia proclaimed its independence in 1945.[21]

Despite massive indoctrination, Pancasila was a contested ideology. Most Indonesians initially bought the idea of the Pancasila principles, and the New Order managed to establish Indonesia as a "Pancasila state" by the mid-1980s.[22] In fact, many PLN employees, as we will see in chapter 3, promoted electricity and electrification using the language of state ideology to get support from the government and buy-in from the people. But by the end of the Soeharto era in 1998, many Indonesians came to loath the state ideology because it was deemed a cover for Soeharto's authoritarian rule.[23] Some of the expressed ideals of Pancasila remained merely words on paper. The touted ideals of a Pancasila economy to have state-owned companies, private corporations, and cooperatives working together to economically develop the nation were barely realized in the electricity sector. Because of the favor given to the state power company, private companies and cooperatives could never break the dominance of PLN. As we will see, three electric cooperatives established in the New Order ended up bankrupt and their assets and customers transferred over to PLN (chapter 6).

Besides Pancasila, the other important keyword for the New Order government was *pembangunan* (development).[24] In Soeharto's mind, his New Order government's priorities were to develop the country because growing the economy and lifting millions of people out of poverty would be the sources of his legitimacy to rule. His hope was that using money and material benefits would get citizens to forget or accept the violent nature of his regime's rise. Thus, many Soeharto government programs were carried out in the name of *pembangunan*. Countless speeches made by government officials tied the regime to development; *pembangunan* also became one of the key terms of the New Order's development-speak. For example, the first cabinet that Soeharto formed in June 1968 was called the First Development Cabinet (Kabinet Pembangunan Pertama). One of the civil awards bestowed by the government on civil servants (including PLN employees) was called the Satyalancana Pembangunan (Development Medal). The New Order regime carried out five-year development plans (REPELITA). In the Pancasila moral education textbooks that school children were compelled to learn, Soeharto was portrayed as the head of a family who worked justly to bring welfare to the entire family.[25] It was no surprise that most Indonesians readily accepted it when Soeharto was conferred the title "Father of Development" (Bapak Pembangunan) by the People's Consultative Assembly in 1983. *Pembangunan*, in short, became the justification for his regime's existence and the legitimacy to rule.

Moreover, Soeharto's fondness of Javanese philosophy infused his leadership style and, to a large extent, shaped the patrimonial character of the New Order state. In his 1989 autobiography, he narrates and interprets major life events through the lens of Javanese philosophy and peppers it throughout with Javanese sayings.[26] One Javanese adage he claims to have lived by is *mikul dhuwur mendhem jero* (literally, "raising high, burying deeply," meaning: one needs to maintain one's parents' good names and suppress their weaknesses).[27] As the "Father of Development," Soeharto considered himself the nation's patriarch who worked steadily to make Indonesia a prosperous country. Consequently, his patriarchal leadership style mirrors the relationship of a Javanese father and his children. Just as good Javanese children are taught to show reverence for their father, Indonesian citizens as "children" of the nation must show respect to the "father" of the nation who ostensibly knew what was best for them. In this regard, Soeharto expected his "children" to maintain his good name and bury his shortcomings.

The New Order political climate and bureaucratic mechanism did not encourage people in village administrations to send their input back up the chain of bureaucracy.[28] Because of the "father knows best" mentality, villagers were rarely enrolled in the New Order's development projects. Instead, development projects were "handed out" to them in return for their acquiescence to the regime's sociopolitical order. As a result, the New Order government distributed development benefits and, using PLN as a conduit, brought electricity to rural areas.

New Order's Village Development

At the time Soeharto began his New Order regime, around eight out of ten Indonesians lived in rural areas. Soeharto claimed that his rural roots made him sensitive to the poor lives of villagers and motivated him to modernize the countryside.[29] What he didn't admit was that he knew that Indonesia's rural population could be an asset or a liability, depending on how his regime treated them. For an army general who rose to power by crushing the PKI, once a legitimate political party with a strong base in the countryside, Soeharto understood that he needed to pay attention to the villagers' welfare, lest they rebel. Ali Moertopo, one of his closest and most influential aides, articulated this rationale explicitly: "Poverty represents a latent danger and from the security angle represents a primordial factor for the vulnerability of the people against disturbances within and without."[30] Because of this, Moertopo asserted, "[Indonesia's] national development can only be successful if it is based on rural development."[31] To this end, Soeharto ensured that he found strong support for his village development project from his most important cabinet ministers.

In September 1971, Soeharto reshuffled his first cabinet to replace four ministers and add two new ones. Four of the six newly appointed technocrats (Mohammad Sadli, Subroto, Widjojo Nitisastro, and Emil Salim) along with Ali Wardhana—appointed the Minister of Finance by Soeharto in 1968—came to be known as the "Berkeley Mafia" after the University of California, Berkeley, where they all received advanced training in economics.[32] These men became highly influential technocrats in the New Order.[33] Following internal debate and deliberation, the group recommended a development agenda focusing on the rural areas. Subroto recounted this episode:

> The idea of developing the agricultural sector first was discussed intensively among the five economic technocrats. A popular model of development was the Indian model which from the beginning emphasised the development of heavy industry. Our emphasis, however, was to begin by developing the rural sector. Fortunately, in promoting this idea we had a very sympathetic ear from President Soeharto because of his background. Our simple model was based on the assumption that an "upward spiral movement" would result from increased effective demand by the agricultural sector and from the increased supply of agricultural inputs to stimulate the growth of the industrial sector. The industrial sector would make use of the agricultural inputs to produce outputs which would in turn be used by the agricultural sector as inputs.[34]

Thus, Soeharto's priorities to improve the socioeconomic conditions of the villagers had the support of his highly trained economists.

To develop Indonesia's then estimated 60,000 villages,[35] the Soeharto government categorized them into one of three types according to their stage of development: a *swadaya* (self-attempting) village was the least developed, a *swakarya* (self-working) village was somewhere in the middle of transition, and a *swasembada* (self-supporting) village was the most developed. The New Order used several factors, such as the villagers' way of life, educational and economic levels, and adoption and use of technology to determine the village level. Thus, in a *swadaya* village, people were still thought to be "traditional," and local customs strongly governed their relationships. Their livelihood was typically homogeneous and only to subsist. Less than a third of the population had primary school education and the annual per capita income was under Rp 12,000. Village infrastructure was lacking and communication with the outside world was limited. In a *swakarya* village, the local customs were undergoing a transition from outside influences, and people's livelihoods were more diversified. Between 30 and 60 percent of its population had completed primary education, and the annual per capita income was around Rp 12,000. In a *swasembada* village, people earned their living in a variety of occupations. More than 60 percent of the population had completed primary education, and the annual per capita income was more than Rp 17,500. Local customs did not strongly bind people's relationships. Their adoption of new technology was high, and adequate infrastructures (e.g., roads, irrigation systems, schools, health centers, and electricity) were in place.[36]

To quantify the qualitative description of the three village types, the research and development arm of the Ministry of Education and Culture wrote a document listing the criteria by which to evaluate a village's stage of development and guidelines for assigning a numerical value to each criterion. The first category of criteria considered a village's human capital, its natural resources, and its distance from and accessibility to the provincial capital and other towns. The second category considered variables such as commodities produced by the village, villagers' livelihoods, and their levels of education. The third assessment includes sociocultural characteristics of the village such as belief systems, village institutions, cooperation among villages, and village's facilities. When the numbers are tallied up, villages that scored seven to eleven were categorized as *swadaya* villages, twelve to sixteen *swakarya* villages, and seventeen to twenty-one *swasembada* villages.[37]

Although the three village types were too tidy and linear (many villages had hybrid characteristics and did not neatly fit the classifications despite the quantitative assessments), they provided the New Order government with a language and a plan for its village modernization program. One of the main objectives for each REPELITA development agenda was to transform as many lower-ranked villages as possible to the next level and transform all into *swasembada* villages by 2000.[38]

Initially, the village improvement program consisted mainly of rolling out agricultural intensification projects. The top two were called the "Mass Guidance" (Bimbingan Massal, Bimas) and "Mass Intensification" (Intensifikasi Massal).[39] Through these projects, farmers were free to sell their rice to any buyers, although special government cooperatives would purchase their rice at a guaranteed minimum price, ensuring a minimum income. However, when the

Soeharto government evaluated its overall village development program after two successive Five-Year Development (Pembangunan Lima Tahun, PELITA) periods, it was disappointed to find it had not transformed as many villages into *swasembada* villages as it had hoped. At the end of the first PELITA on March 31, 1974, there were 3 percent *swasembada*, 53 percent *swakarya*, and 44 percent *swadaya* villages. By the end of the second PELITA on March 31, 1979, there were 9.2 percent *swasembada*, 50.9 percent *swakarya*, and 39.9 percent *swadaya* villages.[40] In other words, after ten years, the bulk of the villages still fell into the lower categories.

Because its goal fell short, the Soeharto government began to systematize its village development endeavors. Initially, during the first two PELITAs, Soeharto's Three Principles of Development (Trilogi Pembangunan) aimed to sequentially (1) secure national stability, (2) increase economic growth, and (3) equalize the benefits of development. Starting in the third PELITA in April 1979, Soeharto reversed the second and third goals. The objective was to achieve equality and social justice across the archipelago by transforming more villages into *swasembada* villages. Equalization (*pemerataan*) became another term of the regime's development-speak, and the Eight Paths to Equalization spelled out areas that government programs must address. The paths aimed to achieve equities in eight areas. It sought to provide equity for (1) meeting basic needs in food, clothing, and housing; (2) accessing education and health care; (3) distributing income; (4) obtaining opportunities for employment, (5) getting involved in entrepreneurial activities; (6) accessing law and justice; (7) participating in development (especially for women and youth); and (8) spreading development projects across the country.[41]

Noting that the equalization agenda would be more effective if it targeted the countryside, the New Order government launched four improvement programs designed to bring information and infrastructure to the villages. The two information projects were the Newspaper Entering Villages (Koran Masuk Desa) and the Television Entering Villages (Televisi Masuk Desa) programs. The latter began after the launch of the Palapa communication satellite in 1976.[42] One infrastructure program called Electricity Entering Villages (Listrik Masuk Desa, LMD) functioned to electrify the rural areas. The second infrastructure program called Armed Forces Entering Villages (Angkatan Bersenjata Republik Indonesia Masuk Desa) sent the Indonesian Armed Forces to work with villagers building roads, irrigation, and sanitation facilities. The projects were rolled out to support the New Order regime's belief that village development was the "backbone of national development."[43]

Out of those programs, rural electrification became the government's leading village improvement project. The United States' financial and technical assistance to electrify rural areas in Java, Lombok, Sumatra, and Sulawesi in the later 1970s (detailed in chapter 6) helped launch a nationwide rural electrification program, which would be prioritized in the Third PELITA period starting on April 1, 1979.[44] In the subsequent years, the Soeharto government invested heavily in the endeavor and helped turn PLN into one of the largest public utilities in Southeast Asia.[45]

Many government officials supported this project, believing that electricity was a desired symbol of modernity: a well-lit country symbolizes a modern state. In 1970, Soedharmo Djajadiwangsa, the director general of Village Development of the Department of Home Affairs, asserted that village development and modernization could not be imagined without electricity.[46] Ir. Prayitno, PLN Disjaya chief in the late 1970s, once said, "Progress, modernization, and welfare seem difficult to imagine without electricity."[47] In other words, electricity not only served to energize and illuminate Indonesia's villages. Electricity was also supposed to create a pathway for Indonesia's journey toward a bright future.

Overall, the village improvement programs served dual purposes for the New Order government. On one hand, they did as they were intended and opened village life to the outside world by bringing information, electricity, and roads. On the other hand, the Soeharto government used the programs to broadcast its development projects to rural residents, control the flow of information, indoctrinate citizens on Pancasila, and, in the case of electricity, persuade villagers to vote for the government's political party during general elections. I now turn to this technopolitical characteristic of the rural electrification.

The Technopolitics of Soeharto's Rural Electrification

The case of technopolitics or "the strategic practice of designing or using technology to constitute, embody or enact political goals," was most apparent in the case of electricity and the New Order's electoral politics.[48] The Soeharto government held its first general election in 1971. Ten political parties contested the election. The government's party, Golkar, short for Golongan Karya (Functional Groups), won the most votes and seats in the legislature. Two years after the first general election, Soeharto ordered several parties to merge so that a total of only three political parties participated in subsequent elections. Thus, since the general election of 1977, in addition to Golkar, there were the Islamic-oriented party United Development Party (Partai Persatuan Pembangunan, PPP), and the Indonesian Democratic Party (Partai Demokrasi Indonesia, PDI), which was the product of a forced merger between the nationalist and Christian parties after the 1971 general election.

The New Order regime used several strategies to ensure that its political party Golkar kept winning the general elections. Scholars have noted that Soeharto created the Indonesian Civil Servants Corps (Korps Pegawai Republik Indonesia, Korpri) to enforce civil servants' "monoloyalty" to the regime,[49] put labor associations and professional organizations under the umbrella of Golkar,[50] prevented political activities at the village level, and imposed a uniform village administrative structure across the country while creating a passive political citizenry called the "floating mass" (*massa mengambang*).[51] In short, Soeharto created a "hegemonic party system" with Golkar in control.[52]

Golkar's hegemony notwithstanding, villagers had some degree of freedom to choose their preferred political party during a general election. Of course, there were attempts by village administrators loyal to the regime to persuade villagers to vote for the ruling party. Still, many followed the advice of noted figures such as their religious leaders. Unlike government employees who were expected to vote for Golkar because of their affiliation with Korpri, people in rural areas had a range of reasons for casting their ballots. In his 1992 study of Javanese voting attitudes, Afan Gaffar divided the voters he surveyed into two socioreligious groups of *santri* and *abangan*.[53] The devout Muslim *santri* preferred to vote for the PPP. The *abangan* followers of the syncretic Hindu-Javanese tradition were inclined to vote either for the PDI or Golkar.

Gaffar showed that people who voted for PDI either disliked both the PPP and Golkar, were pressured by their peers, or identified PDI with Sukarno, who remained beloved to them.[54] Those who voted for Golkar fell into three types: the first identified Golkar as the party of their village officials, who persuaded them to vote for Golkar in the months before a general election; the second chose Golkar because the venerable Sultan Hamengku Buwono IX of Yogyakarta was a Golkar member; the third type regarded Golkar as a party that successfully "promoted development not politics" as illustrated by the presence of roads, bridges, dams, and markets.[55] To this list I would add electricity. An electrified village was material "evidence" that the New Order regime was doing all that it could to develop the countryside. Golkar and the New Order regime became synonymous with development, which gave Soeharto's rule a form of legitimacy.

The main strategy for securing votes was to electrify dozens of villages just before a general election. In some cases, villagers received instructions to build diesel power plants using generator sets donated by the president. Four University of Indonesia (UI) social science researchers conducted a study of rural electrification in 1979 and wrote, "On the eve of the 1977 general election, there were some villages in Java that, without prior consultation [with PLN] were ordered to receive an electrical generator machine to be used for the villagers' benefit."[56] A district head (*bupati*) of Ponorogo instructed a village leader (*lurah*) in his district to install a donated diesel set from the East Java provincial governor's office in his village in 1972. The *lurah* followed the order but because, according to him, the operator lacked technical skills, the electricity was unreliable. As a result, not many people wanted to become electricity customers.[57] Two villages in the Bantul District of Yogyakarta had a similar experience. They received one of Soeharto's diesel generator sets in 1977, just before the general election. All the subdistrict head (*camat*) cared about was that the presence of these distributed diesel sets would persuade villagers to vote for Golkar. The electricity supply lasted for two years until it became unreliable, presumably because of shoddy construction. A Chinese Indonesian businessman from Yogyakarta took over the effort, although only for three months. Afterward, a group of residents of Karangtalun and Imogiri villages managed electricity generation and distribution for the two villages. In exchange for their work, they received free electricity. The UI social scientists concluded that this scheme of receiving free electricity was not "healthy" financially; their calculations indicated that the effort was not profitable or sustainable.[58]

In my interview with a former PLN president director, he suggested that the New Order government's real motivations for installing diesel-powered electric generators was to win elections. I asked him whether there were any discussions about generating electricity using the villages' available energy resources, to which he replied, "No, back then it was more about accomplishing a target. The timing of village electrification was tied to the general elections and villages needed to be electrified quickly."[59] When I pressed him to elaborate, he said, "Well, the idea was that after electricity was provided, people would vote for Golkar. [People would think that] Golkar was great."[60]

The provision of electricity in the Aceh province also seems correlated with voting patterns. A 1998 commemorative book documenting and celebrating the province's forty years of development presents a table of general election results from 1977 to 1997 and a graph of the number of electricity subscribers.[61] When the two are compared, there is a correspondence between total votes for Golkar and the number of PLN customers. More voters in devoutly Muslim Aceh supported the PPP than Golkar or the PDI in the 1977 and 1982 elections. It was not until the 1987 general election that Golkar won the most votes in the region: 804,121 against 659,505 for the PPP and 78,219 for the PDI. In the 1992 and 1997 elections, Golkar secured more than a million votes, while PPP votes were 630,368 and 663,010 and PDI garnered 126,498 and 71,811 votes, respectively.[62] The shift to more Golkar votes correlates with greater electrification coverage in Aceh. Between 1984 and 1996, the number of electricity subscribers jumped from about 50,000 people to slightly above 300,000, a sixfold increase in twelve years. In contrast, between 1969 and 1984, the number increased less significantly, from about 10,000 to about 50,000, a fivefold increase in fifteen years.[63]

Historically, the people of Aceh had resisted the New Order regime. Between 1976 and 1982, separatist rebels opposed Jakarta's attempt to control the resource-rich province.[64] The Indonesian army eventually suppressed the rebellion, and after 1982 the New Order government began to electrify Aceh's countryside. The role of Ibrahim Hasan, Aceh's "extraordinary governor" at the time, proved instrumental.[65] Under his leadership, the provincial government provided the funds to install electric generators and erect power lines across rural regions in the central, southeastern, western, and southern parts of Aceh. As a result, the number of electrified villages in the province almost tripled in less than five years. In 1985, only 664 out of 5,463 villages were electrified. Four years later, the number jumped to 1,951. In addition, Hasan managed to persuade many Acehnese to support the New Order government without sacrificing Acehnese identity and Islamic values. He argued that a vote for Golkar "is not apostasy," and when the government party wins, "it will mean more and faster material progress" for the Acehnese people.[66]

Similar stories of a strong correlation between electrification and electoral politics occurred elsewhere in Indonesia. For example, an unpublished report prepared by the West Java branch of PLN in 1976 mentions that President Soeharto made a gift of twenty diesel generator sets that the provincial government was eager to use in the villages "so that [they] would have been electrified before the 1977 general election,"[67] and thus be persuaded to vote for Golkar. PLN leaders did not like this practice. In the same report, the power company complained that distributing free electric generators undermined its effort to install a more cost-effective electrical infrastructure. The power company wanted small electric generators to temporarily serve remote and isolated areas until its power lines could reach them. The report stated, "The unwise selection of location [for the installation of diesel electric generators] in areas where the villagers cannot afford to pay [for electricity] is a hindrance [to our efforts], but often the selection of those locations is based on strategic and political considerations."[68] In this case, the patrimonial aims of the New Order regime conflicted with the technoeconomic goals of the PLN. The company was reluctant to supply electricity in the way the Soeharto government provided it. Because PLN was state controlled, it had to follow the government's agenda.

In 1979, the same year the LMD program began, the Soeharto regime enacted Law No. 5 (Village Law) that homogenized Indonesia's diverse village government structures using a Javanese village system as a model. It tried to bring administrative uniformity across all Indonesian villages, much to many non-Javanese villagers' displeasure.[69] Hans Antlöv asserted that the law made village administrations "miniature replicas of the central government, enforcing decrees and policies determined from above," allowing the state to penetrate deep into the villages.[70] Soeharto took advantage of the new village government structure to establish a patrimonial relationship with many village elites, cultivating their dutiful stance toward his regime. The New Order government constantly reminded village chiefs that their loyalty to the regime would benefit their villages. Antlöv, who studied a village in West Java in the 1980s, recounted the following episode relating directly to rural electrification:

> People in Sariendah are told over and over again that the New Order is directed by righteous rulers: they hear it on television, on the radio, at school, at the mosque, at the local *wayang* performance, or whenever they are in contact with one of the 350 persons in Sariendah who have passed the government's Pancasila Promotion Programme [i.e., the P4 courses]. A typical example was when Otong—the chairman of Leumachai—announced that the hamlet was getting electricity. He summoned a meeting with the most important local notables at the Leumachai mosque. Headman Wirahmat was specially invited to provide for the guidelines of the official programme, *Listrik Masuk Desa* (Electricity Enters the Village). Wirahmat started the meeting by saying how grateful (*berterima kasih*) Sariendah should be for having the honour of being chosen for the programme. It was only through the hard struggle of the New Order government that the present level of prosperity could have been attained. Now it was time for people in Sariendah to repay their debt (*hutang*) by being loyal (*setia*) and support Golkar at the upcoming election. The "age of modernity" (*zaman moderen*), he continued, was a creation of the New Order.[71]

Wirahmat, the village head, tried to persuade his fellow villagers to support Golkar and was connecting the provision of electricity with the upcoming election. The village eventually got its electricity, and Golkar won in Sariendah in the 1982 general election. Sariendah was one of thousands of villages electrified before the 1982 election as part of a concerted effort by PLN and the government. A 1980 internal PLN report noted: "It is known that village electrification investment is expensive, but [the project] aims to enter villages where 80% of the population resides, to improve their lives. The 1980/1981 village electrification program in particular must not fail since PLN's main task is to support the government's program that we must safeguard and implement successfully, especially ahead of the 1982 Election."[72]

In that report, PLN leaders acknowledged that rural electrification was connected to the government's electoral politics. It was a program that PLN had to support because it functioned as a state-owned enterprise that received government funding.

Lighting Up the Villages, Electrifying the Villagers

The Soeharto government spent huge financial resources to electrify new villages. For the 1980/1981 fiscal year, for example, the designated rural electrification funds for a "crash program" to electrify 1,000 villages were around Rp 62.66 billion.[73] Soeharto then sent his cabinet ministers to inaugurate newly electrified villages across the country, occasions they used to campaign aggressively for Golkar. In this sense, villagers not only got electricity in their homes, they were also "electrified," so to speak, to cast their ballots for Golkar.

To give some examples, on the eve of the 1982 general election, junior minister for Women's Affairs and Golkar cadre Lasiah Soetanto presided over an inauguration ceremony on March 22, 1982, to celebrate the electrification of thirty-four villages in Bali.[74] On March 15, 1982, Minister of Labor and Transmigration and former West Sumatra governor Harun Zain inaugurated fifteen electrified villages in the province. On March 25, Minister of Industry A. R. Soehoed inaugurated twenty-five recently lit villages in West Sumatra and donated some equipment for Bung Hatta University.[75] On the same day in Central Java, 142 newly illuminated villages were celebrated in a ceremony attended by Coordinating Minister for People's Welfare Surono, Central Java Governor Soepardjo Roestam, and PLN President Director Sardjono, among other important officials.[76] Minister of Finance Ali Wardhana was in Tolo, South Sulawesi, to usher in the era of electric lighting in fourteen villages on March 25, 1982.[77]

There were countless celebrations inaugurating recently illuminated villages during the New Order. These ceremonies were usually attended by the villagers, PLN representatives, the governor of the province, district heads, and village chiefs, along with a crew from national television and journalists to cover the event. In many cases, a large banner advertising the event would be placed strategically for many people to see. The banners had different wording, but they all convey hopefulness and gratitude. One such banner reads "Habis Gelap Terbitlah Terang Listrik Masuk Desa" (Out of Dark Comes Light Electricity Entering Villages).[78] Another says "Listrik Masuk Desa Membuat Desa Banyak Berkarya" (Electricity Entering Villages Make the Villages Productive).[79] It was not uncommon to connect the event directly to New Order. One banner displays the phrase "Listrik Masuk Desa Salah Satu Perwujudan Pemerataan Hasil Pembangunan" (Electricity Entering Villages One

Figure 5. A stone inscription of several electrified Balinese villages.
Source: Photo by Anto Mohsin, April 2012.

of the Embodiments of Equitable Distribution of Development).[80] One banner expressed the villagers' explicit appreciation. It says unabashedly, "*Terimakasih Bapak Menteri Listrik Sudah Menyala*" (Thank You Mr. Minister for Turning On the Electricity), thanking the Environment and Forestry Minister Emil Salim who came to the village of Motoling in North Sulawesi to officiate the inauguration of thirty-nine electrified villages.[81]

The inauguration ritual typically included speeches from a PLN official, a provincial governor, and a cabinet minister in attendance (though not always in that order). The PLN representative usually provided the electrical infrastructure statistics: the kilowatts of electric power installed, the total circuit kilometers of distribution lines erected, kilovolt-amperes of substations built, and the total funds needed to construct it all. Afterward, the governor would speak, and then the designated cabinet minister would give a speech and turn on an electric light to symbolize the beginning of an era of electricity. The speeches were followed by the signing of a large stone inscription (*prasasti*) with the name of the electrified villages by the highest-ranking administrative official in attendance. For example, Ida Bagus Oka, Bali's governor in the mid-1990s, signed his name on the *prasasti* inaugurating several electrified Balinese villages on August 11, 1995 (figure 5).

During the ceremony, cabinet ministers repeatedly credited Golkar and the New Order government with the electrification program's success. When Sudharmono, Soeharto's State secretary and the head of Golkar's Central Leadership Council (Dewan Pimpinan Pusat), inaugurated eighty-four newly illuminated villages in Central Java in March 1982, he was reported to have chatted with villagers about which political party they would choose in the upcoming election. *Kompas* noted that most people there shouted the name of Golkar's banyan tree symbol and held up two fingers to denote Golkar's number in the election.[82] Similarly, on March 30, 1982, Dr. Subroto attended a ceremony in East Kalimantan where he donated a television to fourteen newly electrified villages. *Berita PLN* reported that after the ceremony, Subroto "accepted the determination (*kebulatan tekad*) of the villagers in attendance to appoint General (Ret.) Soeharto to serve as Indonesia's next president for the 1983/1988 period and to name him as the Father of National Development."[83]

Perhaps in trying to provide a more balanced account, *Berita PLN* quoted some villagers, too. A village elder in Sidogiri, for example, told the magazine that Subroto's presence with his entourage was "like a lightning flash during daylight giving him and his fellow villagers an overflow of joy (*luapan kegembiraan*)."[84] Dr. Subroto confirmed this when he said that he had the same impression of the villagers' happiness for the "gift" that they had just received from the New Order government.[85] PLN Rural Electrification Chief Ir. Johannes J. Rumondor was quoted once: "I felt and witnessed it myself, how pleased, satisfied and happy the villagers were after receiving electricity."[86]

The villagers' satisfaction helped Golkar win votes. In the 1982 general election, M. C. Ricklefs noted that Golkar won most votes in all provinces but Aceh and managed to regain the national capital after losing it to the PPP in the previous election. PDI's and PPP's total votes fell by some 8 and 28 percent, respectively.[87]

In 1986, a year ahead of the 1987 general election, Soeharto repeated the strategy. Throughout the year, *Berita PLN* wrote that Golkar chairman Sudharmono inaugurated 326 electrified villages in Central Java, West Java, South Sulawesi, Yogyakarta, East Java, and Irian Jaya.[88] In Irian Jaya, Sudharmono delivered a speech connecting rural electricity and electoral politics by saying that the fruitful results of this program were due to everyone's hard work, "especially those who channeled their aspirations through GOLKAR."[89] Meanwhile, Subroto inaugurated 208 electrified villages in East Java on two separate occasions in 1986.[90]

Sudharmono and Subroto were by no means alone. In the same year, Junior Minister for the Promotion of Domestic Products Ginandjar Kartasasmita inaugurated five electrified villages in West Java. Minister of Forestry Soedjarwo inaugurated thirteen villages in East Kalimantan. In the next year, *Berita PLN* announced that Sudharmono inaugurated fifty neighborhoods in Jakarta, a story that opened the introduction of this book;[91] Subroto 256 electrified villages in West Nusa Tenggara, East Timor and East Java;[92] and Minister of Communications Roesmin Nurjadin seventy villages in South Sulawesi.[93] By April 1987, Soeharto's cabinet ministers had inaugurated hundreds of electrified villages. This feat, coupled with the decision by Nadhatul Ulama—one of two Islamic organizations that made up the PPP—to withdraw from the party, and the resultant fall in PPP votes, helped Golkar win the 1987 election. The Nadhatul Ulama's vote deflation tactic was advertised to exert its independence as one of the largest Islamic organizations in the country. However, according to Liddle, it received government largesse for its schools and teachers in return.[94]

In December 1991, several Fifth Development cabinet ministers simultaneously inaugurated dozens of electrified villages in several provinces.[95] During one of these inauguration ceremonies, the governor of North Sulawesi asked villagers in his province to make the 1992 general election successful, "for the sake of continuing development" (*demi kesinambungan pembangunan*).[96] This line was a coded phrase urging those who heard it to vote Golkar. Saadillah Mursjid, the cabinet secretary, apparently uttered the same phrase when he inaugurated twenty newly electrified Balinese villages in 1991. *Berita PLN* reported that Mursjid hoped that villagers would help make the upcoming general election successful "for the sake of continuing development."[97]

Conclusion

Using village electrification and other development programs, Golkar projected an image of a "caring" political party, which left the PPP and the PDI at a competitive disadvantage in the general elections. By 1997, the last general election of the New Order, many villagers identified programs that brought "things" to their villages—including electricity, television, and newspapers—as the result of the Soeharto government largesse, for which they should be thankful.

Two PLN employees explicitly told me the linkage between providing electricity and electoral politics. One of them said, "The aura of rural electrification in the Orba [Orde Baru or New Order] era was filled with the political interest of the Orba regime. After Orba, this 'aura' stopped. Although it seems to start again."[98] He added, "Back then village electrification was always connected to the Golkar's campaign."[99] He volunteered this information in light of the planned village electrification inauguration ceremony to be held in Kintamani, Bali, in early May 2012. Indonesia's minister of Energy and Mineral Resources at the time, Jero Wacik, was originally from this region and presided over the celebration. Here, a strategy that Soeharto practiced widely in the past was replicated and produced a similar result. Wacik was a member of the Democrat Party of President Susilo Bambang Yudhoyono which, in the gubernatorial race in 2013, nominated Made Mangku Pastika, the incumbent governor of Bali, who had been previously nominated by a different political party. Wacik's presence during the ceremony projected a strong image of the president and his political party as caring for the people by giving them electricity and a new deep water well in the Bangli District. Thus, even though many Balinese usually vote for candidates of the Indonesian Democratic Party of Struggle in provincial elections, Pastika won a second term, this time as a candidate of the Democrat Party.[100]

Another PLN employee admitted that a leading consideration to bring electricity to the villages during the New Order was to help Golkar win elections. He said, "That's the history of village electrification. One of [the regime's] campaign materials (*bahan kampanye*) was rural electrification." Although the regime profited from this endeavor, he quickly added that at least the villagers benefited, too, particularly because many longed to access what was then a new and attractive technology.[101] His sentiment was echoed by Goenawan Mohamad, the poet, essayist, cofounder of Indonesia's highly regarded weekly *Tempo* magazine, and one of the New Order era's leading public intellectuals and critics. He said to me, "At least the villagers got something out of it." He made this remark to contrast the practice of money politics then and now. We discussed Indonesia's post–New Order electoral politics, which sees some candidates literally buy votes from villagers by giving them money before they cast their ballots. Mohamad expressed his frustration with this practice after hearing my story about the connection between New Order village electrification and the general elections.[102]

Indonesian studies scholars have argued that the New Order's patrimonial characteristics were demonstrated by Soeharto's distribution of benefits among high-ranking members of the military and bureaucratic elites.[103] This chapter argues that the Soeharto government extended its patronage to the broader populace by bringing electricity into their villages. Many rural people wanted electricity for the material benefit it brought. Night illumination added time to hold social gatherings and increased safety. Electricity provided villagers with a new form of entertainment by watching television programs. Villagers who received electricity appreciated this technology, and those who did not yet have it waited for the government to expand its coverage to their areas. In both cases, they resorted to supporting Golkar and the New Order to ensure the continuation of the national development program. Soeharto's New Order succeeded in using electricity for a broader purpose than just bringing a new form of energy to the countryside. Soeharto's approach to distributing largesse and material benefits to the populace to earn political legitimacy stood in contrast to other repressive measures his government used to obtain acquiescence in the countryside, such as the military operations in Aceh and East Timor.

PLN, which implemented electrification on Soeharto's behalf, did not always agree with the New Order regime's practices. Still, its contestation was limited, as its principal mission was to support the government's development programs. PLN tolerated Golkar's political use of electrification because it believed it still served its mission of spreading the new energy technology to rural areas.[104] However, as I discuss in the following chapters, in helping the New Order government get votes through electrification, PLN resorted to building an electric infrastructure that relied heavily on diesel that proved costly when the New Order regime collapsed in 1998 and the Indonesian rupiah was significantly devalued against the US dollar. In addition, PLN could not charge profitable electricity prices to its consumers in the countryside. The government determined electricity prices to make it affordable for villagers.

Although the New Order government's patrimonial technopolitical practices drew mild resistance from PLN, they were criticized by other entities. For example, *Listrik Indonesia* once published an article on the eve of the 1997 general elections criticizing all three contesting political parties for lacking clear agendas. Most of what one promised was the same as the other. For instance, they all advocated for an increase in spending in education without elaborating how they would use additional funds. Concerning electricity, the trade magazine was critical, writing that village electrification had been used as a vote generator by a certain political party (it did not name it explicitly, but it strongly implied Golkar).[105] What the magazine suggested was that the New Order regime did not electrify rural areas quickly because doing so would reduce the incentives to persuade the masses to vote for Golkar. PLN was complicit in this act, because, as we shall see in the next chapter, the company was established as a technopolitical patrimonial institution of the New Order regime.

The Electric Bureaucracy

The electrification of Indonesia in the New Order was carried out mainly by the state-owned corporation called PLN (Perusahaan Listrik Negara), whose dominance, which persists to this day, divides electricity providers in Indonesia into two broad categories: PLN and non-PLN.[1] PLN electricity is generated from the company's power plants. Non-PLN electricity is generated from various sources, including power stations installed by local village communities, provincial governments, electric cooperatives, and independent power producers (IPPs) and is used for either local consumption (factories, hotels, cooperative communities, etc.) or sold to PLN at agreed-on rates.[2] PLN then retails the electricity to its customers at prices set by the government. Except in certain cases and in a limited geographical scope, such as in communities served by electric cooperatives, non-PLN electricity is transmitted using PLN's power lines. Thus, to sell electricity to a wider public, non-PLN power producers must conduct business with PLN.

Created as a monopolistic vertically integrated enterprise in the mid-1960s, PLN was tasked with generating, transmitting, distributing, and selling electricity in the country. However, it did more than just build power plants, substations, transmission towers and lines, distribution lines, electrical feeders, and load dispatch centers. The company constructed division headquarters, branch offices, training centers, warehouses, laboratories, and libraries; recruited and trained tens of thousands of employees; and kept fleets of technical service trucks, motorcycles, company cars, and other maintenance and repair equipment.[3] These material assemblages form the New Order state electric bureaucracy PLN. The visible presence of many PLN division headquarters in provincial capitals (figure 6) and branch offices in smaller towns (figure 7) scattered across the archipelago—all emblazoned with PLN's logo—serves as a constant

Figure 6. PLN Bali Division office building.
Source: Photo by Anto Mohsin, July 2019.

reminder of the state power company's role in providing electricity and thus
helping Indonesia modernize.

The Indonesian government's rationale to establish PLN as a monopoly was
primarily legal. The 1945 Constitution asserted that the country's natural and
mineral resources should be placed under the state's control "for the greatest
benefit of the people."[4] Consequently, the state interpreted that affordable, reliable, and good-quality electricity produced using the country's resources should
be provided to all citizens regardless of their socioeconomic status or geographical locations. This ambitious goal was tempered by the reality that the state could
only apportion a limited amount of its annual budget for electrification, thus
making the mandate to electrify the whole country a tall order. Nevertheless,
many Indonesian leaders believed that private companies driven solely by profits could not be trusted to carry out this mission. Unless there was a big economic incentive or a favorable rate of return on their investments, the government believed that private businesses would not invest in electrifying rural areas.

As a state-owned enterprise, PLN received support from and answered to the
Indonesian government. The New Order regime subsidized PLN's operations,

paid the salaries and benefits of its employees, channeled foreign loans to the company, and politically supported many of its electrification projects. Because PLN depended greatly on the government, its maneuverability as a company was limited. For one thing, it had to conform to the New Order's wishes and directives. PLN's board of directors (i.e., its executive team) had always been filled with Soeharto appointees and had to accept that the government had the power to set the electricity tariff structure. Whenever any important events were held in the country (international conferences, big sporting events, People's Consultative Assembly meetings, state visits by foreign dignitaries, etc.), the government expected an uninterrupted supply of electricity to successfully hold the event. Of course, PLN was obliged to provide this service and did all it could to ensure the smooth flow of electric current.

As one of the New Order regime's important technical bureaucracies, PLN did not just work to electrify the country, it also had to channel the state's patrimonial practices. In other words, Soeharto's patrimonial state was connected to the population via electricity. Accordingly, PLN did not evolve as just a technical institution; it had to function as a social organization as well. PLN workers participated in several charitable works, such as giving scholarships

Figure 7. PLN Palopo Branch office building.
Source: Photo by Anto Mohsin, July 2019.

to children, celebrating religious holidays, building houses of worship, donating money to charities and blood to hospitals, and holding other social programs. Their biggest charitable events and ones that were widely reported in the media were usually carried out to commemorate the annual National Electricity Day on October 27.[5]

Although PLN workers were involved in philanthropic works, in their mind their main corporate social responsibility was to bring electricity to the countryside, which they carried out year-round. Electrifying rural areas involved more than extending power lines to the countryside and installing electric meters in households. PLN workers held information sessions on the benefits and dangers of electricity, promoted electricity as a tool to increase villagers' income, fostered small businesses, and campaigned for energy conservation whenever the power company was pinched by rising fuel prices.

To PLN employees, fully electrifying the country (especially the rural areas) was their ultimate social mission, and this goal was on equal footing with their aspiration to turn their company into a modern and profitable utility corporation. PLN tried its best (and sometimes struggled) to balance its social mission (*misi sosial*) to bring electricity to the villages with its commercial mission (*misi komersial*) of making profits from their high-paying customers in the cities. The missions were clearly in tension with one another. To make money, the company needed to either increase revenue, reduce cost, or ideally both. But engaging in village electrification served none of the revenue-generating goals because subscribers in the countryside were not PLN's profitable customers. Ir. Johannes J. Rumondor, the person PLN appointed in 1976 to supervise rural electrification, tried to justify it by saying "rural electrification must be seen from the economic welfare benefits not in the form of cash revenue."[6] PLN leaders did it by calling their organization "an agent of development," that is, an institution that helped drive the government's national development agenda. In any case, PLN had little choice in the matter. The Soeharto government was aware of these contradictory goals but insisted that electrification must be done this way because it understood that it could and needed PLN to channel its patronage to the populace.

As I explain later, PLN also operated as an ideological institution. As a state-owned company, PLN was obliged not only to accept the New Order government's interpretation of the state ideology Pancasila but to disseminate it. To ensure the former, the state required PLN employees to take the mandatory Pancasila courses. The indoctrination proved quite successful. Many PLN workers internalized the New Order's interpretation of the state ideology and linked it with electricity. They used the state ideology to talk about their duties electrifying the country and made Pancasila principles plain to the public by pointing out that delivering electricity was their efforts to achieve "social justice for all Indonesians." Since the organization had a broad reach across the archipelago, it worked quite effectively as an extension of the New Order Pancasila state.

PLN Origins and Early Years

To better understand PLN's existence as a sociotechnical and ideological institution, we need to trace back its origins and evolution. Although PLN claims its founding date as October 27, 1945, when President Sukarno established the Office of Gas and Electricity (Djawatan Gas dan Listrik), the embryonic organization that turned into PLN wasn't established until 1965.[7] The Office of Gas and Electricity was created to coordinate all the gas and electricity installations seized by Indonesian laborers who answered the call by leaders to take over power plants and other Dutch electrical assets after Indonesia's declaration of independence on August 17, 1945.[8] Ir. M. A. Safwan was appointed to head the new office, reportedly because he was able to organize some youths and employees of Seibu Djawa Denki Djigjo Kosha (the West Javan division of the electric company under Japanese occupation) to safeguard several power plants from being destroyed by the Japanese army's scorched-earth policy.[9] However, the office wasn't fully functioning because of a severe labor shortage and uncertainty of ownership over the seized power plants. To the office employees, it wasn't clear which installations would remain in the new government's custody and which would be returned to the Dutch, who tried to regain control over its former colony.[10] During the Indonesian revolution (1945–49), many Indonesian nationalists, including workers in many industries, loudly called for the nationalization of many Dutch enterprises. However, it wasn't until 1958 that all former Dutch electricity companies were nationalized (discussed in chapter 1).

After nationalization, Sukarno established a new electric institution. It underwent several structural and name changes over the years. First, the Central Administering Board for Electricity and Gas Enterprises (Penguasa Perusahaan Peralihan Listrik dan Gas, P3LG) was formed in January 1958 to manage the activities of the nationalized companies,[11] and then in 1961 under the leadership of Ir. Srigati Santoso, P3LG was replaced by the General Management Board of the State Electricity Company (BPUPLN). Like its predecessor, BPUPLN did not exist very long because it relied extensively on government subsidies, practiced an incoherent accounting system, and was beset with internal communication problems, infighting, and regionalism.[12] Sukarno finally dissolved BPUPLN in December 1965, after which two companies, the State Gas Company (PGN) and the State Electricity Company (PLN), were formed

Table 3. Gatrik's symposia

Date	Topic
November 12–15, 1968	Limited seminar on nuclear power for electricity
July 29–August 2, 1969	Limited seminar on electricity
December 1969	Seminar on electricity voltage and distribution system
December 1969	Seminar on the application of electricity
January 19–24, 1970	Seminar on nuclear energy
February 19–21, 1970	Workshop on research
March 12–14, 1970	Workshop on rural electrification

with Ir. Amir Hoesein Abdillah heading PLN.[13] Based on this, PLN was arguably first established in 1965.

In the mid-1960s, PLN was not the only institution established to take care of electricity matters. Another organization, Gatrik (an abbreviation of Direktorat Djenderal Tenaga dan Listrik, Directorate General of Power and Electricity), was established in August 1966 to replace the ministry-level Department of Electricity and Power, which had been created less than a year earlier in June 1965. Gatrik was headed by Ir. Ahmad Mohammad Hoesni. In June 1968, when Soeharto formed the First Development Cabinet, Gatrik was transferred from the Department of Basic and Light Industries and Power to the newly created Department of Public Works and Electric Power (DPWEP), headed by Ir. Sutami. The transfer reflected Soeharto's decision to place both public works projects and power plant construction in a single department under the leadership of a trusted and experienced person. Sutami had worked for Sukarno, but he managed to gain Soeharto's trust to work in his cabinet. Gatrik and PLN worked closely together until Gatrik's formal dissolution in 1973. Gatrik's upper echelon was primarily made up of PLN employees who had been promoted through the ranks, while its middle-ranking officials were, in fact, PLN employees on loan for various tasks.[14]

In many ways Gatrik performed the role of an energy think tank that provided the space and place for PLN and other government employees to discuss all matters related to energy and electricity. During its brief existence, Gatrik organized a series of conferences on energy and electricity, produced voluminous proceedings of those symposia, and even drafted a national energy policy in 1969.[15] Between late 1968 and early 1970, Gatrik held a total of seven symposia (table 3). These symposia were held after two Gatrik officials attended an energy seminar in West Germany. The director general of Gatrik, Ir. Hoesni, sent Dr. Artono Arismunandar and Ir. Sufrani Atmakusuma to West Germany to participate in a seminar on Energy Policy and Economy in Berlin between October 9 and November 2, 1968. Arismunandar and Atmakusuma's report on the seminar exemplifies a transfer of critical electrical knowledge, which arguably played a part in prompting Gatrik's activities holding seminars and workshops for the next year and a half.

According to Arismunandar and Atmakusuma's report, the German Foundation for Developing Countries (GFDC), which was founded by the West German parliament members to help develop the Global South, organized the seminar. The GFDC held eighty seminars between 1960 and 1966, attended by delegates from eighty-seven countries with Indonesia attending since 1960.[16] In the 1968 seminar, the Indonesian delegates listened to presentations by several German experts, presented a country report on energy, and visited several sites, including the Walchensee hydropower plant in Bavaria, two load dispatching centers, four factories, two models of electrified farms, two hydropower resources, a nuclear research facility, and two federal ministries in Bonn.[17]

In their report, Arismunandar and Atmakusuma wrote four conclusions about their visit. First, Indonesia's participation in the seminar was vital, and they recommended the country ensure funding to continue sending delegates to workshops. Second, they acknowledged that although the knowledge and insights they gathered from the Germans were valuable, they were mindful that the developing world could not just copy what the Germans did because the developing countries had different systems and conditions. Third, although Asian countries had similar energy challenges, their capacities to develop their power sector varied. Fourth, they recommended that Indonesia produce a better and more systematic plan to mine its primary energy resources, draw up a better energy policy, electrify rural areas, and involve energy economists in formulating a national energy policy.[18] Their last recommendations became the themes discussed in several Gatrik symposia.

Gatrik's Demise

A labor–management conflict in late 1968, which turned into a crisis of confidence in the leadership of Gatrik and PLN, provided a pretext for removing the organizations' top leaders in 1970 and for ridding both institutions of alleged communist personnel and Sukarno-era influence. It began with a move made by the PLN board of directors to investigate alleged corruption by some PLN employees over the medical benefits they received. The decision by the board to suspend reimbursements to PLN employees for using medical services outside of PLN's internal facilities and to ask Hoesni to investigate the fraudulence angered some employees. The employees wrote and sent a letter of objection to PLN management and copied it to several outside agencies. Hoesni met this move by forming an investigative team that found two people were implicated in the wrongdoing. The employees, in turn, launched a counter-attack by writing another letter that criticized Hoesni and PLN executives for their handling of the matter and their poor performances as managers.[19]

This early dispute then evolved into a wider feud following another letter signed by seventy-seven Gatrik and PLN employees in November 1968 complaining about the general leadership of the two organizations. In the letter, the employees requested that Gatrik and PLN leaders explain the rationale for their unclear budgetary and personnel policies. The letter received wide support from many people inside PLN and Gatrik, including some senior people in the two organizations.[20] It appeared that their dissatisfactions with Gatrik and PLN management had been felt for some time and stemmed not only from their resentment of unclear promotion mechanism but also from other alleged corrupt practices that included PLN's so-called Consulting and Contracting (C and C) scheme, the acquisition of portable diesel generators, and Hoesni's home purchase in Bogor using state funds. Revenues from the C and C scheme, which was obtained by using PLN resources to give extra services to the public for a small fee, were supposed to benefit the PLN employees, but the details of how the extra income was used were not clear even to the PLN directors.[21] The mobile diesel units were bought in haste on Hoesni's order and bypassed the usual purchasing procedure to complete them by a certain time, and it was later found that "the whole deal could have been arranged more cheaply."[22] As for the third allegation, McCawley writes, "very little information was produced to support allegations of corruption carried out by Hoesni in his use of a house in Bogor. There were nevertheless widespread suspicions held in the PLN and Gatrik . . . that Hoesni had used funds from Perusahaan Gas Negara, of which he was formerly president director, to purchase a house at Bogor in his own name and had only subsequently been forced to return ownership to the PGN. These suspicions may well have been completely unjustified, but their existence was sufficient to give rise to much discontent."[23] In short, Gatrik and PLN employees were very dissatisfied with what they saw as corrupt and selfish management of the PLN-Gatrik complex.

The conflict lasted for months, and it involved investigations carried out by Police Inspector General Ostenrik, who at the time also served as the DPWEP Inspector General, and moves and countermoves launched by the PLN-Gatrik management and the seventy-seven workers and their allies (the press sided more with the workers than with the management, for example). But Hoesni's initial response to the letter, which included firing two and transferring eighteen of the signatories (some to remote posts), did not bode well. Two newspapers, *Kompas* and *Harian Kami*, and the Jakarta branch of the Indonesian Graduates Action Association (Kesatuan Aksi Sarjana Indonesia) protested this decision and called for Sutami to take firm action against Hoesni. As time went on, the conflict widened and charges of communist influence in the group were launched by both sides. At some point Hoesni's decisions were supported by another investigating team called Team SPRIN 85 formed by the Inspector General Ostenrik and by extension by Sutami. But when Sutami made the announcement of his decisions on February 21, 1969, he was met with strong criticisms by the employees. They refused to accept the minister's conclusions. Both sides tried to settle their dispute with members of parliament but to no avail.

The arrest of Colonel Soekarno, an army officer, a Gatrik official, and an adviser to Hoesni on charges of being a communist didn't help the situation. This arrest was a blow to Hoeni because Soekarno had supported Hoesni's decisions to punish the signatories of the letter. Because Soekarno once headed the screening investigations to find communist-leaning PLN employees, Sutami had to set up a new investigation team, and this time it was headed by Ostenrik, which netted more employees identified with "communist elements."[24] Another result of the conflict was Hoesni's and Abdillah's dismissals from their positions in 1970. In his postmortem analysis of the labor dispute, Peter McCawley argued that there was no indication that Hoesni and Abdillah were sympathetic to the Indonesian Communist Party just because they served in the Sukarno administration.[25] But in the broader political context of the time, when Soeharto's New Order was obsessed with eliminating alleged communists from the Indonesian bureaucracy,[26] the removal of Hoesni and Amir suggests a means of ridding Gatrik and PLN of influence of the Old Order regime.

After Hoesni and Abdillah's removal, the Soeharto government subsequently instituted a few changes that would lead to the establishment of PLN as the leading electric bureaucracy. First, after Hoesni's dismissal, Sutami transferred Gatrik's functions to PLN, which reduced the directorate general's role in the electric power sector. Second, Sutami appointed Ir. Abdul Kadir, an experienced engineer and manager, to head PLN in 1970.[27] Third, in 1972, the government changed PLN's status to a Perusahaan Umum or *perum* (state-owned company) by issuing Government Regulation No. 18. A *perum* is a type of Indonesian state-owned business in which the government owns 100 percent of its capital. The regulation legally established PLN as a state-owned enterprise, which authorized it to produce, transmit, and distribute electricity; plan and build electrical infrastructure; develop electric power; and provide services in the electricity sector.[28] In 1973, Soeharto issued Presidential Decree No. 9, which abolished Gatrik and placed PLN within the DPWEP.[29] Two years later, Sutami passed a ministerial decree to reaffirm PLN's status as a government-owned agency tasked with supporting national development in the electricity sector.[30] Sutami's decree put PLN in lockstep with Soeharto's development programs. On one hand, these laws empowered PLN employees to methodically start electrifying the country; on the other hand, its ties to the New Order meant that its electrification policies had to cater to the regime's objectives. This link was further cemented in Government Regulation No. 54 of 1981, which revised Regulation No. 18 to stress the government's authority and jurisdiction on electricity. Thus, the 1981 Government Regulation affirmed PLN as the technopolitical institution of the New Order patrimonial state.

Developing Expertise

One of the foremost concerns of PLN leadership in the early years, especially after PLN was established as a *perum*, was developing the technical expertise and engineering capabilities of its many employees. PLN leaders were aware that their company's credibility as a technoscientific bureaucracy depended on demonstrating their ability to run the organization and carry out electrical projects well. Developing expertise was also a way for PLN to protect the bureaucracy from the intrusion of military personnel, many of whom were placed in the state's bureaucracies during the Soeharto period. The Ministry of Public Works, for example, had one military officer (out of eight total) serving as an upper-echelon bureaucrat in 1981.[31] The Indonesian military accepted this practice because of the prevailing dual-function (*dwi-fungsi*) doctrine they followed at the time, in which they believed they were entitled to serve both in the military and in any state organizations to help maintain the country's political stability. In addition, political scientist Donald K. Emmerson offered three hypotheses as to why Soeharto appointed military personnel in state bureaucracies: "to dominate the bureaucracy [by the armed forces] thoroughly and uniformly," to prioritize the portfolios of the bureaucratic organizations headed by the military officers, and "to reward [the military personnel] and ensure [their] loyalty on a personal basis" by allowing them to enrich themselves using state resources.[32] The third one was a well-known Soeharto patrimonial practice to ensure loyalty of his army officers.[33] Under this challenge PLN saw two interrelated issues: filling the rank and file of its organization with qualified people and developing internal expertise.[34]

One of the strategies that PLN leaders in the 1970s used was to ask elder and experienced employees to delay their retirement or return to service. An example of the former is Soepolo Wiradi, head of thermal power plant maintenance at the PLN headquarters, and of the latter is Achyar Sawijan, a skilled and experienced diesel technician.[35] Wiradi died before he could retire. PLN President Director Prof. Ir. Suryono paid respect by laying wreaths at his funeral on October 3, 1977, and mentioned that the company lost a much-needed skilled and valued colleague.[36] Sawijan received his training in Singapore during the Japanese occupation, was later employed by OGEM as a machinist, and then worked as head of a DPP until 1969. PLN leaders valued his knowledge and expertise on diesel generators and continued to employ him to fix and maintain old diesel machines. He tried to instill confidence in the younger employees by saying, "Our experts are not inferior to foreign experts. . . . If we want, we can fix our own devices and machineries."[37]

As the years went on, PLN recruited more employees. However, the bulk of the company's new employees were not university graduates but graduates of technical high schools or the equivalent. This trend persisted even more than two decades after PLN was established. The World Bank reported that "As of March 31, 1989, PLN had about 51,200 employees, of whom about 37,300 are employed on the permanent payroll. PLN has no difficulty in recruiting staff educated at levels up to technical high school, but less than 4% of the staff have university degrees."[38]

The high school graduates that PLN recruited were trained at one of PLN's four Center for Education and Training Units in Cibogo, Ancol, Slipi, and Tanjung Priok (all in Jakarta). At these training centers, selected PLN employees learned about diesel engines, how to operate and maintain them, and how to manage a small, remote PLN branch office where a diesel power station was located. Some recruits were trained on a combined-cycle power plant basics, while others were schooled on accounting. Throughout the 1970s and 1980s, different cohorts of PLN employees were regularly trained at these centers. Ir. Dudung Yachyasumitra, director of PLN Education and Training Center in the late 1970s, regularly delivered opening speeches to inform these trainees that their skills would be of valuable importance to the company. In one such speech, he said that even though ten weeks is short for the training course, it is important for the trainees to be properly trained because PLN was growing.[39] In addition, some qualified PLN employees were sent to get on-the-job training abroad, as was the case for a cohort of PLN workers who were sent to France to study the operations of a load dispatching and distribution center.[40]

As for recruiting university graduates, PLN hired many graduates from Indonesia's most prestigious engineering school, the Institute of Technology in Bandung (Institut Teknologi Bandung, ITB). There are two reasons for this.

First, in the 1970s and 1980s, there were still very few technical graduates in the country to fill the positions at PLN, which relied on only a few technical institutions, ITB among them, for their supply of engineers. Second, many ITB graduates were already employed by PLN since the 1950s. Given this situation, ITB students leveraged the alumni network to find positions at the state power company. PLN did hire engineering graduates from other Indonesian universities but disproportionately recruited from ITB. At one point, PLN even built an electrical engineering lab at ITB with funds and assistance from the French government.[41]

Talented university graduates were usually put on a management track and had several assignment rotations throughout their careers. It was not uncommon for would-be managers to be posted in three or more different PLN branch offices. They were to be ready to be placed in any one of PLN's divisions and branches at any time (table 4, figures 8 and 9). Former PLN President Director Ir. Sardjono called it the "zigzag career pathway."[42] The rotations served two purposes: to understand and get experience managing operations in different areas and to instill a strong sense of national unity among PLN leaders, a practice modeled after the Indonesian military, which rotated assignments of its commissioned officers. The rationale was that when people are assigned to a branch office outside their hometown, they would be exposed to the people, customs, cultures, and conditions in the new areas and these would motivate them to serve the company better and appreciate the diversity of Indonesian peoples.

The makeup of Indonesia's heterogeneous societies means that fostering national unity is one of the foremost concerns of the nation's leaders. One way to address this concern was to expose PLN employees to cultures outside of their own. Hence, a Javanese served not only in Java but also on other islands. Likewise, a Balinese obtained experience working outside Bali. As an illustration, Ir. Djiteng Marsudi, a Javanese, was a 1962 graduate of ITB with a bachelor's degree in electrical engineering. He received further training in England in 1972 and France in 1978; he served in several of PLN's offices in Java and Sumatra before he was appointed PLN's director of finance in 1993 and finally as PLN's president director in 1995. Ir. Ipung Purmowarmanto, a PLN Bima Branch manager, acknowledged that he liked "learning the characteristics of each regions [where he had been sent to work] including each region's customs and the habits of its people."[43]

When it came to developing inhouse expertise, PLN gave their employees specific project assignments or supported their doctoral education. One example of a PLN employee who became highly knowledgeable in a particular area was Ir. Vincent T. Radja. He became a well-known expert on geothermal energy, which he developed by serving as the project leader for the Kamojang Power Plant, Indonesia's first geothermal power plant (GPP).[44] Another example is Ir. Januar Muin, who successfully completed two hydropower projects in West Sumatra: Batang Agam and Maninjau hydroelectric power plants. A few ambitious and talented employees received financial support to complete their doctoral degrees in a university in Indonesia or overseas. The percentage of PLN PhD employees by the mid-1980s was a small fraction of PLN's total labor force, but they constituted some of the top experts.

One of PLN's highly trained engineers was Dr. Ir. Artono Arismunandar, who served as the director of PLN Power Research Institute (Lembaga Masalah Ketenagaan, LMK) in the late 1970s and once proposed to create an extra high voltage (EHV) transmission line to transmit electricity economically.[45] His proposal was realized when Indonesia built its first 500 kV interconnected system stitching the regional networks in Java in the 1980s (detailed in chapter 4). Dr. Dipl. Ing. Nengah Sudja developed expertise in regional development and in 1992 was appointed to head PLN LMK.[46] He supported Arismunandar's proposal and once recommended interisland electrical interconnectivity between Java and Sumatra to better serve electricity regionally.[47] Sudja thought beyond national borders when he suggested the completion of the Asahan power plan to support a Southeast Asian regional power grid.[48] Dr. Ir. Munawar Amarullah earned his doctorate at the University of Houston with a dissertation titled "The Pricing of Electricity in Indonesia" in 1983. He studied welfare economics, and after several appointments as head of the Ujungpandang and Surabaya branches, he became the deputy director of finance in the mid-1980s. As we shall see in chapter 6, Amarullah was critical of PLN's approach to rural electrification, especially about its collaboration with electric cooperatives.

Because one of PLN's main tasks is to electrify the countryside, the company worked on developing expertise in this area as well. In 1976, PLN created a division called the Sub-Directorate of Village Electrification, headed by Rumondor. Under his direction, PLN sought to increase its skills and knowledge of rural electrification. Through a series of four national workshops held between October 1977 and August 1978, with the assistance of USAID and National Rural Electric Cooperative Association (NRECA) representatives, PLN employees learned how to prepare and produce feasibility studies to determine whether a rural area would be suitable for electrification (elaborated on in chapter 5). Rumondor wrote, "[feasibility study reports] are one key to determining whether a rural electrification project would be successful or not."[49] He also said that the reports would help secure foreign loans and stressed their importance as both a technical and a financial tool. In other words, demonstrating

mastery of creating feasibility studies assures international donors that the Indonesian state power company has the skills and knowhow to carry out rural
electrification projects.

Collectively, employees' knowledge, experience, and expertise facilitated PLN
to turn into a technically capable institution, which helped protect the bureaucracy from the intrusion of the Indonesian military. Unlike some other New
Order–era institutions, PLN saw few military personnel appointed to leadership positions. The specialized knowledge and training needed to build electric infrastructures meant that even though the New Order regime regulated
many of PLN's operations, it left matters of technical affairs to the power company's highly trained and specialized labor force.

Developing Reach

Another big challenge for PLN was developing its bureaucratic reach across the
country. Having a functioning countrywide organization was vital for PLN's
status as a state-owned utility company, and it could not possibly serve the
entire country with just a few offices. PLN leaders addressed this issue by di-
viding their organization into thirteen regional areas (PLN Wilayah), two distribution offices (PLN Distribusi), and one generation office (PLN Pembangkitan) in the 1970s. Table 4 and figure 8 show the sixteen PLN divisions and
their areas of coverage. As can be seen from table 4, not every PLN division
covered an Indonesian province, which shows PLN's priorities and pragma-
tism in creating a nationwide organization.[50] Some divisions' coverage areas
were composed of two or more provinces because of the varied population
density. Several provinces outside Java were more sparsely populated than others, so PLN decided to combine two or more provinces under the jurisdiction of
one region. As the most populated island, Java needed a total of five PLN
divisions.

PLN restructured its regional divisions in the wake of an important transformation of the company in 1994 (figure 9).[51] Following the issuance of Presidential Decree No. 37 of 1992 to invite private companies to invest in the
electrical supply industry, the PLN board of directors lobbied the Soeharto
government to change PLN's status from *perum* to Perseroan Terbatas (PT) or
persero to compete with private companies. As a *persero*, PLN was allowed to
create subsidiaries and sell some of its stocks to the public, although the government still maintained control by owning 51 percent of the stocks. The insti-
tutional change was intended to shift PLN toward becoming a more profit-
oriented company, strengthening its "commercial mission," and to compete
with private companies better. Ir. Djiteng Marsudi, PLN's CEO from January
1995 to July 1998, created the first two PLN subsidiaries.[52] Two PLN units that

Table 4. Sixteen PLN units and their areas of coverage in the mid-1970s

Unit	Area of Coverage
PLN Region I	Aceh
PLN Region II	North Sumatra
PLN Region III	West Sumatra and Riau and district of Sungai Penuh of Jambi
PLN Region IV	South Sumatra, Jambi, Bengkulu, and Lampung
PLN Region V	West Kalimantan
PLN Region VI	South Kalimantan, Central Kalimantan, and East Kalimantan
PLN Region VII	North Sulawesi and Central Sulawesi
PLN Region VIII	South and Southeast Sulawesi
PLN Region IX	Maluku
PLN Region X	Irian Jaya
PLN Region XI	Bali, East Nusa Tenggara, and West Nusa Tenggara
PLN Region XII	East Java except for the district of Bojonegoro
PLN Region XIII	Central Java, Yogyakarta, and the district of Bojonegoro
PLN West Java Distribution	West Java except for the district of Tangerang (only distribution)
PLN Jakarta and Tangerang Distribution	Special capital area Jakarta and the district of Tangerang
PLN West Java and Jakarta Generation	Special capital area Jakarta and West Java (generation and transmission)

had been overseeing electricity generation in eastern and western parts of Java became two separate companies. The two subsidiaries, called generation companies, were to operate and maintain several large power plants in Java and Bali and they were to compete with each other in selling electricity from their generators.[53] Because of these changes, by the mid-1990s, PLN had reduced its regional areas from thirteen to eleven, added a special area of operation for the island of Batam, and transformed PLN regions XII and XIII into PLN Distribution East Java and Central Java, respectively, and PLN West Java and Jakarta Generation became PLN West Java Distribution.

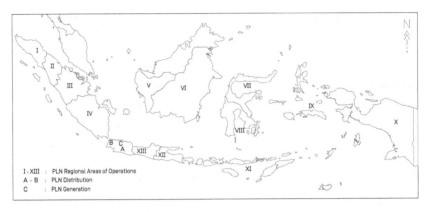

Figure 8. PLN regional areas of operation in the 1970s.
Source: *PLN in 1975/76* (Jakarta: Dinas Humas dan Protokol PLN Pusat, 1976).

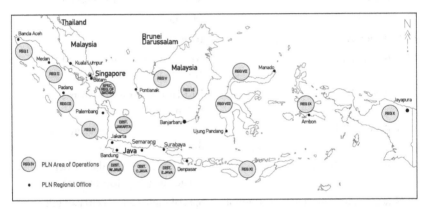

Figure 9. PLN regional areas of operation in the 1990s.
Source: *PLN Company Profile* (Jakarta: PLN Publication and Documentation
Subdivision, 1996).

In both instances, PLN structure reflected both the centralized and decentralized characters of the organization. It was centralized because the operations carried out by PLN offices across the country followed the plan set by headquarters in Jakarta. The appointments of regional managers were also made by PLN executives in the capital city. PLN headquarters published a monthly magazine called *Berita PLN* (PLN News) that communicated policies, important messages, stories, and updates to employees across the nation. Copies of *Berita PLN* were disseminated widely to its division and branch offices. At the same time, PLN regional and branch offices functioned autonomously in many aspects. They worked independently to attract and enroll new electricity subscribers, respond to customer complaints, operate power stations in their jurisdictions, and maintain the local electric facilities. PLN dubbed these branch offices the "spearhead" (*mata tombak*) of the power company and stressed their crucial role in creating a good corporate image among electricity customers because this image would reflect PLN's overall identity.[54]

PLN as a Social Institution

As mentioned already, PLN operated not just as a technical institution but also as social one, channeling the New Order state's largesse to its employees and people in the villages. Even after becoming a *persero*, PLN continued its mission to electrify rural areas, which was the most visible social work the state power company did. PLN President Director Dr. Ir. Zuhal stressed PLN's dual role in an article published in 1994.[55] His successor Djiteng Marsudi underscored it further in 1996 when he wrote, "PLN as a *persero* still has both social and commercial tasks. A social mission such as village electrification must still be done by PLN even though commercially this is not profitable, but this is a duty that the government gave to PLN as an agent of development."[56]

Besides electrifying the countryside, PLN distributed state patronage in other significant ways. Managers who worked at branch offices played a crucial role disseminating benefits to their workers and electricity customers. In many ways they acted as an extension of PLN leadership in Jakarta and to a large extent of the New Order government. Their charitable works were reported in *Berita PLN*, in PLN regional publications, and in the local print media.[57]

There were two categories of government largesse that PLN branches distributed: internal and external. For the internal type, we need to understand that many PLN leaders saw and treated their employees as a family, an approach that was more prominent in branch offices. One leader of the Biak Branch in the early 1990s admitted that he used the "persuasiveness and familial" strategy to manage his employees (including the Papuan natives) at his branch.[58] He continued, "Frankly, we involved them without discrimination. To use an analogy, if they lift one rock, we also lift one."[59] As such, PLN tried to increase the skills of its employees by giving them additional training, education, and even scholarships. Two "local sons" (*putra daerah*) from the Biak Branch passed the national test and were admitted as fulltime PLN employees.[60] Likewise, the Bima Branch recruited undertrained and undereducated workers as fulltime employees to work as drivers and staff for the company's cooperative.[61] The Bima Branch leader in 1995 did inhouse training to motivate his employees to improve their skills by rewarding accomplished workers annually.[62] In another case, PLN West Java Distribution division gave scholarships to forty-nine orphaned students whose parents had belonged to the "big PLN family."[63] These examples illustrate that the power company acted as a vector of educational patronage of the New Order government by giving their employees opportunities to complete or further their studies and trainings.

The second type of government handouts that PLN transmitted was external. There was an official program called Guidance on Weak Economic Entrepreneurs and Cooperatives (Pembinaan Pengusaha Ekonomi Lemah dan Koperasi). PLN branches selected and fostered small businesses by giving them financial and other supports. PLN Tanjung Karang Branch, for example, delivered capital assistance in the amount of Rp 1.25 billion to 224 small businesses and cooperatives in the Lampung province in December 1995. Twenty percent of the capital was allocated as educational aid delivered as a grant for sixteen foster coops.[64] Also in December 1995, the Fakfak Branch allocated Rp 127,500,000 to eight small entrepreneurs and fourteen company cooperatives.[65] In another case, PLN donated several electric motors and helped construct a pump system for farmers in the Bajo district in Sulawesi to help irrigate their fields during the prolonged draught in the region. PLN's prior assistance to the Bajo farmers had helped them produce crops in their otherwise dry lands.[66] In these examples, PLN channeled government's financial donations to small enterprises.

PLN cemented its image as a social institution when it decided to adopt a march and a hymn following common cultural practices among many Indonesian organizations with a strong social component.[67] To do so, it launched a contest in December 1996 to attract music composers to create a song for each. Two music teachers won the competition: Jerry Silangit for the march and Oktovialdi for the hymn.[68] The lyrics to the march stress the duties of PLN employees as civil servants who work responsibly to provide electricity to create a prosperous and just society. The march aspires to make "PLN advanced, modern, and independent" and claims that PLN's achievements are the nation's accomplishments. PLN's hymn thanks God for his blessings, calls for an effort to increase excellence, and encourages PLN employees to serve the country by building a modern Pancasila nation.[69]

PLN as an Ideological Institution

The Soeharto regime mandated all civil servants, including PLN employees, complete the two-week-long P4 courses at their respective institutions. Consequently, throughout the 1980s and up to the early 1990s, successive cohorts of PLN workers took the P4 courses. During the training period they were freed from their regular duties because they were required to attend classes from 8 a.m. until 6 p.m. so they could focus and pass the courses. The course materials consisted of three books on Pancasila, the 1945 Constitution, and the GBHN.[70] Seven relevant speeches, remarks, and thoughts of the president on Pancasila were included as reference materials.[71] Trainees read and discussed the materials and were tested on their knowledge at the end. To enliven the participants in absorbing and understanding the largely dry course materials, they were allowed to choose their "favorite, funniest, and serious" instructors.[72]

News regarding PLN employees taking the Pancasila courses periodically appeared in the company's internal magazine throughout the 1980s. The articles usually include either an excerpt from or the entire opening remarks given by a government official and an announcement of which cohort of employees were enrolled in the courses. Many speeches delivered at the opening of the P4 courses reminded employees about the importance of Pancasila, the 1945 Constitution, and GBHN and how they are connected to the New Order development agenda. Government officials used the state ideology to excite PLN employees about their role in the nation's development. For example, when Mining and Energy Minister Dr. Subroto delivered his opening remarks before the very first P4 courses for PLN employees on March 6, 1979, he stressed the importance of "sharpening" employees' understanding of Pancasila and for them to "dig deeply into the meanings of Pancasila, UUD [the 1945 Constitution] and GBHN" so that they were armed with the knowledge of the country's important texts.[73] He used the state ideology to rouse PLN workers about their important job electrifying the Pancasila state. To him (and many other government officials), PLN employees must first be Pancasila workers to be effective as utility workers. In fact, one PLN executive, Administrative Director Ir. Mohammad Singgih, said in his remarks to the twenty-first cohort of P4 students on October 3, 1985, "only Pancasila people can build a Pancasila-based society. Those who don't have Pancasila, who don't understand Pancasila, who don't internalize Pancasila, who don't love Pancasila will be difficult to build an Indonesian Pancasila society. Only Pancasila people can make the journey of development toward our desired goal."[74]

Many scholars who have analyzed Pancasila critically rightly pointed out that under the New Order regime, "it became a cudgel for control and conformity."[75] They reached this conclusion with the benefit of hindsight, looking back how the New Order state used Pancasila to make Indonesian citizens conform to its will. But there is one dimension that is often overlooked, which was the effects of Pancasila and its mass dissemination on civil servants in the early years. Michael Morfit, who analyzed the Pancasila indoctrination efforts in the early 1980s, wrote:

Pancasila, according to the New Order government, is an ideology of containment rather than one of mobilization. That is, it is conceived in such broad and general terms that it can embrace the wide cultural and religious diversities of the Indonesian nation. While it provides an encompassing umbrella of unity, it is not designed to excite mass participation in the development process or galvanize the nation into action.[76]

While Morfit was correct to show that Pancasila provided a tool to unify the nation, he didn't allow enough time to see how the indoctrination efforts unfolded and how they in fact "excite[d] mass participation in the development process" among many state employees. PLN workers became the mouthpiece of the Soeharto government's understanding of Pancasila and unabashedly linked the state ideology with electricity every chance they had.

On many occasions (village electrification inauguration ceremonies, flag-raising ceremonies, interviews, etc.), New Order officials and PLN employees used the state ideology to animatedly talk about electrification. Soeharto often said that his regime's development agenda aimed to transform Indonesia into a "modern, just and prosperous society" based on Pancasila and the 1945 Constitution.[77] Whenever Soeharto inaugurated PLN electrification projects, he explicitly reinforced this connection. For example, in 1986, during the launching ceremony of the Cirata hydroelectric power plant (HPP), Soeharto said, "Without sufficient electrical provision, it would be difficult to realize our goal of creating an advanced, prosperous, and just society based on Pancasila."[78] In another instance, so exciting was electrification for the PLN Director of Planning Ir. Ketut Kontra, he could not stop talking about how virtuous it was, using the language of state ideology. In a 1982 speech, he talked about drawing up the policies of electrification using Pancasila as the underlying foundational text of these policies.[79]

Many PLN employees and Department of Mining and Energy (DME) officials believed that electricity played a vital role in realizing the national dream and often invoked Pancasila in their rhetoric. Rumondor, PLN's rural electrification coordinator, once said in an interview, "The target of village electrification is to improve the lot and welfare of people in the villages, to equalize development benefits, and to stimulate economic activities in the villages in order to achieve the national end, which is a just and prosperous society based on Pancasila and the 1945 Constitution."[80] To many PLN leaders, electricity was a vital technology to transform Indonesia into a modern Pancasila state. Similarly, the last two lines of PLN's hymn: "Towards modernization / based on Pancasila" (*Menuju Modernisasi / Yang Berdasarkan Pancasila*) explicitly linked Pancasila with their efforts illuminating the country. In this sense, the electricity bureaucracy became the vector of state ideology and helped energize the state's ideological program. It did so not just by delivering public goods and services but also by helping convince the populace that the New Order Pancasila interpretation was the correct way and that oppositions and deviations from this understanding would be deemed as anti-Pancasila and by extension antigovernment and antidevelopment.

Conclusion

As I have discussed, the New Order government founded and nurtured PLN to become the monopolistic electric bureaucracy to channel various state's largesse. PLN did so by delivering electricity to the villages and distributing social benefits to its employees and customers. This resulted in PLN functioning as a techno-social utility company. The state power company received huge financial, political, and material support from the government, but with the understanding that the company needed to always do what the state asked them to do. This includes accepting appointed leaders, following the government's electricity pricing structure, and doing all the things the government asked, including transmitting the state's patronage. PLN tried to become more independent from the government's interference by developing its own technical expertise and successfully lobbied to change its status from *perum* to *persero*, but it was still bound to carry out its biggest social mission of electrifying the rural areas. Bringing electricity to the villages was one of the New Order's biggest patrimonial practices, and PLN became the regime's technopolitical institution.

The power company also served as a conduit of the Soeharto government's interpretation of Pancasila. Its employees were required to take the mandatory Pancasila courses, and they used the state ideology to discuss their duties. On many occasions, PLN's efforts to expand its organization, develop its technical capabilities, and grow the country's infrastructure were made in the name of Pancasila. The language, promises, and ideals of the state ideology became PLN's ammunition to motivate employees and customers about the supposed virtues of the state ideology understood by the New Order state. In carrying out their double goals, PLN played a central role in making the Pancasila principles plain to the citizenry and, as a result, Pancasila-based development and ideology became a legitimizing discourse for the regime.

One consequence of having a state company monopolizing the country's electrification business was uneven electrical coverage. Constrained by limited workforce, capital, and technological resources, PLN had little choice but to prioritize its electrification schemes to serve highly populated areas. This blueprint was aligned with the government's priorities to stay in power because more densely populated centers meant more voters served. Thus urban areas and more populous islands became better electrified than the countryside and less densely inhabited areas. Remotely located communities such as the ones on a small or isolated island, in the mountains, or along the country's borders received the least attention when it came to electricity provision. Another implication of PLN's electrification strategies was a low participation of private companies in the Indonesian electricity business.[81] Other results of PLN-dominated electrification include citizens' heavy reliance on the state power company to meet their electricity needs even though the company could not always keep up with their demands. As a result, PLN often bore the brunt of people's complaints and ire when there was a long wait for a household connection, a rolling blackout, a power outage, or any poor services the customers experienced. Consumers complained in newspapers and directed their frustrations at PLN, usually unaware that many of PLN's decision-making processes were dictated by or at least required government involvement.

Java-Centrism and the Two Grid Systems

A T THE START of the New Order regime (1966), many of the country's electricity and gas installations required major repairs, including a few power plants from the Sukarno period that were only half-finished. In 1968 the Soeharto government identified twenty-four priority projects (table 5), for which the DPWEP set aside nearly Rp 4.4 billion and the state allotted almost Rp 2 billion.[1] The funds were allocated, for example, to repair and complete fourteen power stations and install DPPs in several provincial and district towns. The Jatiluhur (a.k.a. the Juanda) hydroelectric plant had been operational since 1967, and funds were earmarked to finalize the project. Similarly, the funds for the completed Asahan and Batang Agam HPPs were appropriated for maintenance only.

These residuals and some new projects occupied PLN throughout the 1970s. Tabulated data in PLN's annual reports from 1975 to 1979 indicate that the company steadily increased the number of power stations, substations, and electricity customers and expanded its transmission and distribution networks. The reports include images of PLN branch offices and various parts of the electric infrastructures. Some photos show PLN employees at work installing household connections or maintaining power lines. One can also find tables, graphs, and maps in these reports. In short, the colorful and glossy annual PLN publications in the later 1970s conveyed the idea that the company was hard at work electrifying the nation.

A closer look at the reports, especially the maps, reveals two different system-level designs for generating electric power in Indonesia: scattered DPPs and an interconnected grid. One can see, for example, many red dots sprinkled on the regional maps in the PLN 1975–1976 report. These red dots represent DPPs installed in towns along the coasts or in high-population centers inland. The only exception to this is maps of Java, where one can see other

Table 5. PLN Priority Projects in 1968

	Name	Place	Starting Year	Planned Year of Completion
1	Asahan HPP and transmission	Sigura-gura (North Sumatra)	1961	1970
2	Riam Kanan HPP	Bandjarbaru (South Kalimantan)	1961	1969
3	Sources of Energy Surveys[a]	Larona (South Sulawesi), rivers (West Sumatra), other places in Indonesia	—	—
4	Power Research Institute[b]	Jakarta	—	—
5	Rehabilitation of gas transmission and gas equipment factories	Jakarta	1965	In phases
6	Gas Research Institute	Bandung	1965	In phases
7	Gas field surveys	Bongas (Cirebon) West Java, East Java, Madura	1965	In phases
8	Batang Agam HPP	Batang Agam (West Sumatra)	1961	1970
9	Tonsea Lama HPP	Tonsea Lama (North Sulawesi)	1954	1968
10	Garung HPP	Garung (Central Java)	1962	1969
11	Ngebel HPP	Ngebel (East Java)	1959	1968
12	Palembang SPP	Palembang (South Sumatra)	1963	1970
13	Semarang NGPP	Semarang (Central Java)	1966	1968
14	Medan NGPP	Medan (North Sumatra)	1966	1968
15	Palembang NGPP	Palembang (South Sumatra)	1966	1968
16	West Java transmission network	West Java	1965	1970

Table 5. (*continued*)

	Name	Place	Starting Year	Planned Year of Completion
17	Makasar SPP including transmission	Makasar (South Sulawesi)	1965	1968
18	Scattered DPPs	Singkawang, Watan Soppeng, Banda Aceh, Tahona, Lubuklinggau, Palu, Bima Raba, Ampenan	1960	1968
19	Electric power repair shop	Klender	1962	1968
20	Rehabilitation and repair	Entire Indonesia	1966	In phases
21	East Java transmission	East Java	1965	1970
22	Priok SPP units 1 and 2	Jakarta	1960	1968
23	Jatiluhur HPP	Jatiluhur (West Java)	1955	1968
24	Karangkates HPP	Karangkates (East Java)	1962	c

Notes: DPP, diesel power plant; HPP, hydroelectric power plant; NGPP, natural gas-fired power plant; SPP, steam power plant.

[a] These surveys consisted of several projects, some of which were the continuation of surveys started in 1967, such as the Larona and West Sumatran rivers surveys.

[b] Laboratories of the Power Research Institute would be built as needed to support research in electricity.

[c] No year given.

types of power plants dotting the island: HPP, natural gas, and steam. There are a few HPPs in Sumatra, Kalimantan, and Sulawesi, and a gas power plant each in Medan and Palembang, but DPPs dominate the maps of the islands other than Java.[2] A few such power plants were connected by high-voltage transmission lines (70 kV or 150 kV) four years later, but these regional grids are few and far between; the most networked power plants are on Java.[3]

PLN continued the trends of this infrastructure growth, and by the mid-1990s, numerous DPPs dotted the country. This information can be gleaned from another set of maps produced by PLN, this time included in the commemorative volume *50 Years of PLN Dedication*. The book narrates PLN's journey electrifying the nation since Soekarno created the first electrical agency in October 1945. It contains twenty-two colorful maps of PLN's areas of operations, each displaying major power plants, substations, and high voltage transmission lines (both built and planned). Electricity produced by diesel power plants, this time represented by little red squares, predominates the country, including in Sumatra, Kalimantan, Sulawesi, Maluku, Nusa Tenggara islands, and Papua.[4]

Another PLN publication, *PLN Statistics 1995*, quantitatively supports the visual representations of the dispersed DPPs, reporting that at the time there were a total of 3,646 diesel units in all of Indonesia, most of which (3,539 units) were outside Java.[5] The total rated capacity of all these diesel generators was 2,265.4 MW, constituting a mere 15.12 percent of the total electric power generated in the country in 1995.[6] The bulk of electric power produced came from steam-powered (32.16 percent) and combined cycle (29.46 percent) power plants, which were built primarily in Java and Bali.[7] Despite the small percentage of power generated by the DPPs, they formed a crucial component of Indonesia's electric power infrastructure. Outside Java, they powered many localities, and without them electricity would only be available in about a dozen limited regional networks. These DPPs stood alone, unconnected to any grid, and when they broke down, electrical services were disrupted for days and sometimes weeks.[8]

The separate and detached DPPs are symbolic of the political challenges of New Order Indonesia as a modern nation: a country with a vast territorial expanse administered by a centralized authoritarian regime attempting to exert control over its disparate domains, many of which were out of reach of the state and some threatening to secede and fragment the country. Just as the New Order state used its powerful military, large bureaucracies, and Pancasila ideology to oblige order from Indonesian citizens and stitch together far-flung regions into a unified whole, PLN similarly employed its technical knowhow and organizational reach to keep all these isolated DPPs "integrated" despite being physically disjointed. In Java, however, PLN successfully bound the island's regional grids into a unified grid linked by the country's first EHV (500 kV) power transmission lines. This electrical backbone is known as the Java-Madura-Bali (Jamali) interconnected system, or the PLN grid (figure 10), and it established Java as the most illuminated island in the country.

I argue in this chapter that the creation of Indonesia's two power grids (the Jamali system and scattered DPPs) is a concrete realization of the fledgling nation's Java-centric governance generally and its approaches to electrification in particular. The electrification schemes of postindependence Indonesia followed the path dependency set up by the colonial-era electrification. Despite

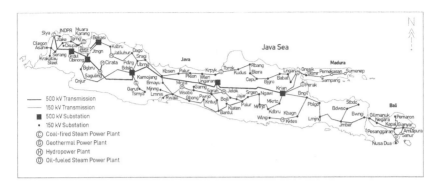

Figure 10. Java-Madura-Bali interconnected transmission system in 1989.
Source: Perusahaan Umum Listrik Negara, "Program Pelaksanaan Pembangunan REPELITA V Sistem Kelistrikan Jawa-Bali Dalam Rangka Peningkatan Pemasaran, Efisiensi, Mutu & Keadilan dan Pelayanan" (unpublished manuscript, 1989).

the social justice ideals of Pancasila and the government's rhetoric of equality, a lopsided Java-centric development persisted. The imbalance meant that more electric power and better-quality electricity services were provided in Java than on other islands. Java's better electricity provision translated to better educational, political, and economic opportunities, and the island became the main destination for many Indonesian citizens who lived elsewhere and sought upward social mobility.

In developing the Java-focused electric infrastructures, PLN resorted to building two main types of power plants in the country. The first was largescale, economical, and more fuel-efficient power plants, which required sophisticated technical and managerial expertise to operate and maintain. These largescale plants harnessed Indonesia's nonoil resources. The second type were more easily constructed diesel-fueled, small to medium scale power stations, which did not require sophisticated technical knowhow to run. These two kinds of power plants make up Indonesia's electric landscapes to this day. The decision to construct these DPPs, as I explain later, was based on interrelated political, technical, financial, and geographical reasons. Their existence provided cheap electricity to many village households, a tangible, material benefit the New Order regime delivered to establish their visibility in the villages to secure political support. PLN's numerous DPPs are visible, material representations of the New Order state's patrimonial technopolitics in the countryside.

Java-Centrism in the New Order

The New Order government focused many of its development programs (including electrification endeavors) on Java for several reasons. First, for pragmatic and political reasons, Java was (and remains) the most populated island and the Javanese constitute the largest pool of potential voters in the general elections.[9] To be sure the Balinese, the Bugis, the Madurese, the Minangs, the Bataks, and a few other ethnolinguistic groups combined make up a sizable percentage of the population, but when faced with the challenges of creating an integrated power grid spanning the archipelago, the New Order state invariably chose the island with the highest population density. Extending PLN transmission lines from any Javanese provincial and district capitals to the surrounding countryside would connect more customers than on other islands. Plus, the support of the Javanese voters in general elections would benefit the New Order government greatly (see chapter 2).

The second reason had to do with the results of colonial-era electrification. As I describe in chapter 1, at the end of Dutch colonial rule, Java was the best electrified island in the Netherlands East Indies. The largest three Dutch companies electrified Javanese urban areas largely because the highest concentration of Europeans were found there. Javanese cities like Jakarta, Bogor, Bandung, Surabaya, and Semarang were among the earliest towns to be illuminated in the late colonial period. The preexisting electric infrastructure facilitated easy expansion compared with building new networks elsewhere. Moreover, Java has several rivers and abundant geothermal energy that could be harnessed to generate electricity. Growing Java's electrical network was easier and more expedient than constructing one from scratch outside Java. Consequently, by the mid-1970s, the four largest cities in Java (Jakarta, Bandung, Surabaya, and Semarang) had a good transmission network in place.[10]

Third, a historicopolitical reason figured in the Java-centrism of the New Order. For centuries Java has been the center of several political entities. Two kingdoms in particular exerted considerable sociopolitical influence over most of Java and other parts of the archipelago. They live in the memory and imagination of many Indonesians today. The first, the Majapahit empire, an East Javanese, Hindu-Buddhist kingdom of the thirteenth to sixteenth centuries, is considered one of the two greatest precolonial Indonesian polities.[11] The second, the Mataram sultanate, founded in the sixteenth century and located in the interior of Central Java, produced Javanese dynasties whose descendants still rule four of its successor kingdoms today: the Sultanate and its minor princely state the Pakualaman of Yogyakarta and the Susuhanate and its minor princely state the Mangkunegaran of Surakarta.[12] This is not to say that other Javanese and non-Javanese kingdoms were not important. Several, such as the Sunda Kingdom and the Banten Sultanate in western Java, the Srivijaya Empire in southern Sumatra, the sultanate of Aceh, the Gowa and Tallo kingdoms in southern Sulawesi, the sultanates of Tidore and Ternate in northern

Maluku, and other sovereignties played roles in the complex political history of precolonial and colonial Indonesia. However, the legacies of the two Javanese kingdoms mentioned above seemed to hold strong sway on Sukarno (who was half-Javanese) and Soeharto (who was full Javanese).

As national leaders, Sukarno and Soeharto influenced how Indonesians perceived their country and their duties as citizens. Sukarno, for example, often invoked the Majapahit in his speeches, suggesting that modern Indonesia should aspire to the same kind of territorial unity that Majapahit rulers established within its domains, which stretched from Sumatra to New Guinea, with Java as its center of power.[13] Considering that the means by which Majapahit rulers achieved such unity were mostly by conquest, Sukarno emphasized the end point of unity and not its messy pathway. This notion of Majapahit being the precursor of the modern Indonesian state still lives in the imagination of many citizens, in part, to revive a sense of "glorious" past and find a local political model to emulate.

Sukarno's fascination with Majapahit's "unification" of the archipelago was small in comparison to Soeharto's deeply influenced Javanese view of life. Born in the village of Kemusuk, Yogyakarta, Soeharto loved Javanese philosophy and even professed to live by it. He believed in the idea of power as a zero-sum entity which, when accumulated by one, is lost to others. This is different from the way power is conceptualized in the West. Political scientist Benedict Anderson analyzed the modern Western concept of power as "an abstraction deduced from observed patterns of social interaction; it is believed to derive from heterogeneous sources; it is in no way inherently self-limiting; and it is morally ambiguous."[14] The Javanese understanding of power is diametrically opposed to this, "as something concrete, homogeneous, constant in total quantity, and without inherent moral implications as such."[15]

The Javanese conceptualization of political power is analogous to the law of conservation of energy (a.k.a. the First Law of Thermodynamics). One aspect of the Javanese perception of political power is that "its total quantity does not change, even though the distribution of power in the universe may vary."[16] This is similar to the idea expressed by the First Law of Thermodynamics in that the total energy in the universe is constant (i.e., it cannot be created or destroyed) and can only be transformed from one form to another. Likewise, the Javanese believe that power exists in the universe in a certain quantity and "that concentration of power in one place or in one person requires a proportional diminution elsewhere."[17] Moreover, in "Javanese traditional thinking there is no sharp division between organic and inorganic matter, for everything is sustained by the same invisible power."[18] It is not too farfetched, then, to surmise that for someone who viewed political power as concrete and in fixed quantity also regarded electrical power (or more accurately electrical energy) as constant and must be amassed and concentrated in one area.[19] For Soeharto, it would make the most sense to focus on Java, the center of his political power. It is akin to the Javanese old tradition for the ruler to "concentrate around him any objects or persons held to have or contain unusual [political] Power."[20]

The Jamali Interconnected Grid

Starting in the early 1980s, PLN began building several largescale steam power plants (SPPs), GPPs, and HPPs. A list of these power plants, types, and their locations in and outside Java are found in tables 6 and 7. When Dr. Subroto, then minister of Mining and Energy, inaugurated the start of the Mrica power plant project in August 1982, he said that Indonesia's hydroelectric contributions was 20.7 percent (~ 516 MW) of the total energy output at the time, but he hoped that it would increase to 32 percent (~ 1,999 MW) of the projected total output in 1988.[21] Many of these power plant projects were financed by international financial institutions. For example, the Suralaya, Saguling, Kamojang, and Cirata were funded in part by World Bank loans.[22] There were several power plants constructed outside Java, but not all were considered largescale plants. The Bakaru HPP, for example, had a total capacity of 126 MW.[23] The power capacity of the Sikunang-Dieng and Lahendong GPPs was very small compared with the other three built because they were experimental plants. When completed, the Gresik combined-cycle power plants complex would be the largest in the country and became the backbone power supply of the Jamali interconnected system.[24]

The high considerations of developing power generations on Java was perhaps best illustrated by the Suralaya power plant (figure 11), Indonesia's first largescale coalfired SPP. The Suralaya plant was designed to use coal extracted from the Bukit Asam coalmine in the province of South Sumatra. However, instead of building it near the mine to accommodate easier transportation, the Soeharto government decided to construct it in Merak on the northwestern coast of West Java. Why did PLN decide to build Suralaya in Java instead of in Sumatra? There were three main reasons, two economic and one technical. First, another coalfired SPP in Bukit Asam was simultaneously being constructed starting in 1983 and would be completed in February 1988. This plant also used coal from the Bukit Asam mine and provided southern Sumatra with a sizable generation. A 150 kV transmission line delivered electricity from Bukit Asam power plant to the provincial capital Palembang. This project was awarded to four Indonesian companies (PT Waskita Karya, PT Hutama Karya, PT Panca Makmur, and PT Buana Power) to complete the civil

Table 6. PLN's power plants in Java

Name	Type	Location	Total Capacity (MW)
Sikunang-Dieng	GPP	Central Java	2
Gunung Salak	GPP	West Java	110
Kamojang units 1, 2, 3	GPP	West Java	140
Darajat units 1, 2, 3	GPP	West Java	145
Mrica	HPP	Central Java	184.5
Cirata units 1, 2, 3, and 4	HPP	West Java	500
Saguling	HPP	West Java	700
Suralaya units 1 and 2 (first phase)	SPP	West Java	800
Gresik	CCPP	East Java	1,500

Notes: CCPP, combined-cycle power plant; GPP, geothermal power plant; HPP, hydroelectric power plant; SPP, steam power plant.

Table 7. PLN's Power Plants Outside Java

Name	Type	Location	Total Capacity (MW)
Lahendong	GPP	North Sulawesi	2.5
Maninjau	HPP	West Sumatra	68
Bakaru	HPP	South Sulawesi	126
Belawan	SPP	North Sumatra	130
Bukit Asam	SPP	South Sumatra	130

Notes: GPP, geothermal power plant; HPP, hydroelectric power plant; SPP, steam power plant

engineering aspect of the plant.[25] Second, one of the coal transportation hubs from Bukit Asam to Suralya would be the port of Tarahan in Lampung and the Indonesian government hoped that this port would stimulate the economy of the local area and province in general. Third, PLN engineers reasoned that erecting the Suralaya SPP in West Java and transmitting the electric power using an EHV transmission line was more cost-effective than building it in South Sumatra and sending the electric current across the Sunda Strait using a high-voltage direct current submarine cable.[26] Although PLN's technoeconomic calculations may have justified the project, this decision robbed Sumatra of a chance to connect the island to Java for a more integrated system. To

Figure 11. Suralaya power plant. Source: Photo by Satari, December 2007, courtesy of Wikimedia Commons.

this day, Sumatra is still unconnected to Java, and discussions about connecting the islands electrically are ongoing.[27]

How was the coal transported from Sumatra to Java? A combination of land and water coal supply lines was built from the hinterland of South Sumatra to West Java. A set of coal trains would carry 2,080 tons of coal from Tanjung Enim coalmine to the Tarahan port on a 420-km railway, followed by a bulk carrier shipping the coal to Suralaya on a 100-km shipping route.[28] At one point, there was an issue building these logistical lines. Dominion Bridge and Balfour Beatty, the chosen contractor to build the coal port at Tarahan, encountered a land subsidence issue for the onshore part of the port. The Indonesian government installed a temporary coal-loading facility and imported coal from Australia as a stopgap measure to start the Suralaya power plant in April 1985.[29] After protracted negotiations, the Indonesian government terminated the contract in March 1986 and hired a new contractor to finish the port.[30] When the Suralaya power plant was inaugurated on August 10, 1985, it was reported that the percentage of power plants using oil dropped from 85 percent to 73 percent after the plant began operations.[31] Despite this reduction of domestic oil consumption, the construction of DPPs continued apace elsewhere.

To integrate the Suralaya power plant and Java's other big power plants with the regional grids, the New Order government constructed Indonesia's first interconnected transmission system. The islandwide electric network was an engineering feat and began operation on April 16, 1987.[32] The network consists of 500 kV transmission lines, several substations, and one main and four regional load control centers. Their constructions were completed in four phases done by Italian, English, and Indonesian companies and was financed by funds from the World Bank, the Asian Development Bank, the state budget, and PLN's internal budget.[33] PLN proudly claimed that its integrated power grid was the first such system in Southeast Asia.[34] The power lines would eventually connect Java's regional networks and those of Madura and Bali as one whole unit. The new network also linked largescale power-generating stations in Java, such as the Suralaya coalfired SPPs, Saguling and Cirata HPPs, and Paiton coalfired power plants. Regulating the energy supplies and demands was PLN's Load Dispatch Center (Pusat Pengatur Beban) in Gandul, West Java.[35] The successful completion of the PLN grid helped the company earn recognition for its increased technical abilities to construct and operate a sophisticated sociotechnical system.

Madura's and Bali's regional grids were connected to Java's power system using underwater cables.[36] By 1989, the integrated three-island grids had been completed. For Madura and Bali, being connected to Java's islandwide grid had both advantages and disadvantages. Populations of the islands enjoyed better electricity provision than many communities on other islands, where there was either too little or no electricity at all. At the same time, this interconnectedness made Bali and Madura highly dependent on Java. For example, when a merchant ship accidentally damaged the Java-Madura submarine electric cable on February 19, 1999, the whole of Madura went dark. Thankfully, PLN had backup diesel generator sets that powered Madura's hospitals and other vital installations.[37] The company later brought in a 10 MW bargemounted DPP to power the island, and electricity was available again on March 20, 1999.[38] It took a few months to repair the damaged underwater cable.

Bali had a few DPPs, but they did not produce enough electricity to meet rapidly growing demands. Java's surplus electricity transmitted via the submarine cables helped Bali meet its electricity needs. Still, there has been a constant anxiety on the part of some Balinese that the Java-Bali undersea cables tethered their island to Java perpetually. In 2009, some Balinese had asked PLN to construct an overland transmission line crossing the Bali Strait called the Java Bali Crossing (JBC) to supply additional power because they were worried that Bali would not get enough electricity if there were something wrong with the undersea cables.[39] Although there was initial support for this idea, some Balinese later opposed it because of cultural, religious, and environmental concerns.[40] I Wayan Koster, one of Bali gubernatorial candidates in June 2018, campaigned against the project.[41] He remained opposed to it after being elected governor, and several Balinese supported him because they said it would violate a provincial regulation on spatial planning.[42] The latest news on this issue shows that PLN had redesigned the concept and instead plan to build an EHV submarine transmission line to be laid underneath the Bali Strait. Citing that it was part of a National Strategic Project, the plan is currently underway with a target of completion in 2025. Using the same acronym as before, the project is now called Java Bali Connection.[43] It seems Bali would continue to be linked to Java well into the future.

PLN's Java-centric approach to electrification helped construct the PLN grid, the electric backbone that combined the regional grids of Java, Madura, and Bali. This interconnection was the first (and so far only) integrated power system in Indonesia and, as a result, the three islands are the most illuminated regions in the country. On Sumatra the brightest spots at night are in provincial capitals such as Banda Aceh, Medan, Padang, Pekanbaru, Jambi, and Bandar Lampung. On Kalimantan, one can see scattered dots of lights along the coast where towns and cities are located. On Sulawesi in urban areas, such as the cities of Makassar and Manado. On Lombok, the southern part of this island is more brightly lit than the northern part. In the other parts of Indonesia, darkness still envelops large areas. Satellite images of Earth at night show this vividly.[44]

Scattered DPPs

Toward the end of Soeharto's rule in 1998, DPPs existed in significant numbers across the Indonesian archipelago. In 1997 there were 3,627 diesel power-generating stations and 111 power plants of other types outside Java. In comparison, there were only 56 diesel-fueled power plants and 177 power plants of other kinds in Java.[45] In other words, there were many more DPPs than all other types of power plants combined. How did Indonesia end up with thousands of diesel-powered generators scattered across the islands, and why did PLN choose this technology to electrify the country? As I will explain, there are several interrelated reasons: (1) the availability of cheap oil, (2) PLN's financial and technical justifications, (3) standardization of construction; (4) pioneer technology and state encroachment; (5) the New Order development progress narrative; and (6) PLN's allegedly corrupt practices.

The Dutch discovered oil in the Netherlands East Indies in the second half of the nineteenth century. The oil drilled from a well in Telaga Said in northern Sumatra in 1885 led to the founding of the Royal Dutch Company in 1890, and by the early 1900s, oil had been found in Sumatra, Java, and Kalimantan. Foreign companies dominated oil production in the first half of the twentieth century. Following Indonesia's independence in 1945, oil production continued, but it wasn't until the Indonesian government passed the foreign investment law in January 1967 and created the Indonesian state oil and gas company (Perusahaan Pertambangan Minyak Bumi dan Gas Negara, Pertamina) in 1968 that joint operations in oil exploration and exploitation began. While the law forbade foreign companies to invest in certain areas (e.g., power generation and distribution and defense-related products), it allowed investment in the oil and gas sector.[46] However, instead of giving foreign enterprises concessions, "with ownership rights to the oil," they were asked to sign "production sharing" contracts that "gave [the foreign companies] rights to part of any stream of oil they discovered. This new type of relationship was pioneered by Indonesia and Caltex in the late 1960s."[47] Along with its foreign partners, Pertamina extracted Indonesia's fossil fuel resources and steadily increased the country's oil production in the 1970s. According to Indonesia's Department of Mining and Energy, foreign investment in oil exploration and exploitation in Indonesia jumped from US$270 million in 1968 to US$4.2 billion in 1984. Indonesia's oil production rose from 468,000 barrels a day in 1968 to 1.68 million barrels a day in 1977.[48]

Windfall from oil revenues allowed the New Order government to subsidize oil for domestic consumption. The subsidies kept the price of diesel oil artificially low—significantly lower than its production and distribution costs—which resulted in "cheap oil." PLN constructed the distribution network to deliver diesel to even the remotest parts of the country. For instance, a remote village in Papua received the fuel by air. A small chartered plane would load barrels of diesel and drop them in one of the lakes for the locals to fish out of the water.[49] The availability of cheap oil and the countrywide oil delivery network facilitated PLN's use of DPPs to electrify many areas of Indonesia.

PLN's financial and technical rationale determined early on that DPPs were the most suitable and cheapest technology for generating electricity. In a 1978 seminar discussing the availability of various energy sources in rural areas, Ir. Suryono, PLN president director between 1975 and 1980, said that among the three types of electric generators PLN considered, the cost of a diesel generator was the cheapest.[50] What he didn't reveal was that the Soeharto government levied no import tax on the machines, which made them cheaper than other alternatives.[51] A DPP also satisfied two of PLN's important technical criteria: variable electricity demands (load) and operational considerations. Ali Herman Ibrahim, a member of the PLN board of directors in the mid-2000s, explains, "a diesel power plant is flexible in meeting an electrical load, easy to maintain, and has a varied capacity from small to large."[52] This flexibility allowed PLN to size the appropriate power capacity to serve the electric power needs of its rural communities, which were not uniform across Indonesia.

PLN's technical and financial rationales were supported by another justification: constructing and operating a DPP can be standardized. There were four important documents related to such standardizations. The first was an operational report on two pilot projects of micro-DPPs written in 1977 by Ir. Tahir Harahap, a PLN employee. The other two documents were PLN standards on village electrification and village electrification construction published in 1987 and 1991. The final document was an operational manual released in 1994. In his 1977 report, *Perlistrikan Desa* (Village Electrification), Harahap detailed his analysis of the Samalanga and Panton Labu power plants in Aceh. He described the investment, electric power produced, number of technicians employed, operational costs, and revenues and profits from both plants.[53] Overall, Harahap advocated using small DPPs in the villages. However, he wrote that similarly detailed studies on wind-powered, ocean tide–powered, solar-powered, and micro-HPPs were needed to have good alternative comparisons.[54] In a section describing the "advantages and disadvantages" of micro-DPPs, he outlined only the benefits: they can be installed anywhere in the country, they are independent of varying seasons and weather conditions, they can be constructed in under one year, they are cheaper to build than micro-HPPs (about a fifth of the cost), and because they can be placed in the center of towns, it would be easy to find qualified personnel to operate them.[55]

Although his calculations of the operations of the two micro-DPPs were incomplete (he didn't calculate the costs of spare parts or operational costs of the local PLN branch overseeing the plants), he argued that this scheme would be more profitable than operating bigger power stations that were already supplying electricity to a few provincial towns: Medan, Palembang, and Ujung Pandang.[56] In short, Harahap's report argued that small DPPs would be an effective investment to electrify Indonesia's villages with minimal cost and careful planning. The report was published as a Power Research Institute publication and widely circulated within PLN.

Ten years after Harahap's report was published, PLN issued the first of its two rural electrification standards. The 1987 document, "SPLN 74: 1987 Village Electrification Standards" (*Standar Listrik Pedesaan*), was followed four years later by the publication of a more detailed "SPLN 87: 1991 Village Electrification Construction Standards" (*Standar Konstruksi Listrik Pedesaan*). Both were written to facilitate the construction of a power system in rural areas quickly and cheaply without compromising technical integrity. In addition, in 1994 PLN issued a manual to care for their DPPs using some testing and monitoring equipment fitted to the generators.[57] The goal of this research was so the company could do more predictive maintenance and, in the long run, reduce incidences of failures. These documents indicate PLN's favored approach of using DPPs for rural electrification. A lot of thought was put into drawing up these documents, and the main idea was standardization to enable PLN engineers, technicians, and contractors anywhere in the country to speedily set up and maintain pioneer DPPs.

Indonesia's highly contoured landscapes meant that many villages were isolated from one another. To string wires from its main transmission lines to these remote villages would require a large sum of money, which PLN was reluctant to finance because of the likely small return on investment. Instead, PLN preferred to build a power station with one diesel generator with a power output of half of what the projected load in the tenth year of operation would be, which could be increased by adding a second generator or replacing it with one with higher capacity later, if needed.[58] PLN's idea was to use this type of power generation temporarily until the area served was connected to the grid so it could move the diesel generator to another location. The company called it Pioneer Diesel Power Plant (PLTD Perintis).[59] Dr. Emil Salim, minister of Communications (1973–78), said at one point that installing what he called "pioneer technologies" in the remotest parts of the country, particularly the eastern part of Indonesia, was urgently needed because private companies were reluctant to invest in these technologies because of a lack of adequate infrastructure in these areas. He writes,

Because of the crucial importance of infrastructure in uniting and developing our country—and because private enterprise was not moving into this field—I felt that government intervention was needed. That is why a pioneer (*perintis*) airline and shipping line were introduced. It was based on the simple logic that if the private sector was not interested in moving into these sectors, the government would have to do so. The government subsidised airline services to distant isolated regions which sometimes had only a football field to serve as a landing strip. This was the only way that medical services could be provided to isolated areas in Kalimantan, Sulawesi, Nusa Tenggara, Maluku, and Irian Jaya.[60]

Unification may have been on Salim's mind, but placing these "pioneer technologies" also allowed the state to encroach into remote places and villagers' lives. Diesel electric generators were relatively easy to install and, in the end, many supposedly short-term power stations became lasting fixtures of the landscape.

At one point, PLN attempted to replace some DPPs but stopped short of doing so, arguing an economic calculus of its return on investment. PLN reasoned that one crucial factor hindering its "de-dieselization" process was the low electricity consumption in many villages, which was "about 45 kWh/customer/month."[61] This small consumption rate coupled with load factor, a measure of electricity usage efficiency, in some systems of about 20–25 percent, resulted in "high long-run cost and low [electricity bill] revenue in the villages."[62] In other words, because not many villagers used electricity as much as PLN would like, the company did not want to bother dismantling the plants and replacing them with different types of power stations. PLN reasoned that to economically install and run a mini-HPP or a small-scale GPP in the villages required a "utilization factor of 70–85% ," or at least seven out of ten villagers need to be electricity customers.[63] But this so-called technoeconomic problem was part of a larger issue with bringing electricity to the villages.[64] The villagers' low use of electricity was tied to their low income, and they did not want more electricity than what they needed.

In the 1970s, several New Order bureaucrats had expressed the goal to completely electrify the county by 2000, the year when the New Order hoped that the bulk of Indonesia's villages would have transformed into *swasembada* villages.[65] To speedily and cost-effectively electrify a village or a cluster of villages, PLN engineers determined that diesel power stations were the most reasonable choice. This way, PLN village electric workers could figure out whether they could meet the New Order's targets during the five-year development plans (REPELITA). For example, in the third REPELITA (1979–84), the government's goal was to electrify 3,700 villages. PLN managed to exceed this target by electrifying 56 percent more villages using a special budget allocated by the New Order government. Similarly, the government asked PLN to connect 7,000 villages and 1.6 million customers in the fourth REPELITA (1984–89) and 2.4 million customers and 9,500 villages in the fifth REPELITA (1989–94).[66] Based on these targets (and achievements), PLN could report the steady increase of the number of villages electrified each year. Likewise, the Soeharto government could announce a continuous upward trend every year, projecting the idea that it led the nation in a steady march toward prosperity, equity, and modernity. As I have explained elsewhere, an electrified village did not mean that all hamlets that make up the village had received electricity. It just meant that an electrical distribution network had reached at least one point in that village. This was a convenient definition of a "lit village" (*desa nyala*) that PLN used.[67] One connection and the power company could check off the village as "electrified."

Finally, a more covert reason that diesel generators became the main choice and continued as they did in the countryside, in the words of one former PLN president director: "it was easy to build and to be corrupted."[68] When Djiteng Marsudi gave this reason to me, I understood him to mean that constructing DPPs was a source of financial and accounting manipulations whereby marked-up expenses allowed people involved in the projects to pocket the difference in prices or take kickbacks from suppliers. The allegedly corrupt practices of PLN officials distributing projects to build DPPs to get payment from small private contractors or business partners may have occurred quite frequently given the culture of the New Order era. Emil Salim, who once served as Soeharto's minister of State for the Improvement of the State Apparatus (1971–73), admitted that he "learned about the various types of bureaucratic corruption," and many wanted to bribe government officials or their families, "especially when [they were] issuing lucrative tenders."[69] I must note that I could not find any hard evidence of this practice in PLN, though given the climate of press censorship and other means of suppressing information, there was very little chance that any of this was reported or investigated at all.

An indication that this corruption may have occurred, however, was revealed in the post-Soeharto period when President B. J. Habibie, Soeharto's successor, granted the press more freedom to investigate and publish previously underreported topics. For example, in an interview between a *Tajuk* journalist and Djiteng Marsudi, the reporter asked him pointedly about money exchanged "under the table," to which Marsudi replied, "You can ask all of the contractors whose contracts I had signed, I never called them and said, 'I sign this, but you give me money.' Never. You can ask." The reporter pressed further: "But the chance to do that [i.e., to receive kickbacks] was high, wasn't it?" To which Marsudi responded, "Oh, if I wanted, yes. In fact, after I was no longer with PLN, I heard that many people whose contracts have not been signed already gave money [to the contract signor]. . . . There were some who told me, 'Your subordinates are wealthier than you.' I replied, 'That's okay, I accepted it (*saya ikhlaskan*)." The journalist further asked: "Don't you feel alienated, while KKN [Corruption, Collusion, and Nepotism] was already widespread at the time?" Marsudi said, "No. . . . It lies on our faith. I concluded that God is just. Our sustenance is not just in the form of money [but also friends and family] . . . My salary as the President Director [of PLN] was enough. I never played around with the contracts."[70] In these exchanges, Marsudi admitted that he was aware of the situations that allowed

PLN officials to award contracts unfairly in exchange for lucrative financial rewards.

The six reasons worked together to advance DPPs as the best option to electrify rural Indonesia. Initially, PLN intended to use them temporarily as a stopgap measure until largescale power plants could be built.[71] But even after the power company had constructed big stations in Java, it continued to install and operate DPPs on other islands. Pertamina President Director Piet Haryono expressed his concern about the country's heavy reliance on oil for generating electricity as early as 1978. He was worried (correctly as it turned out) that oil consumption would increase and pose problems in the future. Haryono said, "The convenience afforded by oil as one energy source and the low price of this fuel led to high use. Another effect of this is that to switch from this liquid energy source to another source of energy would take a long time."[72] PLN President Director Ir. Suryono agreed that "a barrel of oil conserved is as good as a barrel of oil produced."[73] However, he also asserted that in 1978 PLN was using only 12,000 barrels of oil per day or about 4 percent of national consumption, a small percentage. PLN was "entitled" to use more oil,[74] and did so as it built thousands of additional DPPs over the next two decades.

Underdeveloped Alternatives

Indonesia is endowed with both renewable (solar, wind, water, geothermal) and nonrenewable (oil, natural gas, coal) primary energy sources. The Dutch used hydropower energy extensively to generate electricity. Indonesian leaders understood the availability and value of these resources as well. Sukarno, for example, initiated the Jatiluhur Multipurpose Dam for irrigation and electricity production in the late 1950s. The New Order regime, as we've learned, harnessed water by building largescale hydropower plants. However, it did not widely harness waterpower in hydro-rich villages using a micro (up to 50 kW) or a mini (50 kW–5 MW) HPP (MHPP).[75] Nor did it construct solar- or wind-powered plants in areas where these resources were abundant.

There were brief discussions about the feasibility of generating electricity using hydrological sources in the early 1970s, and there appears to have been some efforts to build them in the 1980s. One PLN division called the Master Project for Physical and Supporting Facilities (Proyek Induk Sarana Fisik dan Penunjang) was tasked to develop this technology. Ir. Bambang Prajitno, the division leader in the mid-1980s, reported that during the Fourth PELITA (1984–89), the Master Project was developing MHPPs with a total capacity of 50 MW across Indonesia.[76] However, in the end, the total number of DPPs still far outnumbered MHPPs. A tabulated village electrification plan for the Sixth PELITA (1994–99), drawn up in 1994, showed that many more diesel-fueled power stations (up to 40 MW) than MHPPs would be constructed (10.45 MW).

PLN provided several reasons. First, the company claimed the mountainous areas where it would be suitable to harness the power of falling water were usually sparsely populated and thus it was not cost-effective to build hydroelectric generating units. Second, PLN said there was a paucity of local experts to carry out studies of potential sites, and local contractors were usually concentrated in the cities. Third, the most difficult technical challenge for PLN was to produce affordable water turbines.[77] However, even when one PLN employee invented a mini water turbine and another invented a hybrid machine by connecting a locally made generator to a water turbine using a automotive gear transmission box, PLN's uptake of this technology was low.[78] The power company was not keen on developing MHPPs.

Some communities took the initiatives to build their own MHPPs. In Bali, for example, I Dewa Made Suambara independently came up with a microhydro turbine using simple technologies that took about one to two months to build. By November 1984, it was reported that his creation had been replicated and installed with as many as 39 HPPs built by December 1984.[79] But PLN argued that the quality of electricity from these hydroelectric stations was low and engineers talked about helping them increase their technical knowhow to ensure the electricity produced would be up to PLN's standards. But apart from discussing them in a January 1985 seminar, there seems to be little else the company did to develop it.[80] In short, PLN didn't consider MHPPs a serious alternative. Diesel power stations held more appeal than any other methods of generating electricity for the reasons I mentioned already.

As for nuclear energy, at one point it was part of PLN's plan. In a seminar on national energy diversification in 1980, PLN Director of Production Development Ir. Sardjono described that in 1979 PLN's generating stations were made up mainly of hydropower (28 percent) and diesel (72 percent), and by 2000, the company hoped to have the following energy mix: hydropower (6 percent), oil (2 percent), geothermal (2 percent), coal (43 percent), and nuclear (47 percent).[81] He didn't foresee that Indonesia would get a large percentage of its electric power from hydropower despite having abundant hydro resources to do so. Although he didn't elaborate why, he probably knew that building large dams would have high social costs that he could not predict.[82] Instead, Sardjono put his hope on another fossil fuel Indonesia had in abundance and on nuclear power.

Although PLN managed to construct the country's first largescale Suralaya coalfired power plant, it never got around to realizing its dream of generating electricity from nuclear energy. The PLN upper echelons throughout the early

1980s did not think it was urgent and left it to the New Order government to pursue this course. Plus, there was another government agency, the National Agency for Nuclear Power (Badan Tenaga Nuklir Nasional, BATAN), charged with coming up with a plan to build a nuclear power plant. Founded in 1964, BATAN acquired its nuclear expertise by building and operating three research reactors in Bandung, Yogyakarta, and Serpong.

In the wake of the Chernobyl nuclear disaster in April 1986, a public debate about whether Indonesia should have a nuclear power plant erupted. Ir. Djali Ahimsa, head of BATAN at the time, said in a press conference that his agency would continue to study the possibility of constructing a nuclear power plant and assured concerned citizens that it would not employ a Soviet reactor technology.[83] He also mentioned a plan to establish a center of atomic safety in Serpong, the location of one of the three experimental reactors, to study nuclear accidents with experts from France, Germany, and Canada, deliberately leaving out the United States and the Soviet Union, where two nuclear accidents had occurred.[84]

Ahimsa saw the risk of a nuclear accident mainly from a scientific perspective, in which risk could be calculated, managed, and controlled. His largely scientific-based risk perception was later countered by a group of nongovernmental environmental organizations that called themselves the Group of Ten (Kelompok Sepuluh). The group gained attention by holding its own press conference and arguing that an accident would inevitably occur due to "human negligence" in a technologically risky system such as a nuclear power plant, no matter how "tidy" its safety mechanism.[85] Referring to the Chernobyl accident, they argued that the potential human costs of a nuclear power plant accident outweighed the benefits and asked the government to consider other energy sources.[86] Noticing rising public concern, Subroto finally issued a statement in Jakarta claiming that the government had not made a decision regarding a nuclear power plant and added that BATAN's study was still preliminary and too "far to reach a conclusion [to build one]."[87] To bolster his assurance, Subroto cited some statistics showing that Indonesia's potential to generate electricity from water power (up to 75,000 MW) and geothermal (up to 15,000 MW) had only been developed at a fraction of the estimated numbers (1,000 MW for hydro and 30 MW for geothermal).[88] Subroto's statement helped calm public anxiety about Indonesia's plan to go nuclear.

Four years passed until talks about nuclear energy emerged again. On July 17, 1990, PLN and BATAN signed a collaborative deal to start developing a nuclear power project.[89] Together they developed a plan to construct a nuclear plant in Muria in Central Java beginning in the 1998/1999 fiscal year. However, a meeting between the minister of Mining and Energy and some members of the Indonesian Parliament in 1996 derailed the plan. Both agreed that nuclear power had to be the last alternative to supply electricity since there were other energy resources that Indonesia could use first.[90] The nuclear project was abandoned altogether in 1997 when Indonesia was hit by a financial crisis that saw its currency depreciated up to 80 percent. In the post-Soeharto period, the government's attempt to construct a nuclear power plant was met by resistance by Muria's residents.[91] As of 2023, Indonesia has not built a nuclear power plant.

Conclusion

The New Order state implemented Java-centric electrification and consequently produced two types of power grids: an interconnected system stitching together regional grids on three islands and scattered DPPs in the rest of the country. The Jamali interconnected system relies on high-voltage transmission lines spanning Java and supported by largescale power plants on the island. The New Order regime invested huge resources to developing Java's electric infrastructure because its high population density, its colonial legacies, and its location as the seat of the political power, where electric power to support that political power needs to be amassed and concentrated. Java became the focal point of the unified Indonesia, just like the Majapahit Empire was, and having more electric energy produced on this island would ensure the centrality of Java in Soeharto's conception of the Indonesian nation.

PLN's choice to use DPPs to electrify many parts of Indonesia, as I have argued, rest on six interrelated reasons. First, the provision of subsidized cheap oil for domestic consumption and PLN's logistical infrastructure to deliver diesel oil across the country. Second, PLN justified this technology on techno-economic reasons. A tax exemption on the importation of diesel generators made it the cheapest option, and DPPs were flexible enough to meet changing customers' electricity demands. Third, PLN's rural electrification standards using diesel generators helped spread this technology widely. Fourth, the state power company used PLTDs to encroach on many remote areas of the country and into people's lives there. Fifth, the New Order state was able to show the increasing numbers of "electrified villages," made possible by quickly installing DPPs in many areas, to report progress on its development agenda. Finally, DPPs were a source of corruption for many people involved in the project, as alleged by one PLN former executive.

There were a few alternatives to DPPs, but the New Order government underdeveloped them. Building MHPPs posed several challenges to PLN, such as finding suitable sites, local consultants to do the feasibility studies, and local contractors who wanted to carry out the project. The company also faced some challenges of manufacturing a water turbine even though two employees proposed viable ideas to produce cheaper methods of construction. PLN was lukewarm to their ideas. DPPs were still their number one choice to generate electricity outside Java.

Meanwhile, Java saw and benefited from the construction of several large-scale power plants and, by the end of the 1980s, a sophisticated transmission system linking it with Bali and Madura. The government's reasons for doing this were to reduce oil consumption and harness Java's natural resources to produce electricity economically. Although this may be the case, this strategy was a visible material realization of the Soeharto government's Java-centric electrification policy, which mirrored its Java-centric governance of the Indonesian nation. This policy inevitably produced regional inequalities and undermined the New Order's rhetoric of implementing Pancasila's fifth principle of social justice for all Indonesians.

Java's more developed electric infrastructures transformed the island into a place where Indonesians go to seek better economic and other opportunities. The island has the most developed and well-lit urban areas, which translates to having more better paying jobs available than on the other islands. People from the countryside flock to Javanese cities and towns in search of these jobs. Java also boasts the best schools, universities, and training centers in the country, attracting the most promising and talented students at the expense of educational places on the other islands. As we shall see in the next chapter, when the government recruited seven universities to do rural energy surveys, five out of the seven chosen are based in Java. There are a few bright spots outside Java, but their numbers are not proportionate to the populations they serve. Java's more developed transportation networks, seaports, airports, and bus terminals mean that the movement of people occurs more expediently, and prices of consumer goods and products are generally found to be cheaper in Java than anywhere else. Java has the best equipped and well-staffed hospitals in the country, and it has a wider network of health clinics in its rural areas providing better health care for populations on the island than anywhere else. Jakarta, Indonesia's capital and political, financial, and cultural center, is in Java. The imbalance and uneven development across all sectors can be tied to the Java-centric electrification of the nation, which means the social justice ideals of Pancasila, often invoked by government and PLN officials in the name of electrification, remain unrealized aspirations.

Social Knowledge of Rural Life and Energy Uses

I N THE 1970S, one of the foremost concerns of the New Order regime was providing sufficient and sustainable energy (including electricity) throughout the countryside, where most Indonesians lived. A remark by one government official expressed the issue succinctly: "Indonesia's energy issues are really rural energy issues. Rural energy issues are more complex than urban energy issues."[1] Indonesia's problem of providing enough energy for the masses was underscored by the global energy crisis in 1973. Although Indonesia was not negatively affected, the Soeharto government worried that if questions about domestic energy production and consumption were not addressed, Indonesia's energy problem might turn into a national energy crisis in the long run.[2]

Indonesia's main energy problem in the 1970s comprised of three interrelated issues: (1) it needed to meet increased demands for domestic oil consumption when oil was still the country's biggest export commodity and source of income; (2) it wanted to prevent the overconsumption of firewood and resulting deforestation and reduce the large kerosene subsidy when both energy sources were widely used in villages; and (3) it wanted to cost-effectively electrify an estimated 60,000 villages. In effect, the government's preferred solution to reduce consumption of kerosene, as a costly subsidy, and firewood, as an unsustainable source, was to introduce electricity to the countryside. However, it had to figure out how to do so without overusing oil resources or decreasing its exports. To address these concerns, the New Order needed to learn what villagers were already doing with their energy sources.

Indonesian government officials and energy professionals worked collaboratively to investigate rural areas, shared findings in a series of seminars and workshops that included foreign experts, and acquired a new set of methodological tools to understand what villagers were doing to meet their energy needs. In the process, the Soeharto government formulated a national energy policy, produced better knowledge about energy uses in the villages, and learned to better plan for rural electrification. PLN officials also commissioned four UI social scientists to investigate the conditions of several recently electrified villages. All the work that government officials, PLN employees, and energy professionals carried out illustrate that providing sustainable and economical rural electrification required more than innovative engineering. Engineers and bureaucrats needed knowledge of the social.

In this chapter I argue that in its efforts to improve the welfare of rural populations by providing cheap and reliable energy, the New Order regime realized it not only needed the technoscientific knowledge about how to find, extract, harness, and distribute energy sources, it also needed access to the social knowledge of rural life and energy uses. The Soeharto government invested money and time to produce such knowledge. Collectively, the data produced, including firewood and kerosene consumption patterns, the Village Master Archive, and the UI researchers' final report, rendered the rural areas more legible to the government.[3] By understanding the rural energy landscapes better, the New Order regime was able to draw up an energy policy framework to address the energy issues and craft an argument for the importance of village electrification, especially about its positive transformative effects, which it linked to its political legitimacy. The state's discourse about rural electrification, however, was not without criticism; several social scientists who examined the rural electrification program challenged and complicated the government's discourse. Their studies demonstrated that electrified villages did not always produce desired outcomes. In one case, electricity exacerbated existing inequalities. The studies also challenged the government's narrow focus on growing rural electric infrastructure without also building or integrating it with other vital infrastructures, which resulted in a disconnect between the aims of rural electrification and the actual needs of villagers. In what follows, I examine the formulation of Indonesia's national energy policy, the implementation of rural energy surveys, the creation of rural electrification feasibility studies manuals and reports, and the production of the UI researchers' report. In the last section, I bring in and discuss a few critical studies of village electrification that challenged PLN's conception of productive and consumptive users.

National Energy Policy Formulation

The energy crisis of 1973 resulted from embargoes on oil exports from several oil-producing Arab nations to the United States and other countries that supported Israel in the Yom Kippur War. The Organization of the Petroleum Exporting Countries increased the price of crude oil fourfold from $3 per barrel in 1973 to almost $12 per barrel in 1974.[4] Although the price increase brought windfall profits to Indonesia as an oil-producing nation, the country was worried about meeting growing domestic demands. Oil and gas exports had been the primary sources of revenue and foreign exchange income since postindependence Indonesia invited foreign companies to extract its fossil fuel resources in the 1960s. Indonesia's account balance moved from a US$289 million deficit in 1970 to a US$2 billion surplus in the 1979/1980 fiscal year. Its percentage of oil and gas exports increased from 40 to 65 percent in the same period.[5] In other words, Indonesia had been relying heavily on oil and gas exports to fund the country. The government used the oil profits to pay for, among other things, the salaries of civil servants, operational funds for state-owned enterprises, and costs of infrastructure projects. Realizing the importance of this significant source of income, Indonesia wanted to export as much of its crude oil as possible. At the same time the country's domestic oil consumption was rising due to increased economic growth. This scenario created tension between government officials and energy industry practitioners; the former wanted to increase oil exportation while the latter expected more allocation for domestic uses.

Following the 1973 oil crisis, Indonesia held its first nationwide energy seminar in July 1974, organized by the KNIWEC, the London-based international organization's Indonesian branch. The Indonesian officials who served as leaders of the committee were the country's most well-known energy professionals. Ir. Abdul Kadir, then the head of PLN, served as the KNIWEC chairman and Dr. Artono Arismunandar, director of PLN Power Research Institute, was its secretary. Ir. A. Suhud from the Directorate General of Mining served as the first deputy chair, Ir. Sumbarjono and Ir. Widartomo from the Directorate General of Oil & Natural Gas served as the second deputy chairs. Budi Sudarsono from BATAN was the third deputy chair.[6] Minister of Mining Dr. Ir. Mohammad Sadli and Minister of Public Works and Electric Power Ir. Sutami served as honorary chairs.

Members of the KNIWEC consisted of representatives from key energy and professional institutions including PLN, PGN, the Indonesian Chamber of Commerce and Industry, the Association of Indonesian Engineers, the Indonesian Economists Association, and three directorate generals (Water Resource Development, Basic Industries, and Education). The makeup of the organization's key players indicates the complex nature of the energy issues that needed to be examined from several perspectives.[7] This interorganizational structure received strong endorsement from minister of Research and Technology, Dr. Sumitro Djojohadikusumo, who said in the 1974 seminar, "The development and management of energy sources is the management of the world economy's bloodline. Thus, the pattern of future energy develop-ment must be based on a set of three types of benchmarks: technological solu-tions, economic realities, and ecological and environmental considerations."[8]

The 1974 KNIWEC seminar was well funded and attended, as many par-ticipants agreed that it was time to thoroughly discuss Indonesia's energy problems and make recommendations so the government could create a more coherent national energy policy. A major point of agreement was that for Indonesia to solve its energy challenges, it had to increase its social knowledge of rural energy practices. In his opening remarks, Sutami said that Indonesia's energy issues revolved around its imbalance between energy production and consumption, increased domestic energy demands, and the paucity of data on commercial and noncommercial energy sources.[9] This was reiterated by Abdul Kadir, who said that any national energy policy framework must rest on two pillars: (1) balanced energy development so that production would meet demand and (2) additional government policies to support such develop-ment.[10] In other words, the two contributing factors to Indonesia's formula-tion of a national energy policy depended on getting better knowledge of Indonesia's energy resources and patterns of domestic energy consumption. Partial information of the current state of Indonesia's energy landscape was already available, but better data were urgently needed.

Two seminar participants stressed the importance of developing a national energy policy by drawing some lessons from the experiences of the United States. M. T. Zen, an official at the State Ministry of Research, argued that the main reason the United States, despite having the largest reserves of energy sources and being one of the biggest exporters of energy, was experiencing an energy crisis in the 1970s was because "the United States does not have a national energy policy."[11] Dr. Arismunandar quoted Dr. Ellis L. Armstrong, then chairman of the US National Committee of the World Energy Confer-ence who explained the reasons for the American energy crisis: "we [Ameri-cans] have not been farsighted enough to adopt policies to meet increasing needs . . . [and] we, as a society, have not understood and appreciated the scale of the energy problem . . . [which resulted in] our sad failure to develop a ratio-nal, long-range energy policy, with intelligent, balanced and effective organiza-tion structure."[12] Based on what Zen, Arismunandar, and others said at the con-ference, the top recommendation was to create a "rationale, integrated, national in scope, comprehensive, and long-term" energy policy.[13]

In 1976, the New Order government created the Technical Committee on En-ergy Resources (Panitia Tehnis Sumber Daya Energi), an interdepartmental team tasked with formulating Indonesia's energy policy. Some of their recommen-dations were sent directly to the government, while others were workshopped in the 1977, 1978, and 1979 KNIWEC seminars.[14] The discussions held at the second KNIWEC seminar in 1977 produced recommendations that informed the second GBHN, signed into effect by the leaders of the People's Consultative Assembly on March 22, 1978. On the topic of energy, the 1978 GBHN mentioned four directives: develop energy by balancing the dual needs of exportation and domestic consumption; conserve oil as fuel by harnessing other energy sources; provide cheap alternative energy in rural areas to prevent deforestation; and enact policies in other areas to support a national energy policy by, among other things, increasing training of experts, research and development, and uses of technology.[15] By the time KNIWEC held its fourth conference in April 1979, the Indonesian government had formulated a national energy framework that included four interrelated mandates: conservation, diversification, indexation, and intensification. Conservation entailed conserving domestic energy consumption and finding ways to increase efficient uses of energy. Diversification aimed to reduce internal oil consumption and increase the energy mix. Indexation referred to finding a good match between a specific energy need (e.g., building a new nonoil largescale power plant) with the corresponding energy source (e.g., coal or geothermal). Finally, intensification meant conducting more surveys and explorations to find new energy sources.[16]

The mechanisms by which Indonesia would need to implement its national energy policy were further elaborated in later symposia. Out of the four mandates, conservation and diversification received more attention than indexation and intensification. Energy conservation especially was thought to be the low-hanging fruit and was comprehensively discussed in a seminar in 1979 held by the Directorate General of Power. The event was one of the largest seminars held by the Indonesian government in the 1970s and was attended by 280 participants who discussed more than four dozen papers addressing the practical and policy-related aspects of conserving energy.[17] They divided the seminar into four different panels, each discussing different areas of energy conservation: industry, transportation, households, and supporting areas (e.g., trade regulations, energy conservation campaigns, oil prices) that would help conserve energy. For the first time, women participants were invited to share their input on conserving household energy. For example, Erna Witoelar and T. Slamet Danusudirjo actively participated in the panel discussions.[18]

Energy diversification in the electricity sector formed the theme of KNIWEC's 1980 seminar. PLN Development Director Ir. Sardjono's paper provides insight into what the company was thinking and planning. In 1977 Indonesia used 86 percent oil-fueled and 14 percent HPPs to generate the country's electricity, Sardjono's paper reports. Decreasing the percentage of oil-fueled power plants was one of PLN's aims for diversifying the use of primary energy sources. The fuel types PLN was seriously considering included natural gas, hydropower, geothermal, coal, and nuclear. Although the New Order government did eventually build coalfired SPPs, two GPPs, and a few HPPs in the 1980s, as we learned in chapter 4, many power stations that PLN installed across Indonesia up to the late 1990s still used diesel.

Energy indexation and intensification were touched on in these and other seminars, but were less debated than the other two pillars of the energy policy. For one thing, the Indonesian government already knew what it wanted to do as far as indexing energy was concerned: it needed to reduce domestic oil consumption to increase oil as the leading export commodity. Intensification required larger sums of capital investment than what the government could afford at that time. Nonetheless, the four pillars were eventually incorporated into the General Policy on Energy Sector (Kebijakan Umum Bidang Energi) published in 1981 by the National Energy Coordination Agency (Badan Koordinasi Energi Nasional). Hence, by the early 1980s, Indonesia had drawn up a national energy policy.

Rural Energy Surveys

Soeharto created the Department of Mining and Energy (DME) when he announced the formation of his Third Development Cabinet in 1978. The new ministry was likely the result of energy concerns discussed in earlier years, but Soeharto decided to add the mining industry to the DME's portfolio. Consequently, the new ministry was charged with overseeing five state enterprises in the energy and mining sectors: PGN for gas distribution, Pertamina for oil and gas exploration and mining, PLN for electricity generation and distribution, and Perusahaan Negara Tambang Batubara (State Coal Mining Company) for coal mining, which shortly split into Perusahaan Negara Tambang Batubara (State Coal Mining Company) and Perseroan Terbatas Tambang Batubara Bukit Asam (Bukit Asam Coal Mining Limited Liability Company). One of DME's divisions was called the Directorate General of Power (DGP), headed by Stanford-educated electrical engineer Dr. Samaun Samadikun.[19] Under this new arrangement, the PLN president director no longer reported to Ir. Sutami but to Dr. Samadikun.

Soon after the creation of the DME, the DGP embarked on a project to solve the government's concerns about the shortage of firewood and unsustainable kerosene subsidies, which were estimated at US\$3 billion a year.[20] These subsidies were so high that in the 1981/1982 fiscal year, the allotted US\$3.4 billion kerosene allowances constituted 15 percent of the national budget.[21] To address this issue, the government needed to find out how much firewood and kerosene people in rural areas were consuming, for which the DGP requested assistance from USAID. The project officially began after the Indonesian and US governments signed a project grant agreement on August 29, 1979.[22] The Indonesian Steering Committee consisted of six people from the DME. Samadikun served as the deputy chair and Ir. Wiyarso, the director general of Oil and Natural Gas, served as the chair. USAID assembled a list of US project participants that consisted of people representing five organizations: Energy/Development International, Development Sciences Inc., GSA International, International Science & Technology Institute, Inc., and Olympic Associates. A total of eleven representatives from these five firms worked with a team of twenty-five Indonesian participants from different agencies. There was also a seven-member Rural Survey Advisory Committee from four Indonesian universities: ITB, Bogor Agricultural University (Institut Pertanian Bogor), Hasanuddin University, and Diponegoro University.[23]

The project, officially named "Energy Planning for Development in Indonesia," sought "1) To foster a better understanding of the effect of energy and economic development plans and programs on the energy situation of the country, as well as the social, economic and environmental consequences of decisions concerning energy pricing, energy technologies and resource development; and 2) To enhance the capabilities of Indonesian planners to analyse the role which energy plays in development, and to plan a national energy program."[24]

To achieve these objectives, the teams planned and implemented several tasks: run pilot surveys of firewood and kerosene use in the rural areas, conduct energy demand analyses that draw on the results of the fuelwood-kerosene surveys, and assess technologies of nonoil energy (resources considered: coal, small-scale hydropower, geothermal, wind, solar, biomass; not considered: nuclear and largescale hydropower).[25] The intent was less to complete a project than to "begin the process of national energy planning and policy analysis" in Indonesia.[26] In other words, the project aimed to show Indonesians the importance of planning for a long-term energy development.

According to the report produced by the US consultants, energy consumed in Indonesian rural houses accounted for "approximately 65 percent of total energy consumption, and 25 percent if only commercial fuels are taken into account," and kerosene was being increasingly consumed throughout the 1970s.[27] Although there had been earlier small-scale regional surveys on this, there had not been one carried out on a national scale. Moreover, data from previous surveys show wide variations, such that very little confidence could be attached to their results or to their extrapolation to a national scale.[28] Thus, the DGP set out to produce new national data that could serve as a baseline for future surveys.

The DGP organized a two-part symposium in conjunction with this project. The first, held September 1–11, 1980, in Jakarta, laid out the methodological foundations of and plan for the pilot surveys. The initial questionnaire was drawn up by the US project staff "based on previous surveys in other countries," but the final one was a collaborative effort between the Americans and Indonesians.[29] Both teams worked together to prepare and train interviewers and data collectors for fieldwork, including how to interview villagers and measure firewood and kerosene consumption.[30] Eight institutions (seven universities and the Forest Products Research Institute) were enrolled to do the fieldwork surveys. The initial plan was to have each institute interview 100 households in their respective areas of coverage to produce 800 data points. The study sample was taken from a larger sample produced by a national survey that Survai Sosial Ekonomi Nasional (National Social Economic Surveys) performed in 1980. This was because the parties involved wanted "to limit field work to a one month period, within regions defined by considerations of accessibility. One hundred households were randomly selected within each of the eight regions contiguous to the university locations."[31] In practice, the samples taken by field surveyors in each region would be increased to 120 households to account for faulty data. This proved to be a good decision. Although the initial plan was to collect data on 800 households, that final number was reduced to 783 because not all questionnaire responses could be used for analysis.[32]

After the September 1980 seminar, in October and November the pilot surveys were carried out in eight regions, covering six provinces (table 8). The goal of the pilot surveys was to create a baseline household energy use profile for three income groups. The hope was to use the survey results as an opportunity "to develop an appropriate survey instrument and methodology for future application in a representative national sample."[33] The institutes covered a total of fifteen districts, three of which (Deli Serdang in North Sumatra and Gowa and Maros in South Sulawesi) are outside Java.[34] In other words, most of the data produced would come from Java, where most rural dwellers lived. In each district, subdistricts for the surveys were selected randomly. The surveyors covered different types of villages in their areas, including farming and coastal villages. Three university teams indicated which village typologies (i.e., *swadaya*, *swakarya*, and *swasembada*) they surveyed.[35] The other institutions did not clearly mark the typologies of villages surveyed, suggesting varying standard operating procedures.

After the surveys, the DGP held a second seminar February 3–5, 1981, to hear presentations on their survey results and feedback. Their presentations were broken into three panels, the first of which shared their findings on timber

Table 8. Surveyors of firewood and kerosene use in rural areas

University/Institute	Regions Surveyed	Province
North Sumatra University (Universitas Sumatera Utara, USU)	Deli Serdang	North Sumatra
Forest Products Research Institute (Lembaga Penelitian Hasil Hutan)	Bogor	West Java
Bogor Agricultural University (Institut Pertanian Bogor, IPB)	Bogor	West Java
Institute of Technology in Bandung (Institut Teknologi Bandung, ITB)	Bandung	West Java
Diponegoro University (Universitas Diponegoro)	Semarang, Demak, Kendal	Central Java
Gadjah Mada University (Universitas Gadjah Mada, UGM)	Gunung Kidul, Sleman, Bantul, Kulon Progo	Yogyakarta
Ten November Institute of Technology (Institut Teknologi 10 Nopember, ITS)	Surabaya, Lamongan, Sidoarjo	East Java
Hasanuddin University (Universitas Hasanuddin)	Gowa and Maros	South Sulawesi

plantations, farming and cattle areas, and horticultural farming communities.[36] Overall, they carried out the surveys satisfactorily and managed to overcome a few challenges in the field. Their number one feedback was that while the survey methodology was good, the way the questions were asked varied among the surveyors.[37] The second panel's findings had a high standard deviation because of the wide range of village types surveyed.[38] One was a fertile area (Sleman), and the other one was barren (Gunung Kidul). They also said that the questionnaire was prepared well, but it would have been better if they had implementation instructions (*petunjuk pelaksanaan*) to carry them out, which supported the feedback of the first panelists.[39] The third panel mentioned a few challenges they faced in the field.[40] One was the difficulty finding respondents from the Survai Sosial Ekonomi Nasional data, and they suggested improving the sampling method. They offered some constructive feedback about the questionnaire, such as asking about household incomes early on and differentiating the type of stove (open or closed) a household uses.[41] Another important input was for all institutions to hand over their raw data of 120 households (oversampled to make up for any bad data) to the DGP so it could reduce them to 100 samples for each institute. Relatedly, they recommended doing preliminary analysis of data to sort out good and bad data when selecting which ones to keep for further analysis.

Following the surveys, the American and Indonesian teams conducted a three-phase data analysis and reported their findings.[42] The report states, "On average, among all regions studied the annual consumption of all fuels for cooking and lighting amounted to 6.99 boe [barrel of oil equivalent] per household. This is equivalent to a per capita consumption of 1.33 boe per year."[43] Breaking it down into two categories (fuelwood and kerosene), the report states that the yearly per capita consumption of fuelwood "of 0.93 boe is equivalent to a level of approximately 0.88 kg per day per capita. Per capita [total] kerosene consumption of 0.40 boe annually is equivalent to approximately 0.2 liters per capita per day."[44] The numbers of annual per person consumption may seem small, but when multiplied by millions of people, they become significant. Overall, fuelwood for cooking accounted for about 70 percent of total domestic annual energy consumption, kerosene for lighting 16 percent, and kerosene for cooking for 14 percent.[45]

The DGP seminar offered a few conclusions from the pilot surveys. First, they discovered a trend among higher-income households of switching from fuelwood to kerosene. Second, they found out many rural stoves were very inefficient and required more wood to burn. Third, they determined that the firewood the villagers used did not come from well-planned sources. Fourth, the percentages of kerosene (19 percent) and fuelwood (81 percent) consumptions confirmed the government's concerns that villagers used firewood in high proportion, which can lead to deforestation unless a better plan to supply this fuel more sustainably was provided.[46] In short, fuelwood was a basic need for villagers, much like food, but how the fuel was sourced and used became a real threat to forest sustainability, particularly in Java.

A few proposals to reduce firewood overconsumption were discussed in a June 1981 KNIWEC seminar. They included supplying surplus firewood from outside Java, reforesting government lands in Java, planting quick-growing trees, supplying alternative energy sources such as agricultural wastes, and providing more efficient stoves.[47] It is difficult to know to what extent the firewood problem in Indonesia was successfully addressed in the New Order since I could find no data to analyze. But when I visited a village in Yogyakarta with a Gadjah Mada

Figure 12. Cooking fuels in a Yogyakarta rural house. Source: Photo by Anto Mohsin, January 2010.

University academic and his undergraduate research assistants in 2010, I saw some rural households still stocking and using firewood alongside kerosene and coconut husks as cooking fuels, suggesting that the issue persisted beyond the Soeharto regime. A kitchen of one such rural household can be seen in figure 12.

Finally, in their report, the American consultants proposed to extend the pilot surveys and include other areas not yet examined. They noted that a pilot urban energy use survey should be carried out as well to determine "energy consumption as a function of income."[48] They recommended that Indonesia should consider alternative fuels to fulfill domestic energy demands, lest oil for exports would be significantly reduced and that energy conservation should be part of a strategy in Indonesia's energy policy.[49] These recommendations echoed the pillars of Indonesian energy policy of diversification and conservation. The consultants also suggested extending the network of universities involved in the rural energy surveys in DGP's future activities.[50]

Rural Electrification Feasibility Studies

In a 1978 KNIWEC seminar PLN's president director at the time, Prof. Ir. Suryono, stressed the role of planning in rural electrification. He wrote that before an investment was made to construct electrical infrastructure in one area, PLN would need to conduct a feasibility study. If the study indicated that there would be no return on investment, no distribution lines would be built there.[51] Many rural areas in Indonesia were sparsely populated, and hence villages were located remotely from one another. Thus, it would be better to electrify a cluster of villages instead of just one village at a time. To do this effectively, PLN engineers needed to assess the viability of a given area to be electrified by conducting a study.

According to PLN Village Electrification Chief Ir. Johannes J. Rumondor, producing a feasibility study report was aligned with a program approach (versus a project approach) to rural electrification. To assess whether a particular area is suitable for electrification, employees of the state electricity company would need to do more than technical, financial, and economic analyses. They would also need to obtain demographic, geographical, and sociological data to better analyze existing and future electric power load demands.[52]

Following Rumondor's trip to the Philippines in early 1977 to visit nine rural electric cooperatives and learn about feasibility studies (see chapter 6), PLN began a series of workshops to train its workers to create similar studies (table 9). The four workshops were held in big cities on different islands covering western, central, and eastern parts of Indonesia. The different locations were meant to showcase PLN's nationwide network which, by the mid-1970s, had established a vast bureaucracy spanning the entire archipelago consisting of thirteen regional areas (*wilayah*) each with a headquarters in a provincial capital (table 4).

The first workshop was held in October 1977 in Semarang, Central Java. PLN Wilayah XIII served as the host and delegations from selected divisions participated as invitees.[53] Examining the list more closely, we can find one delegation each from Sumatra, Sulawesi, Java, and the Nusa Tenggara, an attempt to invite nationally representative PLN divisions. Three representatives each from the USAID and NRECA also attended.[54] Ir. Rumondor and

Table 9. PLN's workshops on feasibility studies

Dates	Place
October 17–22, 1977	Semarang, Central Java
December 5–10, 1977	Denpasar, Bali
January 23–28, 1978	Manado, North Sulawesi
July 28–August 3, 1978	Medan, North Sumatra

Ir. Moeljadi Oetji of PLN served as the workshop trainers. They taught PLN employees the basics of conducting a feasibility study using the concept of "areawide coverage," combining several nearby villages into one area.[55] The participants drafted a manual to codify the skills and knowledge gained in the workshop. Realizing that all knowledge involves tacit components that cannot be fully written down, the trainers asked the attendees to practice their newly gained knowledge to produce feasibility study reports for two areas: Magelang and Pekalongan.[56] A note from the sole delegate of PLN Wilayah XI in this workshop mentions that PLN aimed to complete feasibility studies in all its regional areas of operations by 1981.[57]

PLN followed up the first workshop with a second session in December 1977. This time it was held in Denpasar, Bali; PLN Wilayah XI served as the host; and the chiefs of all PLN regional areas and distribution offices were invited to attend, as well as one NRECA and five USAID representatives. In this workshop the participants revised the draft manual from the first session and named it the "Guidance and Instruction for the Creation of Rural Electrification Feasibility Study" (Buku Pedoman dan Petunjuk Pembuatan Feasibility Study Perlistrikan Desa). To gain practical knowledge, workshop participants again carried out a feasibility study exercise for the district of Tabanan in Bali.[58]

During this second workshop, USAID representative David Devin delivered a keynote address on December 5, 1977, in which he shared his rationale for conducting feasibility studies. He said that there are four reasons to do feasibility studies: (1) "to design projects that will both serve the people and which will pay for themselves and grow," (2) "to give PLN a number of project proposals to present" to foreign donor countries that are interested to help Indonesia with electrification projects, (3) "for planning purposes" and (4) "we hope that the preparation of good feasibility studies will attract the financing necessary to electrify Indonesia."[59] Devin mentioned one interesting note in his speech. He said:

> I would also like to remind you that rural electrification is a very political program and as good government workers we have to be very concerned as to how the program is implemented. Rural electrification is like building a fire, if properly controlled it can be an excellent tool for wining [sic] the people's support for your government. But if not, it can cause great social unrest and political difficulties. Professor Suryono, your President Director, recently briefed your legislature (MPR) and afterwords [sic] he said that most of the questions asked by these politicians, were about rural electrification. On a lower level I am sure you [sic] Wilayah chiefs have all experienced a growing number of raquests [sic]

for electricity by the rural people in your areas. To help solve this problem what we suggest is the preparation of time phased plans at the local and national level based on good feasibility studies. Then when a Camat or Bupati requests electricity you can show him your plan. When people can see that there is a plan for electrification then it is easier for them to wait.[60]

It seems that Devin made the link between electrification and politics for two reasons. He was aware that rural electrification was political in Indonesia (and perhaps elsewhere, too), and he wanted to convince PLN employees of the importance of mastering the skills of producing feasibility studies to continue receiving support from local politicians, the people, and ultimately the New Order government.

The third training session occurred in Manado in January 1978. PLN Wilayah VII hosted the event and, again, representatives from all PLN divisions across Indonesia were invited to participate.[61] Workshop participants shared their knowledge and experience electrifying rural areas in their regions and came up with a more concrete plan for rural electrification. They concluded that they would need to draw up construction standards, learn to interpret and evaluate feasibility study reports using three criteria (socioeconomic, physical, and financial), and simplify the fee structures for villagers to connect to the grid. For the latter, seminar participants proposed to offer two "electrification packages," whereby prospective rural electricity subscribers could choose between two options: (1) 100 VA connection with two light bulbs and one outlet for Rp 30,000 or (2) 450 VA connection with four light bulbs and one outlet for Rp 90,000.[62] It appears that the workshop adopted this idea after learning about PLN Denpasar Branch's "village electrification package" (Paket Kelistrikan Desa, PKD), which had been quite successful in Bali.[63] PLN later slightly modified its PKD and provided more options on the loans it offered customers. In this case, the power company acted as a generous creditor giving small loans to would-be electricity subscribers, channeling the government's financial aid.

The fourth and last workshop on feasibility took place in Medan between July 28 and August 3, 1978. They amended the feasibility study manual produced in the previous workshop with more detailed instructions. Building on what they discussed earlier, they drew up additional standards for rural electrification to further minimize construction costs. They recommended abolishing the household wiring connection fee to allow more villagers to become electricity subscribers and proposed five categories to differentiate rural customers: households, agriculture, village industry, streetlights, and social function. They suggested enlisting village heads to read electric meters and report them to PLN and create an "information package" for village communities to introduce the benefits and dangers of electricity, installation procedure, electricity prices, and electric bill payment.[64] In other words, PLN employees discussed more things to do to attract and retain potential rural customers beyond assessing the practicality and desirability of building a power system in an area. Additional knowledge of rural populations and their villages was needed.

Through these four workshops, PLN acquired the techniques to do feasibility studies and realized that it needed more vital information about rural areas to support future feasibility studies. Rumondor reported in 1980 that by that year PLN had acquired basic information on all the approximately 61,000 Indonesian villages. This information included the location code, name, level of development, PLN *wilayah*, electrical conditions, management, population, number of households, number of electric consumers, natural resources, and types of distribution lines of each village. The database was called the Village Master Archive (Arsip Induk Desa) and since the data were stored digitally, the information could be updated easily.[65] This database and the PLN-produced volume of feasibility studies formed technologies of surveillance that made Indonesian villages more visible to the New Order government. With these data, the government could quickly generate a profile of any Indonesian villages, which it then used to determine the feasibility (or desirability) of electrifying those villages in order to quell any potential uprisings or extend its patronage to the countryside.

Social Knowledge of Rural Electrification

As I have described, there had been a flurry of activities since the mid-1970s to better understand Indonesia's energy landscapes and gain more social knowledge of rural energy consumers. In addition to the activities of KNIWEC, the DGP, PLN, and other institutions, there was an interest from the academic community to investigate the effects of rural electrification. After hearing news coverage about the launch of the Listrik Masuk Desa (LMD) program in April 1979, four UI researchers became interested in examining the "cultural shift" (*peralihan kebudayaan*) in rural areas from the pre-electrified to the postelectrified period.[66] Initially, they planned to do an academic study of the social and economic effects of rural electrification but soon realized the insurmountable challenges for such an undertaking. They realized the villages they would need to examine were too numerous, and most had just recently received electricity.[67] Instead, they responded to the foremost concerns highlighted by the government and the media about the program by focusing their study on "how electricity can bring the greatest benefit to people in rural areas."[68] In other words, they modified their study plan to address issues deemed more urgent by the government, and they earned political and financial support as a result, a common move during the New Order era, "the development of Indonesian social science—its very nature and character—is inextricably linked to the shifting requirements of power over time."[69]

After discussing their idea with several PLN officials, the UI scholars decided that they would visit several villages and conduct unstructured and open-ended interviews with villagers and government officials to learn about the conditions on the ground. They promised to produce a report and write recommendations for the government to better electrify the countryside. On June 8, 1979, PLN and UI signed a collaboration charter (*Piagam Kerja Sama*) to formalize their joint effort. The PLN team was represented by the company's chief executive, Prof. Ir. Suryono. The UI academics were led and represented by Prof. Dr. Selo Soemardjan, a sociologist and chair of the Social Sciences Foundation.[70] The charter details the tasks, scope, locations, payments, deliverables, time commitment, and implementation of the research.[71] The Department of Education and Culture, the ministry that regulates K–12 and higher learning institutions, funded the research. PLN knew that the undertaking and the final report would produce more social knowledge for rural electrification and agreed to fund the study.

The UI researchers visited fifteen villages in four provinces (East Java, North Sulawesi, Central Java, and Yogyakarta), although the focus of their study was Javanese villages because they were connected to the grid earliest. Dr. Soemardjan and his team carried out group discussions with residents of each village and interviewed "resource persons," such as village heads and their staff, subdistrict heads (*camat*), local electricians, and, in some places, housewives.[72] After carrying out fieldwork, Dr. Soemardjan drafted an initial report, which was distributed to his and PLN's team members for input to draft a second report. Afterward, they held a seminar with several UI academics, PLN officials, and representatives of government ministries to revise and produce a third and final draft, which is what I reference here.[73] The iterative process shows the meticulousness with which the investigators carried out their work.

The final report contains the researchers' ten recommendations to improve the LMD program, commentaries, analyses, observations, short profiles of each village visited, and, unsurprisingly, justification of Soeharto's RE program.[74] They believed the program was a promising way to achieve social justice, a "strategic means to achieve modernity," and an instrument for transforming rural communities from the "realm of darkness to the realm of light [and enlightenment]."[75] Their understanding of social justice, however, differed from that of the government. The government's concern was to make electricity as widely available as possible, but the UI researchers emphasized making electricity affordable for people in the villages. Consequently, three of their recommendations focused on ensuring that electricity prices would be affordable for the average villagers. They recommended producing electricity using the economy of scale, reducing the costs of electric construction, and implementing cross-subsidies. These suggestions came from their observations that many people in the countryside did not necessarily have the financial means to become electricity customers, although they needed the new energy technology. The UI social scientists observed that children became more motivated to study at night with electric lighting, youths in the villages stopped going to towns for entertainment, many watched entertaining TV programs to escape from their daily lives (they didn't like to watch the news bulletins), illuminated villages became safer, and electric speakers used by a village mosque amplified the sound of the call to prayer (*azan*) reaching the community further.[76] In other words, they noticed positive changes in the villages they visited.

The village profiles provided important knowledge of the Central and East Javanese as well as North Sulawesian countryside and peoples in relation to electricity. Although the investigators didn't explicitly mention this, their data are similar to that collected for PLN's Village Master Archive. Most likely this is because PLN officials accompanied their visits to the villages and suggested acquiring these data during their interviews. For all but two villages, the report includes the following information: village name and location, villagers' livelihoods, first time it received electricity, type of electricity it gets (PLN versus non-PLN), type of power generator, number and types of electric consumers, electricity prices, and other miscellaneous information. The miscellaneous information is most revealing because it contains more stories about how electricity is used in the villages and the commentaries of the social scientists. For example, in Blawong Village, they noted that electric lighting cost Rp 1,500 per month, ten times the price of a kerosene lamp. But those who could afford it obtained it because electric illumination is more stable, cleaner, and easier to handle.[77] In another case, the social scientists observed that the village chief in Karanganom made available two electrical appliances to his fellow villagers for free: a TV set (to watch programs together in his house) and an iron (any villager could borrow it). The television programs were enjoyed most by women and children.[78]

The UI researchers' investigation was one of the earliest social studies of rural electrification in Indonesia. Their report contains some interesting information about several electrified villages in the late 1970s. Some data were particularly revealing in terms of villagers' behaviors when they first received electricity and how they enjoyed the conveniences it afforded. For example, night times became livelier than before, and villagers became more accustomed to using electrical devices and enjoyed entertaining programs on television. Although the researchers were critical of the government not ensuring the affordability of electricity in rural areas, for the most part, their report helped justify the New Order rural electrification program by linking it to the government's national development agenda.

Other Social Dimensions of Rural Electrification

Electricity so energized Indonesian society that it provoked an ongoing debate about its value. Indonesian political and technical elites believed in the transformative effect of the technology in shaping socioeconomic changes in the countryside. Many government officials thought (and hoped) that once the new technology was introduced to the villages, a reordering of rural societies would take place. They presumed that electricity would inspire many to start businesses and increase their economic activities, a reality that did not always happen as they envisioned.[79] Rather than using it to increase their capital, many rural people who received electricity in their homes were content to use it to simply power their light bulbs, radios, TV sets, and other simple electrical devices.

Relatedly, PLN classified its rural electricity customers into two categories: productive and consumptive users. The former refers to people who use their electricity "productively," that is, to generate income, increase revenue, or add economic value to their activities, whether farming, raising livestock, fishing, or selling goods. Using this definition, PLN automatically deemed retail stores, handicraft shops, restaurants, and other businesses (including homebased businesses) as productive users. Farmers and fishermen who used electric machines to increase their yields or income also fell into this category. The state power company preferred this type of user because they contributed to its steady stream of revenue. Small business owners might switch to become PLN's commercial customers to get more electrical power and pay higher prices.

Consumptive electricity users refer to customers who strictly use electricity for passive consumption, such as to power light bulbs and household electric appliances. They may produce income elsewhere, not necessarily at their home, but PLN didn't consider these consumers to be productive. Children who study at night using electric lighting and become more productive students were not considered productive users either. Such a narrow definition of "consumptive users" is problematic because PLN managers and New Order bureaucrats viewed them as "bad" consumers because they used subsidized electricity not as the government intended. Ironically, the state electricity company disregarded its own sponsored 1981 study that showed that the biggest motivating factors for using electricity to run businesses were less about the availability of electricity than a business owner's entrepreneurial spirit (*jiwa wiraswasta*).[80] The study also noted that some villagers wanted to use electricity for their enterprises but couldn't because PLN's distribution lines had not yet reached their villages.[81]

Fortunately, not everyone saw villagers who used electricity consumptively as "wasting" it. A non-PLN-funded critical and insightful study about the effects of electricity in Belacatur village (Yogyakarta) by three researchers from Gadjah Mada University's Center for Population Studies argued that there was another equally important, noneconomic benefit. Electricity benefited the sociocultural lives of the villagers, too.[82] Belacatur villagers who had access to electricity were more informed, more entertained, and more educated and felt more secure than villagers without electricity. They used electricity to power their radios and TV sets and consequently received more information from the outside world, which broadened their knowledge and horizon. As a result, they developed a "global consciousness," becoming more aware of the world outside their village. They also received and enjoyed a variety of entertainment from their electric devices. Children in electrified households managed to put more hours into their studies, and streetlights powered by electricity helped increase security, which made them feel safer at night. An area that was once thought to be "haunted" when illuminated by electric light became less scary. Thus, many young people in the village developed a cognitive shift and believed less in supernatural explanations and events.[83]

Another widely held assumption that the researchers overturned was that villagers' socioeconomic status would generally increase with electricity. Because of PLN's limited capacities to electrify every single house and the prohibitive connection fees for poor villagers, many became the electricity customers of their richer neighbors by siphoning off power from the neighbors' households. Their well-off neighbors had electric meters in their houses and paid the subsidized rates to PLN, but they then sold electricity to their poorer neighbors at a higher rate. The poorest in the village remained without electricity in their households. As a result, the researchers contended, electricity made the preexisting social classes more visible in Belacatur village. Moreover, the better-off villagers had more and better electrical devices than their low-income neighbors. Thus, in Belacatur, regardless of it improving some villagers' socioeconomic conditions, electricity amplified existing village socioeconomic inequalities.

That said, when villages already had other vital infrastructures such as roads and businesses, electricity played a big role in helping them thrive. For example, Cisande village in Sukabumi, West Java, was located alongside a provincial road with heavy traffic bringing people from big cities such as Bandung, Bogor, and Jakarta. The village already had clothing and other businesses before PLN introduced electricity in 1974. Once the village was electrified, the businesses thrived; tailors could switch to electric sewing machines and increase their output, and retail stores and restaurants stayed open longer into the night. With electricity, restaurateurs could install radios and TVs to entertain guests to stay longer and spend more. These business owners used electricity to power their refrigerators, water pumps, mixers, and electric irons to increase productivity.[84]

Another study on the impact of electricity on villagers' socioeconomic lives in four Balinese villages reported a similar pattern. Made Arka, the study author, described two villages (Mas and Celuk) as "touristic villages" (*desa pariwisata*), where the facilities that supported tourism (paved roads and public markets) had been built.[85] The other two villages (Kapal and Mengwi), although not considered touristic villages, were located along the road connecting the southern and northern parts of the island with "heavy traffic."[86] After these villages were connected to the grid, Arka reported noticeable social and economic changes for all four villages. While residents of the touristic villages used electricity to create handicrafts at night, the nontouristic villagers mainly used it to support their cattle-farming businesses.[87]

The two studies show that the availability of roads and other public facilities worked in coordination with village electrification to support more positive outcomes. In many remote villages, however, such amenities were not always made available by the government. Building good roads is expensive and time consuming. Considering that the Soeharto government's main motive was to light up as many villages as possible to gain support from the people in the countryside, integrated village development for all villages was not its main consideration.

Similarly, a comparative study of two East Javanese villages (one agricultural and one industrial) in the 1980s supports some of the same conclusions mentioned already. Namely, there is very little correlation between electricity and productive uses. Electricity can even sharpen existing social inequalities. Imron Husin, the study author, writes in his dissertation:

This study has found that the length of [time of the] supply of electricity seems to bear no relationship at all to the growth of [the] industry. There is very little evidence to support the proposition that the program has improved income, created employment opportunities or stimulated much industrialization in rural areas. Instead, in the absence of many household activities in the area concerned, electrification has stimulated higher consumerism among electricity consumers. In Pare [the agricultural village], the existence of a variety of household activities prior to electrification has helped to increase slightly the average power consumption for productive activities, while in Pandaan [the more industrial village] the household consumers mostly used the power for consumption purposes. Moreover, the failure to take into account the existing unequal distribution of economic and social power in rural communities has added to greater inequalities.[88]

Husin's study concludes that there was a huge disconnect between PLN's village electrification policy, which aimed to stimulate new productive activities, and the real conditions that neglected to account for a village's economic resources and the availability of other supporting facilities, such as markets and transportation networks.

Although Husin specifically criticized PLN Twelfth Region (PLN Wilayah XII) for its failure to produce more "productive electricity customers" (using PLN's narrow definition), he also blamed the New Order government for not including a feedback loop mechanism and monitoring process to ensure the village electrification programmatic goals were being achieved.[89] One of his recommendations was for the government to move away from simply achieving numerical targets of how many villages become electrified because this "is not a reliable means of assessing whether the government's objectives for the rural electrification program are being achieved."[90] Husin's criticism is valid because the New Order regime's quantitative aim to increase the number of electrified villages every year only bolstered Soeharto's nationalist development narrative. Rural electrification became the proxy for village development and electrically illuminated villages became a key performance indicator of the program's achievements, albeit a narrow one. There was little in-depth examination, like Husin's and that of the Gadjah Mada University researchers, to assess whether the new service of electricity in fact contributed to villagers improving their standard of living.

Conclusion

Indonesia's main energy problem in the 1970s involved three interconnected issues: meeting domestic oil consumption, decreasing firewood and kerosene uses in the countryside, and electrifying villages. These issues warranted the government bureaucrats and PLN engineers to begin systematically thinking about the problem to find viable solutions. They realized that providing affordable and sufficient energy to the population, which was an important way to help legitimize and support the regime, required more than just technical knowledge of energy exploration, production, and distribution. They needed to produce social knowledge of rural life and how villagers use their energy sources. They met and debated these issues in a series of seminars, produced a national energy policy, survey results of energy consumptions in the villages, and feasibility studies manual for PLN engineers to better plan for rural electrification. PLN also produced a Village Master Archive that could generate a brief profile of any village. This profile could be supplemented by a feasibility study report of an area to determine its suitability for electrification. The report generated by the UI researchers provides additional information about recently illuminated villages. Combined, the new social knowledge made the Indonesian countryside more legible to the government and was used to further justify the government's village electrification program.

However, the PLN's drive to electrify as many villages as possible every year without considering the varying basic facilities ran counter to its goal (and hope) for rural electricity subscribers to become "productive users" of electricity. PLN's main goal of bringing electricity to the villages was mostly devoid of other infrastructural considerations because it was not their responsibility to build roads, markets, and other supporting facilities. The state power company's main tasks were generating and distributing electricity, and separate government agencies were responsible for building roads, bridges, irrigations, schools, markets, and other equally needed facilities. Unfortunately, for the most part, the transportation, education, energy, and other government agencies were not networked well to provide the rural areas with well-maintained integrated infrastructures.[91] The government considered the benefits of electricity would be more readily felt by villagers than other types of infrastructures and that villagers who had electricity in their houses would be more thankful and supportive citizens. Moreover, with electric TV sets, the government could ensure that its broadcast development programs would reach people in the countryside and get their votes in the general elections.

As it unfolded, the New Order village electrification program became its leading village development program, but it was done at the expense of meeting villagers' needs for other basic infrastructures. Increasing the total number of electrified villages became the desired goal and justification for the government's development agenda and march toward progress. The New Order regime imagined that electricity in rural households would be visible, material proof of their patronage. Although many villagers enjoyed the benefits of electricity, others (those who didn't yet have it or couldn't afford it) became further marginalized. The New Order regime's patrimonial technopolitics is further brought to light in the next chapter, where I discuss the case of three rural electric cooperatives established in the late 1970s.

Rural Electric Cooperatives

I n November 1975, USAID sent a proposal to Dr. Widjojo Nitisastro, chair of the Indonesian National Development Planning Agency (Badan Perencanaan Pembangunan Nasional, BAPPENAS), to undertake a prefeasibility study on the practicality of electrifying Indonesia's countryside. USAID proposed to have a team from NRECA visit Indonesia and determine the workability of selecting specific sites to be electrified. Dr. Subroto, Indonesia's minister of Manpower, Transmigration, and Cooperative at the time (before he became minister of Mining and Energy in 1978), accepted the offer on November 21, 1975, and appointed Ir. Ibnoe Soedjono the head of the DGC as the study's Indonesian coordinator.[1]

The American NRECA team carried out the study between February and May 1976, visiting thirty-five districts in seven provinces to find suitable locations to establish RECs. The team was enthusiastic about the prospect of expanding RE in Indonesia and believed in the economic benefits of electricity. Drawing on the success of its program in the United States and in aiding the Philippines with its RE program, the team recommended that the Indonesian government create "a new national organization for administering and financing a phased program to provide electric service to the majority of rural Indonesians over a 25–30-year period."[2] For the first phase of the program, NRECA recommended "loans for construction of up to 12 local distribution systems in selected *kabupaten* [district], and that such systems be owned and operated by their members as cooperatives, with strong support and supervision from the national agency."[3] In summary, the team wrote that the project would need:

To provide electrification to Indonesian villagers for small industry, agriculture, home and other uses by establishing a new national agency to provide low int. [*sic*] long term loans and technical assistance to locally owned and operated electric cooperative distribution systems [that] purchase power wholesale from PLN. [To] initiate 12 electric cooperatives costing approx. $4 million (Rp 1,660 million) each initially serving 120,000 consumers [i.e., 10,000 customers for each cooperative] bringing home lighting to ¾ million people which should become 1½ million in 10 years[,] meeting operating expenses 2 years after energization [so that they would be] able to begin repayment of loan in 6–10 years [and] possibly expanding to more than 200 cooperatives within 20 years providing 24-hour, low cost electric power to areas in each *kabupaten*.[4]

In other words, the team provided specific plans and suggestions for the Indonesian government to use cooperatives to electrify the countryside.

The NRECA prefeasibility study was well received by USAID and the Indonesian government and prompted Soedjono to hold a two-day seminar on RECs in Jakarta in December 1976. Participants of the seminar consisted of people from the DGC, USAID, the National Electrification Administration of the Philippines, PLN, and ITB. In his synopsis of the presented papers, Soedjono made six recommendations and observations. Two pertain to RECs specifically: first, to achieve the goal of electrifying most of Indonesia's villages by 2000, the Department of Manpower, Transmigration, and Cooperative (DMTC), the DPWEP, or both ministries would need to start a pilot RE project soon; second, cooperatives would need to play a more active role in rural electrification "to ensure people's participation in electricity development."[5]

Soedjono hoped that establishing RECs would activate people in the villages to take part in and collectively own an electricity business. The thinking was that a cooperative's drive for growth would not be mainly to earn profits but to increase members' welfare. This idea followed Mohammad Hatta's thoughts on cooperatives. Hatta, Indonesia's first vice president and one of the foremost thinkers and promoters of cooperatives, wrote once that there is no class struggle in an ideal cooperative because members voluntarily cooperate to defend the collective's needs and interests. Although cooperative members work in various roles, such as operators, administrators, and managers, all members have the same rights, and ideally all decisions are reached by consensus based on a one-person-one-vote system. Hatta emphasized, "This is the benchmark of the real cooperative (*Inilah patokan koperasi yang sebenar-benarnya*),"[6] which in his mind would elevate members' economic status and increase their self-esteem by organizing a business entity of their own. Hatta warned that creating and operating a successful cooperative would not be easy and that achieving optimal form and function required lengthy education and training.[7]

Following negotiations and deliberations, in the late 1970s the Soeharto government founded three electric cooperatives with USAID's technical and financial assistance. Although these cooperatives operated well in the beginning, they ultimately failed. All three went bankrupt and their assets were sold, auctioned, or abandoned. PLN took over their former customers. I argue that there are four contributing factors of the RECs' collapse: (1) USAID and the Indonesian government's different visions of the function of RECs, (2) the New Order regime's largely hands-off treatment of independent cooperatives, (3) PLN's ambivalent view of and reluctance to work with the cooperatives, and (4) the perceived mismanagement of cooperatives by their members. The stories of the three failed RECs reveal the challenges of creating a fully functioning and sustainable electric infrastructure assemblage and illustrate that a technological need from "below" does not always have to be provided by the community members. Many were quite happy to receive the provision of electricity from "above." For many of them, getting an affordable and reliable electricity regardless of the source was a form of social justice.

Two Bureaucratic Approaches of Rural Electrification

When the Soeharto government accepted USAID's proposal in 1975, it opened the door not just to foreign assistance but to two approaches to RE. One of the stipulations of USAID's assistance was to set up electric cooperatives. Although PLN had already been established, the government thought that all matters pertaining to cooperatives, including the ones selling electricity, should be administered by the appropriate agency, which at the time was the DGC. Consequently, the New Order state used two bureaucratic approaches to rural electrification: PLN, to supply government electricity through its grid and power systems, and the DGC, which was tasked with establishing electric cooperatives. Delegating the DGC to found electric cooperatives in a way followed USAID's recommendations, although at the time the DGC had less experience creating technically based cooperatives.

The New Order government's decision to have two agencies carry out RE reflects its penchant to bureaucratize development projects and divide responsibilities (and access to government resources and largesse) among its bureaucracies. DGC was part of Subroto's DMTC, which handled the New Order's transmigration program to resettle people from the heavily populated Java to other islands.[8] Having the ministry manage electric cooperatives meant that Subroto could prioritize electrifying transmigration settlements to make them more attractive to transmigrants. In fact, two of the three eventual sites were transmigration areas.

To accommodate cooperatives in the electricity sector, the Soeharto government passed Government Regulation No. 36 of 1979 giving permission to cooperatives to participate in the electricity business. At the time there were two main types of cooperatives being developed in Indonesia: village unit cooperatives (Koperasi Unit Desa, KUD) and non-KUD cooperatives. In the former, a cooperative could deal with a variety of businesses, and one example was farmers' cooperatives. The latter specialized only in one enterprise.[9] RECs fell into the second category. Since there are two main categories of cooperatives (KUD and non-KUD), the government needed to lay out four schemes (*pola*) for how cooperatives could work with PLN to deliver electricity.[10] The first scheme (Pola I) allowed KUD members assist PLN in reading and routine inspection of electric meters, maintaining distribution lines and substations, and solving minor technical problems. In Pola II, KUD members could do additional tasks, such as connecting households to the grid, wiring houses, and extending low-voltage distribution lines. KUD cooperatives that chose the third scheme (Pola III) needed to buy electricity from PLN in bulk, take care of all the responsibilities in the second scheme, and collect payments, keep books, and administer an office and storage facility. Pola IV was reserved for non-KUD cooperatives that wanted to own and operate their power plant system independently. They had the freedom to determine their prices and collect bill payments from their customers. At the same time, they were responsible for employee recruitment and training. In short, an REC must manage the electricity business on its own without PLN's involvement. Pola IV cooperatives essentially functioned as a miniaturized electric company where they set up their businesses. The three cooperatives established outside Java with USAID assistance operated using Pola IV.

The decision to involve two bureaucracies for RE didn't quite follow NRECA's initial recommendation to establish a new national body to administer these projects. But the team believed that "Any rural electric cooperatives which come into existence on these islands of the Indonesian Archipelago will be owned by Indonesians, managed by Indonesians, serve Indonesians, and reflect Indonesian needs and conditions, no matter what technical assistance may be offered and accepted from managers, electrical engineers, and cooperative specialists from the rural electric cooperatives in America or other nations."[11] In other words, they accepted the decision to use two separate organizations for RE.

However, NRECA was insistent on implementing what it called an "areawide coverage" approach, which entailed cooperatives serve as large an area as possible "having 30,000 to 50,000 households."[12] According to NRECA, the concept of areawide coverage needed "economic viability" to make electricity affordable to rural residents, "financial soundness" to achieve long-term financial returns on investment, and "productive use of electricity 24 hours/day" to encourage villagers to consume electricity for more than just illumination.[13] Both USAID and

NRECA officials believed that the areawide coverage approach would bring the greatest benefits to the greatest number of rural residents. Specifically, they hoped that the Indonesian RECs would get 50 percent of coverage within the first five years and later 85 percent within fifteen years of operation in the selected REC areas.[14] The Indonesian government agreed to implement this approach.

To better coordinate its RE activities, PLN created a Sub-Directorate of Village Electrification in October 1976, headed by Ir. Johannes J. Rumondor. The DGC also later setup its own team and, in mid-January 1977, PLN and the DGC sent separate contingents to attend a workshop sponsored by the Philippines's National Electrification Administration to further study the viability of setting up electric cooperatives in Indonesia. Rumondor and his colleagues from PLN and Ima Suwandi and his coworkers from the DGC flew to Manila to discuss the steps needed to electrify rural areas. They took an intensive course on creating feasibility studies, went on field trips to visit nine electric cooperatives, and developed a course to train personnel to conduct feasibility studies.[15] Their reports made it clear that the Indonesian delegations were impressed by what they saw and learned. Rumondor, for example, found out that the Filipino RE program received good support from the government, involved rural people, provided personnel training, gained the support of the local construction industry, and implemented standardized construction methods.[16] He also learned the importance of conducting feasibility studies to set technical requirements, prioritize locations, and request funding from foreign institutions, and he suggested that more PLN employees get trained on how to perform them (described in chapter 5).[17] In their report, Suwandi and colleagues noted important factors in organizing an electric cooperative: "a strong National Executive Agency to coordinate the implementation of the projects, variety of population density, income per capita, power installed, capitalization, trained personnel, [the] terrain of the projects, and communication."[18] Key here is that "a strong National Executive Agency," mentioned by Suwandi, differed in structure from "a new national organization" as recommended by NRECA. As we will see, Suwandi's "executive agency" would be an office set up by the DGC.

The December 1976 seminar and the Manila workshop in January 1977 further solidified Indonesia's desire to embark on the RE project with USAID's assistance. Further negotiations between the Soeharto government and USAID resulted in several important points. First, as already mentioned, RE would be carried out using an areawide coverage approach. Second, PLN would handle seven RE projects in Central Java by extending its grid into those areas.[19] Third, the DGC would coordinate the creation of three Pola IV electric cooperatives outside Java.[20] To carry out day-to-day tasks, it created the Project

Development Office (PDO), separate from DGC but chaired by the director general of Cooperative and would be supervised by a team of appointees from PLN, BAPPENAS, and the Departments of Finance, Home Affairs, and Cooperative.[21] PDO project officers would coordinate the cooperatives' daily operations, including approving managers, contracts, and plans.[22] Because of these arrangements, progress at the cooperatives would sometimes be delayed waiting for PDO's reviews and approvals. In addition, as we will see, the responsibilities of PDO-appointed acting manager overlapped with those of the DGC-appointed coordinator and hampered progress. Finally, the USAID grant would be used to provide "assistance in the form of an organizational, management and technical advisory team and an architect, engineering design and construction supervision team" to PDO.[23]

Loan and Grant Agreements and Sites Selection

On September 2, 1977, USAID recommended a loan and a grant to its development loan committee, which was later approved.[24] On March 30, 1978, Indonesia and the United States signed a grant agreement for US$6 million, of which PLN received US$2,375,000 and the DGC US$3,625,000.[25] The USAID grant was earmarked to pay for the American consultants on the project through two three-year contracts. The first contract, signed on August 23, 1978, was to hire NRECA personnel to provide "298 man-months of consulting services in the organization, operation, maintenance of the distribution systems, and training."[26] The second contract, signed on September 18, 1978, was to hire Chas T. Main International, Inc. engineers to provide "467 man-months of consulting services" for the PLN and DGC projects.[27] Main's consulting services included designing and constructing the distribution systems and the headquarter complexes, procuring materials, supervising construction, training, doing site surveys, soil investigation, and engineering.

On May 6, 1978, the two countries signed a loan agreement for US$30 million, of which two-thirds (US$20 million) would be apportioned to PLN and the remainder (US$10 million) to the DGC.[28] The Canadian International Agency for Development (CIDA) also agreed to provide a US$21 million loan and a US$1.8 million grant, while the Netherlands government pledged a US$5 million loan. The Indonesian government allocated US$30 million to fund the project.[29] In the end, CIDA's loan and grant, to buy diesel generators and build substations for the three cooperatives, were canceled for economic reasons. CIDA's cost estimates to install 33 MW generation capacity for the three RECs by their sixth year of operation over time "reached the installed cost per KW of plus or minus U.S.$ 1,200," which was different from their initial estimates.[30] This high cost made the Indonesian government cancel

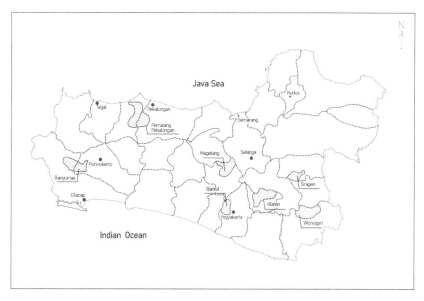

Figure 13. Seven PLN sites in Central Java. Source: Map drawn from Rural Electrification Preliminary Engineering and Feasibility Study Report North Central Klaten, Central Java, Indonesia, August 1977, USAID Development Experience Clearinghouse, PNAAF716.

CIDA's loan proposal in the second half of 1982. To provide temporary generators, USAID earmarked part of its loan to obtain "15 small excess property diesel gensets with a capacity of 100 KVA each and 6 new diesel gensets with a total capacity of 3,200 KW for the three RECs."[31]

The USAID loan and grant funds were used to set up ten pilot RE projects, seven PLN sites in Central Java (figure 13) and three DGC sites in other provinces (figure 14). The selection of PLN and DGC sites was the result of negotiations among several parties. Initially, PLN considered two demonstration projects each in three different provinces of Java, but the company decided to focus its efforts on Central Java for three reasons: compatibility (the constructed regional grid there was financed by USAID), increased accessibility (PLN had not invested enough in Central Java), and exclusivity (other donors were interested in Java's other provinces). PLN chose the seven sites in Central Java using three criteria: "technical (near to the existing grid), economic (complementary to the provincial development plan), and political (the areas whose local leaders have been the most vocal in their demands for electric services)."[32] As for the DGC sites, Ibnoe Soedjono met with the vice

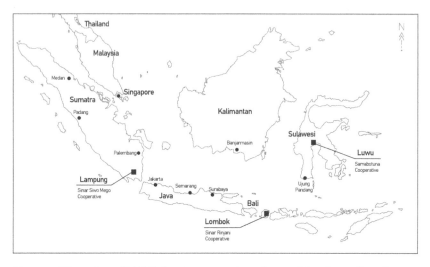

Figure 14. Three sites of DGC electric cooperatives. Source: Map drawn from Report No. 47: Rural Electrification Project—Indonesia, USAID, Loan No. 497-T-052, Project Report for Second Quarter, 1984, USAID Development Experience Clearinghouse, PDAAQ217.

chair of BAPPENAS and USAID director on June 2, 1977, to narrow sixteen potential sites down to three.[33] In the end, they decided on Luwu in Sulawesi, Central Lampung in Sumatra, and East Lombok on the Lombok island. The first two were government-designated transmigration areas.[34]

The seven sites in Central Java encompassed different districts: Klaten, Pemalang, Bantul, Wonogiri, Sragen, Magelang, and Banyumas. Combined they eventually served a total of 511 villages and 114,983 electricity customers by March 1986.[35] The three RECs (Koperasi Listrik Pedesaan, KLP) outside Java were the Luwu REC (founded on December 23, 1978), the Lombok REC (April 21, 1979), and the Lampung REC (April 25, 1979).[36] All were successfully established and initially thrived, but eventually failed. When I visited these three facilities in July and August 2018, they were either sold to or operated by different entities (the Lombok and Luwu RECs) or abandoned (Lampung REC). In the next three sections, I discuss their emergence and collapse using archival sources that include monthly records prepared by NRECA consultants. Led by Peter McNeill, the seven-member NRECA team worked with their Indonesian counterparts to set up the RECs.[37] Their monthly reports detail many cooperative activities, as well as challenges faced and progress made.[38]

The Luwu REC

The REC in Luwu, South Sulawesi, was officially named the Samabotuna REC or KLP Samabotuna for the acronym of the five subdistricts (*kecamatan*) covered: Sabbang, Masamba, Bone-Bone, Wotu, and Mangkutana.[39] The DGC selected the Luwu district because it was a designated transmigration site and PLN electricity hadn't yet reached the area.[40] The headquarters location was remote. It was several hours' drive away from the district capital Palopo, which was itself an overnight bus ride away from Makassar, the South Sulawesi provincial capital.[41] John DeFoor, an RE specialist, was assigned to Luwu REC, and he worked closely with Ramon Garcia, Main's field engineer.[42] In addition to supervising the construction of the cooperative, DeFoor and Garcia gave several training courses. In one linemen course held in May 1981, the consultants praised the twelve participants "to be fast-learners both in the class room [*sic*] and pole climbing techniques."[43] The consultants took a few photos of the trainees and included them in the monthly reports. One such photo shows three young men climbing wooden poles, wearing harnesses and helmets, training their bodies and minds as linemen.[44]

One of the challenges the Luwu cooperative faced, according to the team's reports, was building a functioning cooperative organization from scratch. One early problem pertains to unclear employee responsibilities. The consultants wrote that the forty-three employees of the cooperative did not clearly understand their roles.[45] For example, the five-member board of directors, whose duties were supposed to deal only with policymaking decisions, also served as employees in various roles and thus meddled in the cooperative's daily affairs.[46] Another problem was related to cooperative management. Managerial responsibilities were ill-defined, and consensus about who was running the cooperative was unclear. The government appointed a project coordinator from the DGC Palopo office who acted as the decision maker; in contrast, the person appointed by the DGC's PDO as acting manager did not always perform his role. Finally, in late 1982, the PDO asked Bidullah Hasan, the DGC project coordinator, to replace Waluyan as acting manager, a PDO employee who assumed management function in late 1981.[47] Hasan accepted this dual role (coordinator and manager) after two previous PDO-assigned acting managers "could not meet the challenge of managing [the] REC in a relatively remote location."[48] Earlier issues with unclear employee responsibilities also seem to have been largely solved by this time.

A high rate of employee turnover posed a significant problem for the cooperative, which had difficulties attracting and keeping talented personnel. The position of an accountant was especially problematic and as a result, recordkeeping and reporting fell months behind.[49] The NRECA consultants mentioned

Luwu's remote location and low salary as top reasons.[50] Another contributing factor was the unclear roles of so-called office services. Most departments at the cooperative were "staffed with capable personnel . . . [the] weakness in staff positions relates primarily to 'office services' department, general bookkeeping-accounting."[51] It is not entirely clear what duties "office services" personnel were responsible for, but an incident narrated to me by a former employee illustrates his frustration that led to his resignation when the person in charge of office services wasn't taking care of business. Umar Muktamar started as a bookkeeper and worked his way up to chief of accountant in his five years of employment (1981–86) at the cooperative's Bone-Bone headquarters. He had studied accounting in Makassar and was initially reluctant to find employment in Bone-Bone because of the remote location but was eventually persuaded to join the Luwu REC. At one point in 1986, he wanted to recruit more employees to his division and sent a request to "office services" (Kepala Kantor) to increase his staff. He claims the request went unanswered and was undermined by someone who worked in Kepala Kantor. According to Muktamar, his letter to REC management was never relayed by this Kepala Kantor person despite his repeated requests, and he wasn't sure why. Frustrated and sensing troubles ahead, he resigned. At the end of our interview, he showed me a laminated copy of his letter of employment termination signed by Hasan, which was the only memento he kept from his five years of service at the cooperative.[52]

These initial problems notwithstanding, the construction of the facilities proceeded. Because the REC's headquarters complex was built in Bone-Bone, this subdistrict was prioritized to receive electricity. On August 22, 1981, the cooperative's power plant was successfully energized, and 160 consumers received electricity for the first time.[53] After Bone-Bone, Mangkutana was energized in May 1982 using a USAID-furnished 100 kW generator set.[54] The cooperative suffered construction delays on their main distribution system because a North Sumatran supplier of wooden poles contracted to deliver 3,000 poles by the end of June 1983 had not delivered a single pole by the end of that year.[55] Nevertheless, by the end of 1983, 580 customers in Bone-Bone and 263 consumers in Mangkutana enjoyed twenty-four-hour electricity.[56] By the end of the next year, although its power system was only 25 percent completed (it still awaited the installation of an 800 kW generator that arrived in late 1984), the Luwu REC had 76 employees and 9 board members serving 1,000 customers.[57]

On top of the issues with power generation and distribution, the Luwu REC experienced a financial crisis in 1983. Its revenues were not enough to cover operational expenses. Nonetheless, and despite "NRECA's longstanding plea,"[58] the REC did not change its electricity pricing structure likely because they wanted to retain customers. However, since the government's Daftar

Isian Proyek (Project Content List, DIP) funds, which had funded the REC's operations from the start, "were nonexistent for an extended period during 1983 . . . the REC was forced to raise [electricity] tarif [sic], as cash expenses exceeded revenue month after month."[59] No additional information on the electricity prices could be found in the report.

The cooperative survived the crises of the mid-1980s and continued servicing its members into the early 1990s. At its peak in 1992, the Luwu REC served a total of 15,793 customers in sixty-six villages.[60] From 1984 there was an increase of over 14,000 customers. By this time the cooperative began facing new issues. Its growing customer base far outstripped its generating capacity, and it had trouble collecting payments from customers which, according to people I interviewed, was the result of poor management practices.[61] Fajar newspaper reported that REC customers owed Rp 1 billion of unpaid bills in the early 1990s.[62] One customer said, "how could we pay [the bill] if electricity was only working for 1 hour in three days. Is that fair?"[63] Because revenue was low, the cooperative could not purchase additional generators and was forced to implement rolling blackouts.[64] Darkness returned to Luwu at the end of 1993, and cooperative customers eventually became frustrated with the situation.

One of the earliest signs of troubles started in March 1996 when several Luwu residents complained about their unstable electricity supply to Harmoko, the minister of Information and the chair of the ruling party Golkar, when he visited Palopo to hold a rally. Thousands of Golkar supporters attended the gathering, and Harmoko promised to investigate the matter.[65] In May 1996 people cut down almost all the REC's wooden poles in the Walenrang subdistrict in response to the cooperative's load shedding practices.[66] One Fajar source later estimated it would cost Rp 2.3 billion to fix the damaged transmission lines.[67] Many REC customers were frustrated about the cooperative's poor services and refused to pay their bills. They demanded that the REC be abolished and replaced by PLN. One resident threatened to mobilize his fellow residents to change "color" (i.e., not voting for Golkar) in the upcoming 1997 general election if the ruling party could not resolve their electricity problem.[68] Perhaps as an attempt to dampen Luwu residents' anger, PLN President Director Ir. Djiteng Marsudi promised that PLN would be ready to take over the cooperative's customers if the government ordered it to do so.[69] Unfortunately, Marsudi's words did little to lessen their displeasure. The vandalism continued, and by mid-June 1996, they had damaged 3,033 wooden electric poles (about 33 percent of the total number) in twelve subdistricts, which destroyed 167 km of transmission lines.[70]

Customers' growing discontent was eventually heard by people at the highest levels of government. Golkar officials, sensing the issue might influence the

Figure 15. A former residence of the Luwu REC project leader. Source: Photo by
Anto Mohsin, July 2018.

outcome of the 1997 general election in South Sulawesi, sprang into action.
Harmoko assigned Golkar people in the province to solve the Luwu REC electricity issue, and Golkar branches in South Sulawesi held meetings to discuss the
problem. Ir. Madjid Tahir, the head of the South Sulawesi Golkar Election Winning Bureau, pleaded to the cooperative customers to avoid making things more
difficult for the government to help them.[71] This was coded language asking
people in Luwu to stop damaging the REC's electric infrastructure. In June
1996, PLN began supplying electricity to some former cooperative customers
and promised the remaining customers electricity by December 1996. Upon
hearing this plan, the Luwu district head (*bupati*) joyously exclaimed, "Luwu
residents have been waiting for electricity like rain [after a long draught]."[72]
Finally in July 1996, PLN signed an agreement with South Sulawesi representatives of the Department of Cooperative for the Luwu REC to hand over its remaining assets and customers to PLN.[73] Connecting their electricity issues with
national politics, former Luwu REC members were able to compel the New
Order technopolitical regime to channel its patrimonialism through PLN.

   Out of the three RECs, the Luwu cooperative was the shortest-lived (1978–
96). The former Luwu REC complex is now operated by the North Luwu

district government as a job training center for its Office of Transmigration and Labor. While touring the compound, I observed that one house has been reduced to rubble, although a few houses such as the one occupied by an REC's project leader, still stood (figure 15).[74]

The Lombok REC

Lombok is one of the islands that make up the West Nusa Tenggara province (western portion of the Lesser Sunda Islands). Lombok is divided into four districts (Central, East, North, and West) with East Lombok being the most populated area, which is where Lombok REC was established in Aikmel. It took the official name of Sinar Rinjani REC or KLP Sinar Rinjani (KLP SR) after Mount Rinjani, an active volcano on the island.[75] As we shall see, the Indonesian word *sinar* (ray, beam, or glow) also appears in the Lampung REC's official name, suggesting that the cooperative was viewed as a beacon of hope in electrifying thousands of village households.

The team's reports detail early challenges to establish the Lombok REC, which involved difficulties in recruiting qualified personnel with the key position of accountant the hardest to fill. The team wrote, "In previous NRECA reports, it was indicated that a qualified accountant had been hired. Unfortunately, the person in question reconsidered his proposed move from Jakarta to East Lombok and withdrew his application."[76] No explicit reason was given, although location didn't seem to be a factor. Unlike the remoteness of the Luwu REC complex, the Lombok REC headquarters was within easy reach of Mataram, the provincial capital in West Lombok. When I visited Aikmel in July 2018, it took me about an hour and half by motorcycle to reach the cooperative headquarters from Mataram. One plausible explanation was that big cities like Jakarta were more attractive than small towns such as Aikmel for young graduates looking for a new employment.

The cooperative's easy accessibility, on the other hand, may explain why the Soeharto government and USAID gave extra attention to it. The team wrote, "The Lombok Cooperative continues to be a showplace for rural electrification as numerous officials from national, regional and local government visit the project. Among the visitors during this reporting period [May 1981] was U.S. Ambassador to Indonesia, Mr. Edward E. Masters."[77] It was also for this reason that the team selected Lombok REC as their preferred place to deliver many training courses. The consultants conducted a total of eighteen courses there, the most out of the four locations (Lombok, Luwu, Lampung, and Jakarta) where classes were held.[78] Because of such heightened attention, the Lombok REC showed relatively better progress than the other two coops. In addition, it did one useful thing the other coops did not do to maintain a line of communication with its members. It created a radio station called the Voice of Aikmel, which operated between 5 and 10 p.m. to communicate with the general public.[79] The radio station aired "news about the RE Cooperative, policies and information about the Cooperative's operations, information about the PDO-RE and other governing agencies, local, regional and national news plus the usual welcomed inclusion in radio broadcasts, *music*."[80] Because many members were still illiterate, the radio was an effective tool for communication.

By the end of 1983, the Lombok REC was well on its way to serving an increasing number of customers. Its power plant in Aikmel generated 550 kW of electricity and delivered it around the clock to its 2,000 members. Interest in the REC electricity was high with close to 4,000 new applicants on the waitlist. The cooperative had fifty employees and a PDO-appointed acting manager. Unlike the Luwu REC, the Lombok REC board of directors performed "their functions as 'policymakers,' holding regular Board Meetings, and displaying a sincere interest in the welfare of the REC."[81] The cooperative's finances were also healthy, and there were sufficient funds to buy wooden poles to grow its electrical distribution system.[82]

The cooperative continued to expand and added more customers despite the end of the New Order government's financial support in 1987. In 1992 the cooperative served 16,858 consumers in thirty-seven villages, a similar increase as the Luwu REC customers over about the same time.[83] It managed to continue serving customers for thirteen more years since 1992. When oil prices increased to beyond US$50/barrel in October 2005, the Lombok cooperative began to feel a pinch because it didn't have enough funds to buy diesel oil.[84] When the global crude oil prices rose, the prices of oil sold domestically to unsubsidized industries increased as well. Since the Lombok REC bought diesel oil from Pertamina at an industrial rate, the cooperative needed to take drastic measures implementing rolling blackouts to continue operation. In November 2005, *Lombok Post* reported that small industries were negatively affected by the blackouts and that the cooperative management already "begged" central, provincial, and East Lombok district governments for help, to no avail.[85]

The newspaper coverage and a testament from a former REC manager made it look like the 2005 oil price increase was a turning point in the cooperative's history. Prior to 2005 everything was fine, but the increase in prices significantly hurt the cooperative. For example, Abdul Muttalib, a former cooperative manager, claimed that while he led, the Lombok cooperative managed to break even and occasionally obtain surpluses in revenues.[86] However, a study analyzing the cooperative's financial conditions from 1980 to 2000 concluded that although the Lombok REC was "surviving," it suffered high power and financial losses, especially after the government's DIP funds stopped in 1987.[87] Power losses resulted from electricity theft, meaning a good portion of the power generated and consumed ("around 36% or even more") was uncompensated, and "inaccurate metering and billing might be the biggest [contributor to] nontechnical losses."[88] These conditions led the REC to perform "load shedding for some villages at peak time . . . 6 days on for 24 hours and 1 day off at peak time for about 3 hours,"[89] a situation that worsened considerably when the cooperative could not purchase enough diesel oil to run its generators in 2005. In other words, rather than being a turning point, the 2005 oil prices increase exacerbated an already bad situation.

Meanwhile, an increasing number of REC customers grew exasperated and impatient because of the rolling blackouts. Adam Bahrullah called for boycotting the cooperative by asking his fellow customers not to pay their electricity bills, though not everyone agreed to do so.[90] Then, a breakthrough was made, and after several negotiations, the cooperative managed to get PLN to supply additional electricity temporarily by connecting the PLN grid to its distribution line. PLN electricity was finally delivered on January 7, 2006. But REC customers were not satisfied with this arrangement and demanded to receive direct PLN electricity at its lower rate rather than through an interconnected grid at the higher proposed rate. Disappointed, thousands of people from the villages served by the cooperative descended on the REC headquarters complex on January 11, 2006, and destroyed the buildings and burned much of the equipment and documents. Cooperative employees were chased out of their offices and fled to save themselves. The police officers and soldiers sent to restore order were overwhelmed by the number of demonstrators and could only watch while the destruction unfolded.[91]

It took five years from that unfortunate incident, with protracted negotiations between cooperative management, the East Lombok district government, and PLN, to finally reach a solution. In the intervening years, the East Lombok government temporarily took over electricity management by purchasing and delivering PLN electricity to the cooperative's former customers. PLN sold its electricity to the East Lombok government at Rp 900 per kWh and the government retailed it at Rp 1,200 per kWh to cover billing, collection, and other expenses. The East Lombok government's electricity price was double what PLN sold to its customers in other parts of Lombok at Rp 600 per kWh.[92]

Meanwhile, PLN was facing its own power generation problem. Its DPPs on the island did not generate enough electricity to supply its current customers and the former REC members. Thus, the company implemented load shedding during peak hours between 6 p.m. and 8 p.m.[93] Many cooperative

Figure 16. Agro Selaparang office inside the former Lombok REC complex.
Source: Photo by Anto Mohsin, July 2018.

customers did not fully understand the issue and thought PLN was withhold-ing electricity. Compounded by the fact that they had to pay a higher rate, they became frustrated and demanded to become PLN customers. But it wasn't a straightforward case. The Lombok REC still existed as a valid business entity, and PLN could not take the cooperative's customers legally. In addi-tion, there was a technical issue. The cooperative distribution system at the time was about thirty years old, and because it was not constructed to PLN standards, PLN wanted to replace it. The REC was eventually dismantled, and its assets auctioned off although it wasn't clear where the money went.[94] The complex where its headquarters once stood is now owned and operated by the East Lombok government. One building is occupied by a local government-owned agricultural business (figure 16).

Finally, on March 16, 2011, M. Sukiman Azmy, the East Lombok Bupati at the time, turned on a prepaid electric meter to signal the start of the transfer of cooperative members to become PLN customers.[95] The people who at-tended the small ceremony clapped and were happy to receive PLN electricity after about five years of living with unreliable power. Azmy took advantage

of the occasion by reminding everyone there that one of his campaign promises in 2008 was to provide "electric prosperity" to former cooperative members, which he successfully delivered.[96] Although East Lombok electricity issues predated Azmy's tenure as Bupati, he used them to great effect as talking
points in his political campaigns.[97] Azmy's campaign promises to solve the
electricity issues led to his victory in the 2008 Bupati election. In the case of
the Lombok REC, electricity was tied to local politics. What the former cooperative members wanted most was reliable and cheap electricity, which only
PLN could provide and Bupati Azmy helped deliver.

The Lampung REC

The Lampung REC's formal name was Sinar Siwo Mego REC or KLP Sinar
Siwo Mego (KLP SSM) after Abung Siwo Mego (the Nine-Families Community), the largest local community in Lampung. Headquartered in Kotagajah,
Central Lampung, the REC served the districts of Central and East Lampung
and the city of Metro. Like the Luwu district, the province of Lampung was a
major transmigration area for Javanese farmers who wanted to participate in
the government program.

The Lampung REC faced some of the same problems as the other two RECs
initially, although it managed to overcome them eventually. For example, job
descriptions for its employees were unclear in the beginning, and although
cooperative leaders wrote bylaws that were later approved by members, the
amendments clarifying the responsibilities of board members were not included
in the meeting agenda in March 1981.[98] In 1982 the original members of the
board of directors were dismissed; they were replaced during the 1983 annual
meeting.[99] The team reported in late 1983 that the five new board members had
"gradually accepted their policymaking role in the REC."[100]

Training courses held by NRECA consultants at this REC seem to be more
successful and resulted in better outcomes than the ones held at the other two
RECs. Between 1979 and 1984, a total of fourteen courses were delivered,
including classes on management; accounting; apprentice linemen; electrician
training; distribution system operation and maintenance; meter reading, billing, and collection; power plant recording and reporting; and electric meter
testing.[101] The team was particularly pleased with the test results of a construction cost accounting seminar held in April 1981 and wrote, "In general, it can
be stated that this Cooperative is blessed with qualified personnel in numerous
key positions, an asset that does not exist to-date [sic] at the other RE Cooperatives."[102] These courses may have played a role in staffing qualified people
at the cooperative, but another factor not mentioned may have been access to
a larger and better pool of applicants than at the other two cooperatives.

Overall, the Lampung REC progressed quite well during its early years. It energized its power plant in July 1981, and about 700 families received electricity, which subsequently increased to 2,000 within a few months.[103] By the end of 1983, it served 3,100 customers and had 53 fulltime employees, along with 22 linemen. The PDO-appointed manager, a temporary role that was supposed to be filled with a cooperative-appointed person, continuously served as manager since 1980.[104]

The Lampung cooperative continued to serve its expanding customers until the 1990s; in 1992, it served 14,000 consumers in thirty villages, achieving a similar number of customers as the other two RECs.[105] In 1994, to meet increasing demand, the REC decided to buy electricity from PLN, which treated the cooperative as an industrial customer and charged it accordingly.[106] PLN Fourth Region supplied electric power of 2,770 kVa with a 20 kV, three-phase, 50 Hz frequency specifications.[107] Between 1994 and 2000, the New Order government increased PLN electricity prices a few times, but the REC continued paying the lower 1993 rate. Consequently, PLN claimed the REC owed it Rp 8 billion in unpaid electric bills between 1998 and 2000.[108] When the cooperative's debt ballooned to more than Rp 30 billion because of the unpaid balance, late fees, and fines, PLN Wilayah Lampung (successor of PLN Fourth Region) threatened to cut the currents to the cooperative's 57,000 customers in 2003.[109] The Lampung REC struggled with monthly expenses for operating its six electric generators, maintaining its distribution lines, and paying employee salaries. For example, just to run the diesel generators, it cost the cooperative more than Rp 1.5 billion a month.[110] Consequently, starting in 2003, the Lampung REC's services began to steadily decline, including many blackouts and unstable voltages, which drew the ire of cooperative members, including the residents of Metro.

After failed negotiations with the cooperative, Lukman Hakim, the mayor of Metro, decided to bring his constituents' "aspirations" to PLN. On April 15, 2008, he and his entourage visited the headquarters of PLN Wilayah Lampung in the provincial capital of Bandar Lampung. They met with PLN's executive team and talked for two and a half hours. PLN officials told the mayor that the state power company would help, but only after the cooperative's legal entity had been clarified. In other words, as long as the Lampung REC still existed legally as a business entity, PLN couldn't do much because it did not want to "steal" the cooperative customers.[111] This situation was similar to the Lombok REC after it ceased operations after the destruction of its headquarters complex in 2006.

Cooperative members' demands to become PLN customers grew more vehement, so in late 2008, the director general of Electricity and Energy Utilization signed a letter to form a transfer team to switch the Lampung REC's customers to become new PLN subscribers.[112] A few months passed with little action until in March 2009, Syamsurya Ryacudu, the governor of Lampung, issued a decree establishing the transfer team and specifying its members, which included representatives from the Lampung REC, PLN, and the Lampung provincial and district governments.[113] It took almost a year until the Lampung governor "activated" the team again in early 2010 for things to start moving forward.[114] The key sticking points were the debt that the cooperative owed PLN (Rp 39 billion), unpaid electricity bills (Rp 15 billion), and the listing of cooperative's assets.[115] In a meeting held by the transfer team in February 2010, the cooperative manager reiterated that the "debt" was not really money owed but the difference between what PLN charged the cooperative and the amount the REC paid using the lower rate.[116] Another contentious issue was a disagreement between the Lampung provincial government and the central government over who had the authority to legally dismiss the cooperative. Each insisted that the other had the legal right to do so.[117] In other words, neither party wanted the responsibility of doing it and used the legality argument to avoid accountability.

Meanwhile, cooperative members continued to experience blackouts. For example, five hundred north Metro residents in Purwosari neighborhood had endured a power outage for more than a month by early January 2011. They resorted to using candles and kerosene lamps, and those who couldn't afford kerosene created torches out of bamboo. Children in these households couldn't study well at night, and the neighborhoods appeared unsafe.[118] One resident admitted, "We cannot stand it anymore here. Every night is dark. At nighttime accidents often occur and the children are studying uncomfortably."[119] Even though technically they lived in a city, their area turned into an unelectrified region, not unlike rural areas that hadn't yet received electricity. However, since they had gotten used to having electricity, the forced return to a pre-electrified lifestyle was unbearable.[120]

Finally, on March 31, 2011, the cooperative's electricity business license was revoked by the Lampung governor, which would go into effect on May 1, 2011.[121] PLN announced steps that former cooperative members needed to take to become its customers: (1) pay any debts they owed to the cooperative, (2) pay their electricity bills to PLN starting May 2011 and pay penalties for late payments, (3) pay their bills at post offices and dedicated counters, (4) report to PLN immediately if they are not yet officially registered as a PLN customer, (5) know that their electric energy consumption would be proportional to the capacity installed in their houses, (6) pay connection fees, (7) sign an agreement letter with PLN, (8) become a prepaid electricity customer for those who live near a PLN grid, (9) eventually become prepaid electricity customers, (10) obtain a PLN customer ID by texting to a PLN phone number, and (11) avoid dealing with unknown and illegal entities. Upon receiving the announcement, hundreds of former cooperative customers lined up to settle their debts.[122] After years of suffering through blackouts, they were ecstatic to be PLN customers and believed that they would get better service and more stable electricity.[123]

The Lampung REC laid off 141 employees at the end of May 2011 but retained 45 contractors to work security, finance, and other small administrative functions because PLN agreed to lease the cooperative's electrical distribution lines in Central and East Lampung. PLN needed the lines to supply electricity to former cooperative customers until it completed the construction of new lines up to PLN standards. In the city of Metro, PLN had begun bringing down the electric poles (many of which had decayed) to replace them with their poles.

By June 2011, around 72,000 former cooperative members had become PLN subscribers, many of whom were prepaid customers with household connections fitted with digital electric meters that they could top up when the balance ran low.[124] This new service freed PLN of the hassle of reading electric meters and collecting bill payments. It was the same strategy that PLN used with former Lombok REC members. However, not all consumers could get the digital prepaid meter. Those who didn't were still using the analog version, and during the transition period, PLN instituted a flat average rate to these customers, which meant that some paid for more than what they used and others for less than what they consumed. In short, not all former cooperative customers were pleased with the switch to PLN. In late August 2013, several Metro residents experienced blackouts as frequently as twice a day, experiences that made some nostalgic for REC electricity, which is ironic because they often envied their neighbors who received PLN electricity.[125] Their testimonies, recorded in the *Lampung Post*, show that they simply wanted reliable, stable, cheap electricity. They didn't care who supplied it.

In the end, the Lampung REC became insolvent. When I visited the cooperative's headquarters and power plant facilities in August 2018, the complex had the appearance of having been abandoned for some time. The buildings were deteriorating, and documents were scattered all over the place. I saw rooms with damaged desks, broken windows, and overgrown plants that had encroached on the floors. There was a meeting room with dusty tables and a large map of the Lampung REC area of coverage on the wall (figure 17). The warehouse was still intact with cabinets still filled with materials. It was as if the entire complex was abandoned in a hurry. In comparison, the Lombok

Figure 17. An abandoned meeting room with a map of the Lampung REC area of coverage. Source: Photo by Anto Mohsin, August 2018.

REC headquarters complex looked much better, even though an angry mob had destroyed it in 2006.

Conclusion

All three Indonesian RECs established by the DGC with USAID's technical and financial assistance failed. Even though the cooperatives managed to overcome many initial hurdles to establish a functioning electricity business and expanded to thousands of customers, they ultimately could not keep up with growing electricity demands. They could not increase their generating capacity. Newspaper coverage of the cooperatives reported huge electricity losses due to low infrastructure maintenance and electricity theft that they could not control. Rolling blackouts and brownouts occurred, leaving many customers in the dark for long periods and without reliable electricity. Customers demanded to get PLN electricity and resisted their poor service by refusing to pay their electricity bills which, in turn, decreased cooperative revenues. When the cooperatives folded, their assets were damaged, sold, or abandoned. The cooperative former employees lost their jobs, and eventually all former cooperative members became PLN customers. The stories of the three cooperatives illustrate the difficulty in creating a fully functioning assemblage of power system generation and delivery. A good assemblage requires technical and managerial expertise to implement sound practices of administering a socio-technical system.

Four factors figured into the demise of the cooperatives. The first is two different sociotechnical imaginaries of rural electrification.[126] USAID envisioned electric cooperatives as an effective way to electrify Indonesia's rural areas. The agency provided money, consulting, and materials; trained future cooperative employees, including technical and maintenance operators; and gave courses on accounting and other management aspects. However, using fully independent cooperatives did not align with Indonesia's preferred approach to electrifying the countryside. USAID's vision of what electric cooperatives should be (independent, democratic, and well-staffed) clashed with the New Order government's vision of what electrified villages should be (self-sufficient, supportive of the regime, and compliant with the regime's agenda). The Soeharto government preferred to use PLN to electrify the country. This way the New Order regime could channel its patrimonial largesse to the population in exchange for political support.

The second reason has to do with how the New Order government treated Indonesian cooperatives unevenly.[127] On one hand, it treated KUD cooperatives (such as farmers' and fishers' cooperatives) as small business entities that required constant government attention and controlled (in some cases even meddled in) their operations through the Department of Cooperatives.[128] On the other hand, it left non-KUD cooperatives such as RECs to their own devices after initially supporting them. The Soeharto government stopped supporting them financially and organizationally in mid-1980s once it deemed that the cooperatives could run their own affairs. In contrast, PLN continuously received ample support from the government to function relatively more effectively than RECs. The New Order regime could have helped the RECs by selling diesel fuel at a reduced rate as it did to PLN, but instead treated the cooperatives as industrial customers. One former deputy manager of the Lombok REC told me in an interview that he felt the coop was treated like a "stepchild" by the government. The co-op's appeal to buy diesel fuel from the government at a reduced rate when the price increased significantly in the mid-2000s went unheeded.[129]

The third reason was how PLN saw itself mainly as the rightful electricity supplier in the country and thus viewed rural electric cooperatives as rivals. PLN could have collaborated better with the cooperatives by selling more electricity in bulk and did not have to wait for the cooperatives to be in short supply. At least two PLN employees were critical of PLN's commitment to establish a good working relationship with cooperatives. Haroen, the head of PLN Eleventh Region between 1979 and 1989, strongly suggested that PLN collaborate with cooperatives using the Third Scheme to deliver electricity to rural areas.[130] However, PLN was ambivalent about collaborating with cooperatives using the Third Scheme. Former PLN Deputy Director of Finance Munawar Amarullah highlighted this issue when he criticized PLN for selling electricity to the cooperatives using an unreasonably high price. He argued that it would be difficult for coops to retail electricity at a profit to their potential customers at such high wholesale prices. As for PLN's concerns that delinquent cooperatives would not pay their monthly bills, Amarullah proposed to setup a payment mechanism between cooperatives and PLN or to place a PLN appointee an ex officio member of the cooperative supervising body.[131] When the government neglected to set a price for selling electricity in bulk to cooperatives in the 1989 electricity tariff structure, Haroen was critical of this. But instead of censuring the government, he directed his criticisms to PLN. Citing that the objective of bringing electricity to the villages was for the sake of national interest and not to make a short-term profit, Haroen wrote, "there is no need to fight [for the Third Scheme arrangements] such as PLN holding onto 'plump' villages and not giving it to the Cooperatives; or vice versa the Cooperatives do not want to handle 'lean' villages."[132] Haroen's comment suggests that PLN was unwilling, if not resistant, to working with cooperatives.

Finally, the RECs played a part in their demise as well. Not all management teams put the cooperatives' best interests first. For example, there was alleged mismanagement of cooperative funds with members' observations that management teams lived lavish lifestyles. Because of this widely perceived corruption and alleged embezzlement of funds, people in East Lombok formed a People's Committee (Komite Rakyat) and Communities Alliance for Electricity (Aliansi Masyarakat Peduli Listrik) demanding that the Lombok REC be disbanded and PLN supply electricity to the region.[133] Similarly, one former head of Lampung REC allegedly told two of his employees to sell two generator sets for his gains, which prompted the police to investigate the matter.[134] And the news that a former manager of Luwu REC was charged (and later convicted) with about Rp 1 billion corruption when he worked as the North Luwu district regional secretary didn't generate confidence in his handling of the cooperative in its final years, either.[135]

The villagers just wanted electricity for their houses and businesses. They didn't care who provided this much-needed technology as long as it was made available to them cheaply and reliably. When they no longer enjoyed KLP electricity, villagers demanded PLN electricity. This case shows that a community's need for electricity does not always need to be fulfilled by itself, as they would be fine receiving it from the government. Other villagers expressed the same sentiment in East Java. They received their electricity from the East Java provincial government's collaboration with the Institute of Technology in Surabaya and PLN.[136] The villagers' desire runs counter to Richard Sclove's argument to involve more citizens in many technological decision making and regulations.[137] I do not mean to say that Sclove's contention to bring more democracy into technology is wrong or pointless; it is just that when his idea travels to new locations, it encounters a landscape so different from the one with which he is familiar that citizen participation is not always the same as the one he imagines. The stories of the three RECs illustrate that transferring technologies from one place to another was a messy and unpredictable endeavor. Even well-meaning assistance unfolded on the ground unexpectedly, and one could not always correctly predict the development trajectory of a sociotechnical system.

Conclusion

THE HISTORY OF electrification in the Indonesian archipelago can be traced back to the late colonial period (1890–1942). The Dutch colonial regime and private companies brought the new energy technology to the Netherlands East Indies in the 1890s for the comfort and convenience of the European inhabitants. Dutch private companies spearheaded the endeavors to electrify urban areas by generating their own power or buying it from the colonial government's hydropower plants. They used electricity in extractive industries to exploit the natural resources in the colony to be shipped back to and sold in the colonial metropole. They used it to power their stores and factories and illuminate buildings and places where Europeans lived. The Dutch also sold the idea and machines of modernity via electrical appliances and advertised them openly in a popular and widely circulated periodical called *Alles Electrisch in het Indische Huis en Bedrijf*, targeting mainly white Dutch women in the colony.

My examination of the electric infrastructure built by the Dutch reveals inequality issues in terms of access to and knowledge of the technology. For example, the island of Java, where the colonial capital was located, was the best electrified island compared with other islands in the colony. Even so, one statistic indicates that less than 10 percent of the Javanese population lived in electrified areas and only 5 percent used electricity.[1] The Dutch managed to electrify a few remote areas and small towns outside Java, but for the most part, the countryside was left in the dark. Most ordinary Indonesians could not access electricity because it was unaffordable or unavailable. Not many knew how to run the machines that generated and distributed electricity, either. Most natives worked in European plantations and agricultural estates as contract laborers.[2] The Dutch opened trade schools that trained locals to be mechanics, mostly to fulfill the needs for machine repair and maintenance for the railways and extractive industries, such as sugar and tapioca mills.[3]

During the Japanese occupation of the archipelago (1942–45), Indonesia's leading nationalists, Sukarno and Mohammad Hatta, seized an opportunity to have many Indonesians work alongside Japanese authorities to train as administrators and technical personnel at many institutions, including electrical companies. These trained Indonesians helped fill various positions after Indonesia gained independence in August 1945 and later won Dutch recognition of its sovereignty in December 1949.

In the Sukarno period, electricity played an increasingly visible role in state politics as it energized the new nation figuratively and literally. In the early 1950s, radical Indonesian nationalists, led by labor activist Kobarsjih, demanded the nationalization of the Dutch electric companies. After a protracted process and motivated by a desire to seize West Papua from Dutch control, the Sukarno government finally nationalized all Dutch utility companies by 1958. Sukarno then founded BPUPLN to manage the corporations under one administrative organization, which was later broken up into two state companies in 1965, one that managed gas and other electricity. The latter was PLN, the state electricity company. PLN built new electrical facilities and expanded existing ones. The most notable were the ones used to energize the Fourth Asian Games in Jakarta in 1962. In a speech delivered on the fifteenth anniversary of the National Gas and Electricity Day in October 1960, Sukarno linked electricity with industrialization, socialism, and Guided Democracy. In short, the Sukarno government took over Dutch electric companies and used electricity to unify Indonesia's territorial claims, promote his socialist vision, launch state-led industrialization, and energize the modernization process.

In the aftermath of the September 30th Movement in 1965, Soeharto slowly seized power from Sukarno until he finally gained full authority and was appointed president by the Indonesian legislature in March 1968. Soeharto's rise to power followed the decimation of the PKI, which Soeharto accused of masterminding the September 30th Movement, along with hundreds of thousands of the party's members, sympathizers, and supporters. Soeharto initiated a new kind of era he called the New Order and launched a state-led development agenda to legitimize his rule. He assembled capable bureaucrats (some highly trained) as his aides and made economic development his priority. The Soeharto government's focus was developing the rural areas; to this end, it launched several village improvement projects. One was bringing electricity to the countryside to achieve what was often touted as the national development goal: "a just and prosperous Pancasila society."

The LMD became the New Order regime's leading program to develop Indonesian villages and realize what it deemed its social justice mission: to even out the imbalance between rural and urban areas and Java and the other islands. Even though this project was advertised as increasing villagers' socio-economic wellbeing, Soeharto's program also functioned to secure votes from rural people in the general elections, illustrating a practice I call patrimonial technopolitics. The New Order government electrified thousands of villages and, in the runup to general elections, organized village electrification inauguration ceremonies to persuade people to vote for Golkar candidates. PLN participated in the endeavor, sometimes reluctantly, because as a state-owned enterprise, it had little choice in the matter. As an independent nation, Indonesia spread electricity to the countryside much more widely than either Dutch private companies or the colonial regime, in part because of the work of its electric bureaucracy, PLN.

PLN was founded, supported, and developed to become the New Order's primary electric bureaucracy. PLN increased its organizational reach to encompass the whole archipelago, filled its rank and file with graduates of technical high school and universities, trained its employees, and developed in-house expertise in electricity to gain confidence from the New Order government and maintain independence by avoiding military intervention. PLN electric infrastructures and facilities (power plants, transformers, transmission and distribution lines, substations, fleets of maintenance vehicles, etc.) became visible material manifestations of the New Order state. This visibility extended to PLN as an organization for all its social works in many communities. PLN's monopoly and pervasive presence in the country made millions of Indonesians associate electricity with the company. Everyone wanted and waited for PLN electricity.

The state electricity company played an outsize role not just in illuminating the country but, equally important, as a conduit of the government's largesse and a vector of state ideology. It channeled government patronage to people in rural areas in the forms of subsidized electricity, educational scholarships, financial loans, and other material benefits. State electricity company employees participated in Pancasila indoctrination courses and often used Pancasila to talk excitedly about their duties electrifying and modernizing the country. In this way, PLN employees helped disseminate Pancasila principles to the population and establish Pancasila-based development and ideology as a legitimizing discourse for the New Order government. Electricity became a social good and service. To PLN, realizing Pancasila ideals of social justice meant conceptualizing its organization as an agent of development with the dual goal of becoming a commercially profitable utility company and completing its social mission of electrifying the country.

During the New Order period under Soeharto, PLN carried out many more electrical projects. In the larger scheme, the electric infrastructure constructed during this time was highly Java-centric and resulted in two main power grids: an electric backbone with high-voltage transmission linking three heavily populated islands (Java, Madura, and Bali) and scattered DPPs and a few regional grids in other places. Although more and more standalone DPPs and their limited distribution lines have been stitched together into larger networks, these two main types of power grids continue to make up the Indonesian electrical landscapes today. Java-centric electrification of the New Order was carried out for several reasons. First, electricity was used as a campaign material for Golkar, so the government prioritized electrifying the most populated island, Java. Second, developing the electric infrastructure in Java was easier than constructing new ones elsewhere because the Dutch had built good infrastructure there. Third, it underscored Java as the center of political power in the long history of the islands. Finally, the Javanese conception of power may have influenced Soeharto to concentrate electric power in Java, which was the site of his political power. One major consequence of Java-centrism in the New Order was the continued electrical imbalance between Java and other islands initiated during the colonial period. Instead of realizing equity and balance across the archipelago, electrification in the New Order fell short of the Pancasila social justice ideals many of its proponents invoked.

Rural electrification was one of three main energy challenges that the New Order government faced in the 1970s. Its domestic oil consumption (for transportation, industry, and cooking) was on the rise, threatening oil exports and the country's main sources of income. In addition, people in the rural areas were overusing firewood, which threatened deforestation in rural areas, particularly in Java's hinterlands. To address these issues, the New Order bureaucrats and energy industry practitioners sought to produce the social knowledge of rural life and energy uses to better understand how to decrease firewood consumption, reduce large kerosene subsidies, and effectively light up the countryside. PLN, DGP, a few other government agencies, and some universities were involved in discussing the problems and finding solutions through a series of seminars, workshops, and energy use surveys. The outcomes of these meetings included a national energy policy, feasibility studies manuals and reports, baseline national energy survey results, and assessments by academics both complementary and critical of the government's rhetoric of rural electrification. In addition, employees of PLN, DGP, and other government agencies exchanged information through seminars, gained technical skills in workshops, learned and implemented survey methodologies, and produced knowledge of the social.

As part of the effort to increase wider coverage in rural areas, the New Order government accepted a USAID proposal to study the viability of electrifying villages using cooperatives. The Soeharto government decided to use both PLN and DGC to setup ten electric coop projects, seven in Central Java and three in Luwu, Lombok, and Lampung. The seven Java cooperatives used the Pola III scheme and were largely successful in their operations because PLN was involved as their partner. The independent cooperatives outside Java were successfully established but then faced serious setbacks meeting their members' demands and eventually failed, and their customers switched to PLN electricity.

Indonesia's electrification program in the first fifty-three years after independence produced varied results. By the time of Soeharto's downfall in 1998, PLN had transformed into a semiprivate company, had put in place the infrastructure to electrify big cities and most district capitals, and had electrified 70 percent of Indonesia's villages.[4] Although thousands of villages had been electrified, many more remained in the dark isolated from the centers of electrical and political power. The Indonesian government's insistence on state-led electrification reduced opportunities for public involvement and provided little incentive for private participation in lighting up their regions. Although the Soeharto government was open to the idea of using cooperatives to electrify its rural areas, by 1998 one of three established rural electric cooperatives had closed its business and been taken over by PLN. The other two failed in the post–New Order period. The state power company's reliance on oil to run its numerous DPPs and on government subsidies to fund its operations served as a boomerang that hit it hard following the collapse of the New Order in 1998. Nonetheless, the desire to achieve social justice, realize the dream of establishing a "just and prosperous society based on Pancasila," and build the nation using electricity continues to animate PLN employees and many people long after the fall of the Soeharto government.

The Collapse of the New Order Government

The New Order regime officially ended on May 21, 1998, when President Soeharto announced his resignation to the country in a televised address. Vice President Bacharuddin Jusuf Habibie was immediately sworn in to replace him. Soeharto stepped down in the wake of the 1997 Asian financial crisis that hit several Southeast Asian countries. What started as a monetary crisis quickly turned into a sociopolitical crisis despite government attempts to stabilize the Indonesian currency.

In May 1997, the New Order government held general elections and Golkar predictably won again. In March 1998, members of the People's Consultative Assembly met to reelect Soeharto as president for the seventh term with Habibie as his vice president. Soeharto's appointment and subsequent announcement of cabinet appointees of his cronies and family members disappointed many and prompted student protests. Student demonstrations and dissenting voices grew louder, demanding that Soeharto quit and a new government be formed to reform the social, economic, and political order. Their demands were unheeded at first. But after four students were shot during a peaceful protest at the Trisakti University campus on May 12, 1998, riots broke out in Jakarta. Soeharto's hold on power became untenable as many people he consulted, including those in his inner circle, urged him to resign. When he finally did, it demonstrated students' power to affect change.[5]

The New Order regime's nationalist development made citizens the socioeconomic subjects of government benefits, but also treated them as (largely passive) political subjects it could coerce and persuade to support the regime. In the name of "development," the Soeharto government tried to sell an idea of modernity it purported to be in line with Indonesia's traditional values, encapsulated in Pancasila. It used technologies to create a distinct national identity among the populace as a developing nation laboring hard and playing catchup with the developed world. But the New Order government added a special qualification (Pancasila) to achieving what seemed to be the endpoint of a teleological narrative of the history of nations. In the New Order government's imagination, it wanted to transform Indonesia into a modern Pancasila nation.

Pancasila after the New Order: A Diminished Ideology

The Pancasila ideals were undoubtedly valuable. Soeharto himself wanted many good things for the nation. But Soeharto believed in what Adam Schwarz (borrowing William Liddle's phrase) calls "performance legitimacy," or securing his legitimacy to rule by showing how hard he worked to develop Indonesia economically.[6] In this regard, Nurcholis Madjid has argued that Soeharto suffered from what he called "verbalism—a personal belief that he felt that he had done it because he has said it often."[7] Soeharto did indeed say and repeat many good aspects about his vision of a modernized Indonesia, Pancasila, and the path he wanted the nation to take to reach this envisioned modernity. But his understanding of "development" as largely constructing the built environment, achieving and maintaining a few macroeconomic indicators, imposing narrow interpretations of Pancasila principles, and suppressing dissenting voices undermined the good intentions of establishing a "just and prosperous nation."[8]

Soeharto's upbringing, steeped in Javanese philosophy, and training in the military influenced how he saw the world. He found the state ideology Pancasila most compatible with his worldview and subsequently insisted that other Indonesians learn and internalize its principles according to his interpretations. Using Pancasila, Soeharto created a national identity of a postindependence society aspiring to achieve non-Western modernity. He enrolled high-level bureaucrats, state employees, schoolchildren, and college students in this vision by "educating" them in the Pancasila principles through mandatory courses, for example. In this regard, Pancasila proved quite effective in uniting Indonesia's diverse societies and in moving them to accomplish the one goal the New Order government often repeated: to get to the takeoff stage to create a just and prosperous society. Many social groups in Indonesia worked with a Pancasila frame of mind. It became an ideology of not just the state but also of the citizens. To the New Order regime, Indonesia's answer to its social justice, development, and nation-building challenges was found in Pancasila.

Imposing a uniform interpretation of Pancasila, however, had its costs. Many Indonesians were compelled to think in a rigid Pancasila framework that left little room for other critical interpretations of the five principles. To the New Order regime, the first principle meant that citizens must embrace one of the five state-sanctioned religions (Islam, Catholicism, Christianity, Buddhism, and Hinduism), marginalizing many who adhered to different beliefs. While the regime tried hard to achieve the second principle of a "just and civilized humanity" on the global stage, it turned a blind eye to its own uncivilized treatment of groups in Aceh, East Timor, and West Papua, who were forcibly suppressed because of their criticisms of the New Order and their desire to secede from the republic. The third principle of "Indonesian unity" was mainly translated as Indonesian uniformity, as exemplified by imposing identical village administrative structures across the archipelago in a law passed in 1979. The fourth principle of "democracy by consensus" came to mean cracking down on dissenting voices in parliament and on neighborhood streets, such as in the case of labeling villagers "communists" when they opposed a large dam construction. Finally, the fifth principle, "social justice for all Indonesians," was not always used as the guiding principle of the New Order development agenda, as illustrated by rising inequality in the villages (even the ones that received electricity) and by inequality of electricity coverage among and within regions. Toward the end of Soeharto's rule, Pancasila had turned into an empty slogan wrought with negative connotations and the undesirable implication that if you were not a Pancasila supporter, you could become an enemy of the state. It was immediately abandoned following Soeharto's resignation. When Indonesia held its first post-Soeharto general elections in 1999, political parties of all stripes embraced different ideologies (though none claimed communism as a party platform).

The New Order's Electrification Legacy

The New Order's legacy of electrification produced several unintended consequences. One was that it promoted urbanization instead of deterring it. Currently,

a little more than half of Indonesians live in the cities. These results are contrary to the government goal that electrifying rural areas would encourage
people to stay and develop their villages. But because other supporting and
equally important infrastructures (roads, schools, irrigation, markets, etc.)
were not always built alongside the electric infrastructure, young people left
their villages for the cities to look for better opportunities. The Java-centric
electrification made Java the most illuminated island, where the best schools,
universities, hospitals, and other facilities in the country were located. Indonesian citizens who sought upward social mobility migrated to Java.

Another unintended consequence was the relationship between PLN and
private electric companies. Realizing that PLN could not possibly generate
enough power capacity to meet increasing demands, Soeharto issued Presidential Decree No. 37 of 1992 to entice IPPs to participate in the electricity business. PLN signed contracts with twenty-seven IPPs, although twenty-six "were
concluded without competitive bidding. Not surprisingly, the majority of
these IPPs were connected to Suharto's relatives or close associates."[9] One of
the IPPs PLN signed a contract with was PT Paiton Energy Company (PEC),
which reportedly would build a largescale coalfired power station in East Java
with a projected total electric power output of 1,230 MW, the largest capacity
produced by a private company in Indonesia at the time.[10] However, when the
monetary crisis hit the country in 1997, PLN could not honor its contracts
because electricity usage decreased sharply from the economic slowdown. The
"take-or-pay clause" of the contracts (built in to ensure steady revenues and
profits for the IPPs) required PLN to purchase electricity it was no longer able
to sell profitably. In addition, Wu and Sulistiyanto wrote:

> To make things worse, the payment for many of these IPPs was denominated in
> US dollar while revenues for the electricity companies were in local currencies,
> resulting in skyrocketing financial debts for the electricity companies because of
> depreciation of local currencies. For example, the exchange rate for rupiah went
> down from 2450 to 10000 for a dollar, and the electricity rate would have to
> increase by 70 percent to just stay at its precrisis level. Electricity companies saw
> no way out but to pass on the cost increases to consumers, but the rate hikes
> couldn't have come at a worse time.[11]

Because of this unsustainable situation, PLN eventually renegotiated its agreements with the IPPs. In 1998, the state power company began to hold talks
with PEC. In 2000, it reached an interim payment agreement.[12] It was
reported that in late 2001, PLN and PEC had reached a deal.[13] By the end of
June 2003, PLN completed the restructure of twenty-six contracts while one

contract (with Karaha Bodas GPP) was still going through a litigation process in a US court.[14]

Another unintended effect was PLN's unstable financial conditions. The Asian financial crisis devalued the Indonesian rupiah so much against the US dollar that many businesses lost the value of their savings and reserves.[15] PLN's finances were severely affected, and the company struggled to service its debt obligations. Shortly after the Soeharto regime fell, Kuntoro Mangkusubroto, the minister of Mining and Energy at the time, issued a policy paper in August 1998 proposing to restructure the electricity sector.[16] Citing that one of the main objectives was to "restore PLN's financial viability," he proposed to break up PLN geographically and functionally.[17] For the former, there would be two main subdivisions: PLN in Java and Bali and Regional Electricity Company (Perusahaan Listrik Wilayah) to cover areas outside Java and Bali. For the latter, the government wanted to break up PLN's enterprises into four separate electricity businesses: generation, transmission, distribution, and retail.[18] The policy aimed to do several things, including commercialize electricity provision in Java and Bali, bring more private electricity businesses, introduce a more competitive and transparent market, and slowly increase electricity prices. In short, Mangkusubroto's ministry wanted to liberalize the electricity sector in which there would be multiple sellers and multiple buyers of electricity.

One PLN employee responded critically to this proposal. He released his paper in November 1998.[19] He argued that what Indonesia needed was not a restructure of the electricity sector but a reform of some longstanding unsustainable practices. One of his critical comments concerned government's pressure for PLN to carry its dual role (*peran ganda*) to make profits as a *persero* and to carry out various "nonelectrical" social missions such as financially helping small businesses and "accommodating bureaucrats' interests in developing society in things unrelated to the electricity sector."[20] He is critical of how the government used PLN as a "*political tool*" to avoid unwanted social unrest in the society.[21] Instead, he proposed an alternative suggestion, which includes improving the quality of PLN's workforce, releasing PLN from its "dependency management system" (i.e., having to depend on and receive orders from various government agencies), eliminating PLN's dual role (either treat the company as a *perum* without the expectation of making profits or let PLN function as a *persero* but freed of its social missions), and combating corruption, collusion, and nepotism.

While discussions about PLN's proposed restructuring was ongoing (Mangkusubroto's appointment as PLN's president director in 2000 allowed him to push this agenda further), PLN was forced to reduce its spending, including investing in new power plants. No new electric power while demands continued to increase meant that the country experienced a power deficit in the 2000s. Consequently, PLN was compelled to do rolling blackouts in many cities and regions. At its peak, the power deficit plagued more than two hundred cities across the country.[22] PLN finally managed to solve this issue when the Susilo Bambang Yudhoyono government started to invest in new power plants. The company fixed many of the damaged machines using inhouse (rather than outside) technicians. But it continued to rely on government subsidies because it could not set electricity prices for customers, which meant that for some types of customers, PLN sold electricity below the cost of production.

Amid the power deficit issue, the government enacted a new law in the early 2000s to implement its earlier restructuring policy. Law No. 20 of 2002 tried to break up (unbundle) PLN, which had been operating as a vertically integrated company, into smaller (and purportedly more profitable) constituents. The law facilitated the company to function more like a commercial enterprise than a state-owned and subsidized one by privatizing and divesting its subsidiaries. Using this law, PLN would treat electricity as a commodity from which to profit instead of a public good to be delivered and enjoyed by all citizens. However, several organizations, including the PLN Labor Union and the Association of PLN Retirees, fought this law by bringing it to the Indonesian Constitutional Court for judicial review.[23] The court struck down the law and ruled it unconstitutional. The plan to unbundle and privatize PLN failed, and a new law (not unlike the Law No. 15 of 1985 on Electric Power) was enacted in 2009. The enactment of these laws illustrates the long-standing tension of making PLN a for-profit commercial enterprise versus creating it as a public utility company for equitable access to electricity stemming from PLN's dual mission. Here we can see that the dreams and forces to keep state-led electrification in the name of ensuring equitable access to electricity remain strong.

Law No. 30 of 2009 on Electric Power includes clearer directives regarding electrification than the 1985 law. For example, the 2009 law asserts, "Electric power development aims to guarantee the availability of electricity in sufficient quantity, good quality, and at a reasonable price to improve welfare and prosperity of the people in a just and equitable manner as well realizing a sustainable development" (Article 2). In contrast, the 1985 law merely stated that the goal of electric power development was "to improve the welfare and prosperity of the people in a just and equitable manner and to encourage increased economic activity" (Article 2). The 2009 law spells out explicitly the kind of electricity that would need to be provided to consumers (affordable, reliable, and adequate) as well as how it should be generated in the future, that is, using renewable energy sources. The 2009 law and the Joko Widodo administration's efforts to increase the renewable energy mix into Indonesia's electricity production have produced the country's first largest solar farm and wind farm in Minahasa, North Sulawesi, and Sidenreng Rappang, South Sulawesi, respectively.[24] Both plants were built by private companies, and they sell their electricity to PLN. The choice to construct these power plants outside Java addressed the "in a just and equitable manner" clause of the 2009 law.

Today PLN has grown into a huge corporation with enormous assets but also liabilities. On one hand, it is one of the biggest state-owned enterprises in Indonesia with more than a dozen subsidiary companies that deal with power generation, telecommunication, coal exploration and mining, geothermal energy, engineering consulting, operation and maintenance of transmission lines, and even finance.[25] It controls 80 percent of the country's power generation capacity and 100 percent of the transmission and distribution networks. It is the only buyer of non-PLN electricity generated largely by IPPs. In 2015 it made it onto the Fortune 500 list at number 480.[26]

On the other hand, PLN has also turned into a liability for the government as it has become the main object of criticism by domestic electric consumers. For example, the Indonesian Consumers Foundation (Yayasan Lembaga Konsumen Indonesia), a consumer advocacy group, published an anthology highlighting the many issues plaguing Indonesia's electricity sector, including PLN's low-quality customer service.[27] Indonesians, who have grown frustrated with PLN's monopoly and low service quality, created a pun for the company, calling it Perusahaan Lilin Negara (State Candle Company) for the frequent blackouts they have experienced.

The state electricity company continues to enjoy the political and financial backing of post–New Order governments and, as such, became an unchallenged monopoly in the electricity arena. At the same time, it still carries out its burdensome dual mission and is thus vulnerable to being used as a tool of the government. In the post-Soeharto period, electricity continues to be used as political campaign material. For example, in the 2014 presidential election, Jusuf Kalla, one of the vice presidential candidates, promised to complete electrification of eastern Indonesia, which during the New Order period was largely neglected, within one year if elected.[28] In another case, Prabowo Subianto, the challenger to Joko Widodo's incumbency in the 2019 presidential election, promised to reduce the prices of electricity within the first 100 days of his administration if he was elected.[29] Electoral politics and electricity continue to be intertwined in post-Soeharto Indonesia.

A 2018 report, *Perusahaan Listrik Negara (PLN): A Power Company Out of Step with Global Trends*, paints a pessimistic portrait of PLN as it sought US$1 billion in international bond support. The report states that PLN "fails to recover generating, transmission and distribution costs, resulting in operating losses that have averaged US$ 2.1 billion annually over the past four years," which led the government to give "PLN an average of US$ 4.7 billion annually during this period."[30] In other words, despite its assets and size as a utility company, PLN was operating largely at a loss because it charged customers less than the cost to produce electricity. It could not do much because, as a state-owned enterprise, it was bound by the government's regulations.

Social Justice, Development, and Nation-Building

Electricity still animates Indonesia's desire to achieve social justice, to realize the goal of a just and prosperous society (PLN's motto is "Electricity for a Better Life") and modernize the nation just as these themes continue to influence how electrification is carried out. For example, President Widodo launched an initiative to scale up Indonesia's existing infrastructures by constructing ports, roads, bridges, dams, and electric power plants when he took office in October 2014. He prioritized his national development agenda around these infrastructure projects and was often seen inspecting them around the country, earning him the nickname "the hardhat president."[31] Indonesia's inadequate electricity provision prompted Widodo to announce a project to build 35,000 MW new electric power plant in May 2015. Noticing that many villages in the small islands and border regions still had not received electricity, in August 2018, he instructed PLN to electrify fifty outlying islands and border areas. PLN installed DPPs in these areas. In the East Amfoang subdistrict, one of the electrified regions, a resident was thankful for the better conditions he noticed after the arrival of PLN electricity.[32]

Critical public participation in matters of electricity increased after the New Order, the fall of which ushered in the reformation era, a new period during which Indonesia has been experimenting with a more democratic process of governance and greater freedom to express opinions on various platforms. It is one of the few countries in Southeast Asia where the press currently enjoys a large degree of freedom. Because of this, newspaper and magazine articles include critical reviews of the government's electricity policies, and consumer advocacy groups, such as the Indonesian Consumers Foundation, demand better services from PLN. The government no longer dominates popular periodicals that publish all things electrical, and several other magazines, such as *Listrik Informasi Energi*, *Listrik Indonesia*, and *Energi*, have entered the market. One can find many books written by former PLN employees and other noted experts on electricity.

Public participation has materialized in other forms as well. Greater freedom of assembly has facilitated a few new electrically oriented organizations to spring up. For example, the Indonesian Electrical Power Society (Masyarakat Kelistrikan Indonesia), an umbrella organization for several electrical associations, was founded on May 28, 1998. Another is the Association of Electric Power Generation Experts of Indonesia (Himpunan Ahli Pembangkitan Tenaga Listrik Indonesia), established on March 16, 2017. Granted, these organizations are mainly professional organizations, but they exert some influence in government policy making. Other forms of public involvement include PLN's annual contests to produce the best photographs, essays, or blogs about electricity in commemoration of National Electricity Day on October 27. Since first commemorated in 1960, when Sukarno hoped his nation would become an "electricity-minded" one, Indonesians have been creating stories, meanings, hopes, and dreams around this technology. As they wait for the day when the entire country is fully electrified, a moving target even now, they increasingly realize "the importance of electricity as it connects to their daily lives and to the life of the nation."[33] Electricity and nation-building have achieved greater integration in Indonesia. Likewise, the Indonesian government has increasingly recognized the role of electricity in national development and nation-building. It remains to be seen how the entanglement of electricity and social justice will play out in the future.

Appendix

PLN publications, the division or subsidiary that published them, and their dates of publication (if known). This list may not be exhaustive, but it contains many titles that I came across during my fieldwork research.

1. *Berita PLN*, PLN Headquarters, March 1977 to July 2000.
2. *Buletin Cenderawasih*, PLN Papua Region.
3. *Buletin Enjiniring*, PLN Center for Engineering Services (PLN PPE).
4. *Buletin Jasa Pendidikan dan Latihan*, PLN Educational and Training Services (PLN Jasdik).
5. *Buletin Jukung*, PLN Sixth Region.
6. *Buletin Mentari*, PLN West Sumatra and Riau Generation and Transmission Master Project, PLN Pikitiring Sumbar dan Riau.
7. *Buletin PLN Wilayah IV*, PLN Fourth Region.
8. *Buletin Pusdiklat*, PLN Center for Education and Training (PLN Pusdiklat).
9. *Bungong Jaroe*, PLN First Region, since January 1994.
10. *Cahaya*, PLN Jakarta and Tangerang Distribution (PLN Disjaya).
11. *Cahaya Flobamora*, PLN East Nusa Tenggara Region.
12. *Elektrika*, PLN West Java and Yogyakarta Distribution.
13. *Energi & Listrik*, PLN Power Research Institute.
14. *Floeksi*, PLN Load Dispatching and Transmission Center Java and Bali (PLN Penyaluran dan Pusat Pengatur Beban [Transmission and Load Dispatch Center] Jawa dan Bali).
15. *Fokus*, PLN Headquarters, since August 2000.
16. *HorasJalaGabe*, PLN North Sumatra, Aceh, and Riau Generation and Transmission Master Project (PLN Pikitiring Sumut, Aceh, dan Riau).
17. *ICON+News*, PT Indonesia Comnets Plus.
18. *Indonesia Power*, PT Indonesia Power.

19. *Infodis*, PLN East Java Distribution.
20. *Info Musi*, PLN South Sumatra, Jambi, and Bengkulu Region, since January 2006.
21. *Info Nusra*, PLN Bali, NTB, & NTT Business Unit, June to December 2002.
22. *Info PJB*, PT Pembangkitan Jawa Bali I.
23. *Info PJB ll*, PT Pembangkitan Jawa Bali II.
24. *Informasi Pikit Jabar Jaya*, PLN West Java and Jakarta Generation (PLN Pikit Jabar dan Jaya)
25. *Karimata*, PLN Kalimantan Generation and Transmission Master Project (PLN Pikitiring Kalimantan).
26. *Kilau Borneo*, PLN South and Central Kalimantan Region.
27. *Media PLN Wilayah XI*, PLN Eleventh Region, October 1986 to May 1990.
28. *Menah Tandur*, PLN West Nusa Tenggara Region.
29. *Nuansa Balerang*, the PLN Batam Special Region.
30. *Pelangi Nusra*, PLN Eleventh Region, October 1993 to October 1997.
31. *Pjiar*, PLN Third Region.
32. *Pijar Khatulistiwa (Pikhat)*, PLN West Kalimantan Region.
33. *Pinisi Sulawesi*, PLN Sulawesi Generation and Transmission Master Project.
34. *Sang Bumi Ruwa Juai* or *Saburai*, PLN Lampung.
35. *Suluh Dewata*, PLN Bali Distribution, February 2003 to September 2010.
36. *Suluh Etam*, PLN East Kalimantan Region.
37. *Suluah Nagari*, PLN West Sumatra.
38. *Siger*, PLN Lampung Region.
39. *Sinar Khatulistiwa*, PLN Fifth Region.
40. *Tabaos*, PLN Maluku and North Maluku Region.
41. *Termal*, PLN West Java and Jakarta Thermal Generation Master Project, PLN Pikitterm Jabar dan Jaya.
42. *Terang* Suluttenggo, PLN North and Central Sulawesi and Gorontalo Region.
43. *Varia Elektrika*, PLN Seventh Region.
44. *Visi Pikitiring Jatim & Nusra*, PLN East Java and Nusa Tenggara Generation and Transmission Master Project (PLN Pikitiring Jatim dan Nusra).
45. *Volta*, PLN Second Region, since 1993.
46. *Warta Piring Jabar Jaya*, PLN West Java and Jakarta Transmission Master Project (PLN Piring Jabar dan Jaya).
47. *Warta PLN 8*, PLN South and Southeast Sulawesi Region.
48. *Warta Serumpun Sebalai*, PLN Bangka Belitung.

Notes

Introduction

1. "Walaupun Hujan Lebat Masyarakat Tetap Menghadiri Peresmian Listrik Masuk Desa," *Berita PLN*, January 1987, 19–21.

2. "Walaupun Hujan Lebat," 19.

3. Religions and spirituality are an important dimension of many Indonesians' lives. Invoking God in speeches, such as in this case, is a way to acknowledge that divine forces and interventions matter.

4. "Walaupun Hujan Lebat," 20.

5. "Walaupun Hujan Lebat," 20. Note that the honorific Ir. is short for *insinyur*, an Indonesian word for engineer, which in this case is used as a title for someone who has completed a bachelor's degree in a technical field. This convention followed a Dutch practice and lasted until 1993, when someone who has earned a college degree in an engineering discipline was given the title ST (Sarjana Teknik) after his or her name.

6. Indonesia is a Muslim-Majority country. Houses of worships and religious schools matter to many Muslims. The government was aware of this and provided funds and other assistances to build them to appeal to this large segment of the population.

7. "Walaupun Hujan Lebat," 19.

8. "Kunjungan Kerja Menteri Pertambangan dan Energi Ke Propinsi Nusa Tenggara Barat Pemerintah ORDE BARU tidak jemu jemu menyediakan Tenaga Listrik BAGI RAKYAT KITA," *Berita PLN*, January 1987, 22–24.

9. "Kunjungan Kerja Menteri Pertambangan dan Energi Ke Propinsi Nusa Tenggara Timur 'Bagi Rakyat Yang Belum Mendapatkan Listrik Agar Bersabar,'" *Berita PLN*, February 1987, 23–25.

10. "Menteri Pertambangan dan Energi Subroto Resmikan PLTD dan Listrik Desa di Tim-Tim," *Berita PLN*, January 1987, 25–26. At the time East Timor was a province of Indonesia after its annexation in 1976.

11. "Kunjungan Kerja Menteri Pertambangan dan Energi," *Pertambangan dan Energi*, no. 3 (1987): 14–25.

12. "30,83% Penduduk Jatim Sudah Menikmati Listrik," *Berita PLN*, February 1987, 19–21.

13. "Menteri Pertambangan dan Energi Subroto Meresmikan Listrik Masuk Desa & Kabel Laut Jawa-Madura di Jatim," *Berita PLN*, April 1987, 12–13, 20.

14. "Tambahan penerangan listrik untuk 112 desa di propinsi Maluku," *Berita PLN*, June 1987, 22.

15. "Kabupaten Lahat Mendapat Listrik," *Berita PLN*, April 1987, 22–23.

16. R. William Liddle, "Indonesia in 1987: The New Order at the Height of Its Power," *Asian Survey* 28, no. 2 (1988): 181.

17. Liddle, "Indonesia in 1987," 180.

18. Liddle, "Indonesia in 1987," 189.

19. Liddle, "Indonesia in 1987."

20. "KLP Sinar Siwo Mego Menolak Pailit," *Lampung Post*, March 10, 2010.

21. Komite Nasional Indonesia World Energy Conference, *Hasil-Hasil Seminar Energi Nasional III Jakarta, 21–24 Juli 1987* (Jakarta: PT Melton Putra, 1988), v.

22. Thomas Parke Hughes, *Networks of Power: Electrification in Western Society, 1880–1930* (Baltimore, MD: Johns Hopkins University Press, 1983), 2.

23. John Krige and Jessica Wang, "Nation, Knowledge, and Imagined Futures: Science, Technology, and Nation-Building, Post-1945," *History and Technology* 31, no. 3 (2015): 171–79.

24. World Bank, *Rural Electrification: A World Bank Paper* (Washington, DC: World Bank, 1975), 3.

25. For examples, see Sunila Kale, *Electrifying India: Regional Political Economies of Development* (Stanford, CA: Stanford University Press, 2014); Tanja Winther, *The Impact of Electricity: Development, Desires, Dilemmas* (New York: Berghahn Books, 2008); Leo Coleman, *A Moral Technology: Electrification as Political Ritual in New Delhi* (Ithaca, NY: Cornell University Press, 2017); Christopher D. Gore, *Electricity in Africa: The Politics of Transformation in Uganda* (Melton, UK: James Currey, 2017); Stephan F. Miescher, *A Dam for Africa Akosombo Stories from Ghana* (Bloomington: Indiana University Press, 2022); Ying Jia Tan, *Recharging China in War and Revolution, 1882–1995* (Ithaca, NY: Cornell University Press, 2021).

26. Hughes formulated the sociotechnical system approach in *Networks of Power*.

27. Hughes, *Networks of Power*, 6, 140, 465.

28. Hughes, *Networks of Power*, 461–62.

29. Langdon Winner, "Do Artifacts Have Politics?," *Daedalus* 109, no. 1 (Winter 1980): 121–36.

30. Gabrielle Hecht, *The Radiance of France: Nuclear Power and National Identity after World War II* (Cambridge, MA: MIT Press, 1998), 15.

31. Hecht, *The Radiance of France*, 15.

32. Hecht, *The Radiance of France*, 15. Timothy Mitchell uses a similar term, "techno-politics," but denotes a slightly different phenomenon. See Timothy Mitchell, *Rule of Experts: Egypt, Techno-Politics, Modernity* (Berkeley: University of California Press, 2002). His focus is on the power arising from the interactions among nonhuman nature, humans, and the human-built environment. Hecht notes that the two definitions are compatible, and her edited volume "embraces both in order to explore a range of ways in which technologies become peculiar forms of politics." See Gabrielle Hecht, "Introduction," in *Entangled Geographies Empire and Technopolitics in the Global Cold War*, edited by Gabrielle Hecht (Cambridge, MA: MIT Press, 2011), 3.

33. Jamie Mackie, "Patrimonialism: The New Order and Beyond," in *Soeharto's New Order and its Legacy*, edited by Edward Aspinall and Greg Fealy (Canberra: ANU E Press, 2010), 84. See also Gunther Roth, "Personal Rulership, Patrimonialism, and Empire-building in the New States," *World Politics* 20, no. 2 (January 1968): 194–206 and Max Weber, *Economy and Society: An Outline of Interpretive Sociology*, (New York: Bedminster Press, 1968).

34. Robin Theobald, "Patrimonialism," *World Politics* 34, no. 4 (July 1982): 549.

35. Theobald, "Patrimonialism," 549.

36. Theobald, "Patrimonialism," 558.

37. Karl D. Jackson, "Bureaucratic Polity: A Theoretical Framework for the Analysis of Power and Communications in Indonesia," in *Political Power and Communications in Indonesia* edited by Karl D. Jackson and Lucian W. Pye (Berkeley: University of California Press, 1978), 3–22; Harold Crouch, "Patrimonialism and Military Rule in Indonesia," *World Politics* 31, no. 4 (July 1979): 571–87; Benedict R. O'G. Anderson, "Old State, New Society: Indonesia's New Order in Comparative Historical Perspective," *Journal of Asian Studies* 42, no. 3 (May 1983): 477–96; Donald K. Emmerson, "The Bureaucracy in Political Context: Weakness in Strength," in *Political Power and Communications in Indonesia*, edited by Karl D. Jackson and Lucian W. Pye (Berkeley: University of California Press, 1978), 82–136; R. William Liddle, "Soeharto's Indonesia: Personal Rule and Political Institutions," *Pacific Affairs* 58, no. 1 (Spring 1985): 71.

38. Jamie Mackie and Andrew MacIntyre, "Politics," in *Indonesia's New Order: The Dynamics of Socio-Economic Transformation*, edited by Hal Hill (Honolulu: University of Hawaii Press, 1994), 1–53.

39. Mackie and MacIntyre, "Politics," 6. Mackie further underscores the patrimonial characteristic of the New Order regime in an essay penned after its downfall, "Patrimonialism: The New Order and Beyond."

40. My first use of this term is in Anto Mohsin, "Wiring the New Order: Indonesian Village Electrification and Patrimonial Technopolitics (1966–1998)," *Sojourn: Journal of Social Issues in Southeast Asia* 29, no. 1 (2014): 63–95.

41. Theobald, "Patrimonialism," 549.

42. Sheila Jasanoff, "Technology as a Site and Object of Politics," in *The Oxford Handbook of Contextual Political Analysis*, edited by Robert E. Goodin and Charles Tilly (Oxford: Oxford University Press, 2006), 745–63; Wiebe E. Bijker and John Law (eds.), *Shaping Technology/Building Society* (Cambridge, MA: MIT Press, 1994); Sheila Jasanoff (ed.), *States of Knowledge: The Co-production of Science and Social Order* (New York: Routledge, 2004).

43. The idea of nation as "an imagined political community" is attributed to Benedict Anderson, *Imagined Communities Reflections on the Origin and Spread of Nationalism*, rev. ed. (New York: Verso, 2006), 6.

44. I narrate this in detail in chapter 1.

45. "Pembangunan Kelistrikan oleh P.L.N. Dinas Perentjanaan dan Pembangunan," *Insinjur Indonesia*, no. 8 (August 1960): 4–7.

46. Itty Abraham, *The Making of the Indian Atomic Bomb: Science, Secrecy and the Postcolonial State* (New York: Zed Books, 1998), 11–12; emphasis added.

47. For studies that have problematized technological transfers in development, see Shannon R. Brown, "The Ewo Filature: A Study in the Transfer of Technology to

China in the 19th Century," *Technology and Culture* 20, no. 3 (1979): 550–68; Deborah Fitzgerald, "Exporting American Agriculture: The Rockefeller Foundation in Mexico, 1943–53," *Social Studies of Science* 16, no. 3 (1986): 457–83; Judith Carney, "Landscapes of Technology Transfer: Rice Cultivation and African Continuities," *Technology and Culture* 37, no. 1 (1996): 5–35; Bryan Pfaffenberger, "The Harsh Facts of Hydraulics: Technology and Society in Sri Lanka's Colonization Schemes," *Technology and Culture* 31, no. 3 (1990): 361–97.

48. For technological dialogue, see Suzanne M. Moon, "Takeoff or Self-Sufficiency? Ideologies of Development in Indonesia, 1957–1961," *Technology and Culture* 39, no. 2 (1998): 187–212.

49. Ronald R. Kline, "Resisting Development, Reinventing Modernity: Rural Electrification in the United States before World War II," *Environmental Values* 11, no. 3 (2002): 327–44.

50. Soeharto, G. Dwipayana, and Ramadhan K.H., *Soeharto, Pikiran, Ucapan, Dan Tindakan Saya Otobiografi* (Jakarta: Citra Lamtoro Gung Persada, 1989), 362; original emphasis.

51. W. W. Rostow, *The Stages of Economic Growth: A Non-Communist Manifesto* (Cambridge: Cambridge University Press, 1960), 4–16.

52. Even shortly after its publication, Rostow's work drew some criticisms for its theoretical framing. See for example Yoichi Itagaki, "Criticism of Rostow's Stage Approach: The Concepts of Stage, System and Type," *The Developing Economies* 1, no. 1 (March 1963): 1–17.

53. For critiques of development discourses, see James Ferguson, *The Anti-Politics Machine Development, Depoliticization, and Bureaucratic Power in Lesotho* (Minneapolis: University of Minnesota Press, 1994), and Arturo Escobar, *Encountering Development The Making and Unmaking of Third World*, (Princeton, NJ: Princeton University Press, 1995).

54. Michael Adas, *Dominance by Design: Technological Imperatives and America's Civilizing Mission* (Cambridge, MA: Belknap Press of Harvard University Press, 2006), 238–40.

55. Sukarno, "Speech by President Sukarno on the 15th Anniversary of Electricity Day, Kebajoran Baru, 27 October 1960," Pidato Presiden Sukarno no. 227, ANRI.

56. "Rasa Hormat Yang Setinggi-Tingginya Atas Kesadaran Dan Kesediaan Penduduk Untuk Meninggalkan Daerah Ini Demi Pembangunan PLTA Cirata," *Berita PLN*, May 1986, 3–7.

57. Eka Darmaputera, *Pancasila Identitas Dan Modernitas Tinjauan Etis Dan Budaya* (Jakarta: BPK Gunung Mulia, 1987).

58. Selo Soemardjan et al., *Laporan Penelitian Listrik Masuk Desa* (Jakarta: Direktorat Pembinaan Penelitian dan Pengabdian pada Masyarakat, Direktorat Jenderal Pendidikan Tinggi, Departemen Pendidikan dan Kebudayaan, 1980), 34–35.

59. Susan Leigh Star, "The Ethnography of Infrastructure," *American Behavioral Scientist* 43, no. 3 (1999): 377–91.

60. Paul N. Edwards, "Infrastructure and Modernity: Force, Time, and Social Organization in the History of Sociotechnical Systems," in *Modernity and Technology*, edited by Thomas Misa, Philip Brey, and Andrew Feenberg (Cambridge, MA: MIT Press, 2003), 188. Brian Larkin also criticized the notion of an invisible infrastructure

in "The Politics and Poetics of Infrastructure," *Annual Review of Anthropology* 42 (2013): 327–43.

61. On this see Star, "The Ethnography of Infrastructure," 382.

62. Anto Mohsin, "Lighting 'Paradise': A Sociopolitical History of Electrification in Bali," *East Asian Science, Technology and Society: An International Journal* 11 (2017): 9–34, doi: 10.1215/18752160-3489218.

63. Joshua Barker, "Engineers and Political Dreams: Indonesia in the Satellite Age," *Current Anthropology* 46, no. 5 (2005): 703–27.

64. Mohsin, "Lighting 'Paradise,'" 18.

65. Philip Kitley, *Television, Nation, and Culture in Indonesia* (Athens: Ohio University Center for International Studies, 2000), 56.

66. Kitley, *Television, Nation, and Culture in Indonesia*, 56.

67. Sulfikar Amir, *The Technological State in Indonesia: The Co-Constitution of High Technology and Authoritarian Politics* (London: Routledge, 2012); Moon, "Takeoff of Self-Sufficiency?"; Suzanne Moon, "Justice, Geography, and Steel: Technology and National Identity in Indonesian Industrialization," *Osiris* 24 (2009): 253–77; Merlyna Lim, "Dis/Connection: The Co-Evolution of Sociocultural and Material Infrastructures of the Internet in Indonesia," *Indonesia* 105 (April 2018): 155–72; Abidin Kusno, *Behind the Postcolonial Architecture, urban space and political cultures in Indonesia* (London: Routledge, 2000); Joshua, "Engineers and Political Dreams."

68. Warwick Anderson, "Re-Orienting STS: Emergent Studies of Science, Technology, and Medicine in Southeast Asia," *East Asian Science, Technology and Society: An International Journal* 3, no. 2 (2009): 163–71.

69. Gregory Clancey, "Dangerous, Disruptive, or Irrelevant? History (of Technology) as an Acquired Taste in Asia," *East Asian Science, Technology and Society: An International Journal* 6, no. 2 (2012): 243–47.

70. See David Edgerton, *The Shock of the Old: Technology and Global History since 1900* (New York: Oxford University Press, 2007); Hyungsub Choi, "The Social Construction of Imported Technologies: Reflections on the Social History of Technology in Modern Korea," *Technology and Culture* 58, no. 4 (2017): 905–20; a group of scholars who call themselves The Maintainers have been trying to foreground maintenance in technology studies. See their blog, https://themaintainers.org/blog (accessed November 30, 2020).

Chapter 1. Late Colonial and Early Postcolonial Electrification

1. H. M. J. Maier, "Maelstrom and Electricity: Modernity in the Indies," in *Outward Appearances Dressing State and Society in Indonesia*, edited by Henk Schulte Nordholt (Leiden: KITLV Press, 1997), 185.

2. The regulation was called Indische Staatsblad 1890 no. 190 (*Netherlands East Indies State Gazette*, no. 190 [1890]). See "Electriciteitsvoorziening," in *Encyclopedia van Nederlandsch-Indie Aanvullingen En Wijzingen*, edited by D. G. Stibbe and F. J.W.H. Sandbergen ('S-Gravenhage: Martinus Nijhoff, 1939), 1924.

3. Division of Commerce of the Department of Agriculture, Industry, and Commerce, *1930 Handbook of the Netherlands East-Indies* (Buitenzorg, Java: G. Kolff, 1930), 261.

4. "Electriciteitsvoorziening," 1933, 1935.

5. "Electriciteitsvoorziening," 1936–37.

6. For paper mills, see "Electriciteitsvoorziening," 1928, 1932; for the Malabar radio station, see Division of Commerce, *1930 Handbook*, 394; for Goodyear factories, see "Op bezoek bij de Goodyear—Fabrieken," *Alles Electrisch in het Indische Huis en Bedrijf*, no. 7 (January 1937): 10–11.

7. Division of Commerce of the Department of Agriculture, Industry, and Commerce, *Handbook of the Netherlands East-Indies Edition 1924* (Buitenzorg, Java: G. Kolff, 1924), 217.

8. Djoko Darmono et al., *Mineral Dan Energi Kekayaan Bangsa Sejarah Pertambangan dan Energi Indonesia* (Jakarta: Departemen Energi dan Sumber Daya Mineral, 2009), 102.

9. Division of Commerce, *1930 Handbook*, 247.

10. "Electriciteitsvoorziening," 1925.

11. "Electriciteitsvoorziening," 1924.

12. "Electriciteitsvoorziening," 1924.

13. These oil lamps are called *pelita* in Bahasa Indonesia. In some villages they are still used as a backup lighting. I noticed this when I visited a Balinese village in February 2012 during my fieldwork.

14. H. W. Dick, *Surabaya, City of Work: A Socioeconomic History 1900–2000* (Athens: Ohio University Press, 2002), 163.

15. Nederlandsch-Indische Gas-Maatschappij, *Gedenkboek Nederlandsch-Indische Gas-Maatschappij, 1863–1913* (Rotterdam: M. Wyt & Zonen, 1913), 5.

16. C. Smit, "Review of the History of the Overseas Gas and Electricity Company Limited," in *A Century of Light and Power* (The Hague: Dijkman, 1963), 84–85.

17. NIGM, *Gedenkboek, 1863–1913*, 7.

18. NIGM, *Gedenkboek, 1863–1913*, 13.

19. NIGM, *Gedenkboek, 1863–1913*, 7–8.

20. NIGM, *Gedenkboek, 1863–1913*, 20–21.

21. Smit, "Review of the History," 100–101.

22. An older photo of the building can be found in NIGM, *Gedenkboek, 1863–1913*, between pages 6 and 7 (the second photo plate).

23. See David Edgerton, *Shock of the Old* (London: Profile Books, 2008); Christina Lindsay, "From the Shadows: Users as Designers, Producers, Marketers, Distributors, and Technical Support," in *How Users Matter*, edited by Nelly Oudshoorn and Trevor Pinch (Cambridge, MA: MIT Press, 2003).

24. In *Disenchanted Night: The Industrialization of Light in the Nineteenth Century* (Berkeley: University of California Press, 1995), Wolfgang Schivelbusch wrote that incandescent gas light rivaled electric light because of cost and was even called "electric light without electricity" (48). This innovation along with gas switches developed in 1900 might also have been used in the Dutch East Indies and contributed to the delay of switching to electric lighting.

25. Mohammad Hatta, *Memoir* (Jakarta: Tintamas Indonesia, 1979), 79. A druklicht advertisement accompanied by an illustration of the lamp sold by a Joseph Rute in Surabaya appeared as late as December 1929 on the front page of a Malay-language newspaper. See "Rute Gasoline Druklicht," *Matahari Borneo*, December 19, 1929, 1. https://khastara.perpusnas.go.id/landing/flip_browser/375616_MATAHARI_BORNEO _1929_Desember_19_Tahun_02_No_145_001.pdf.

26. Dick, *Surabaya*, 262.

27. Dick, *Surabaya*, 28.

28. "Electriciteitsvoorziening," 1925.

29. These hanging streetlights can be seen along Haarlemmerstraat, the main shopping street in Leiden.

30. A nice illustration is a photo of the canal Molenvliet from downtown Batavia to the colonial administrative district of Weltevreden, located in what is now Central Jakarta in Division of Commerce, *1930 Handbook*.

31. Besides the NIGM director's house in Jakarta, other extant Dutch-style buildings include the PLN branch offices in Surabaya and Malang.

32. Hughes introduced the concept of "technological style" in his book *Networks of Power* to describe how each of the power systems developed in three different cities was shaped by the city's sociopolitical, geographical, technical, and entrepreneurial characters.

33. Sukarno and Cindy Adams, *Sukarno: An Autobiography as Told to Cindy Adams* (Hong Kong: Gunung Agung, 1966), 34–35.

34. Dick, *Surabaya*, 348.

35. Dick, *Surabaya*, 382.

36. Dick, *Surabaya*, 382.

37. Peter McCawley, "The Indonesian Electric Supply Industry," PhD diss., Australian National University, 1971, 20.

38. In December 1917 Maintz & Co. became NV. Handelsvennootschap v/h MAINTZ & Co. with a registered office in Amsterdam when the two founders of the company, S. Maintz and E. Maintz, decided to retire. See "Inventaris van het archief van de NV Handelsvennootschap voorheen Maintz & Co. te Amsterdam, 1874–1970," Nationaal Archief Ministerie van Onderwijss, Cultuur en Weternschap, 9.

39. Smit, "Review of the History," 129. Smit wrote that there were several names suggested by five different individuals for the new name of NIGM: Nederlandse en Indonesische Gas- en Electriciteits-Maatschappij, Energie-Maatschappij voor Nederland en Overzee, Maatschappij tot Exploitatie van Gas- en Electriciteitsfabrieken, Nationale Industrie en Gas Electriciteit Maatschappij (N.I.G.M.) or Nationale Industrie Gas en Electriciteit Maatschappij (N.I.G.E.M.), and Federale Electriciteit en Gas Maatschappij. In the end it adopted OGEM.

40. Smit, "Review of the History," 103.

41. G. C. Allen and Audrey G. Donnithorne, *Western Enterprise in Indonesia and Malaya A Study in Economic Development* (Norwich, UK: Jarrold and Sons, 1957), 229.

42. Division of Commerce, *1930 Handbook*, 259.

43. Division of Commerce, *Handbook of the Netherlands East-Indies Edition 1924*, 293.

44. Wim Ravesteijn and Marie-Louise ten Horn-van Nispen, "Engineering an Empire: The Creation of Infrastructural Systems in the Netherlands East Indies 1800–1950," *Indonesia and the Malay World* 35, no. 103 (2007): 281.

45. "Electriciteitsvoorziening," 1941.

46. "Electriciteitsvoorziening," 1928.

47. "Electriciteitsvoorziening," 1935.

48. McCawley, "The Indonesian Electric Supply Industry," 8.

49. Adrian Vickers, *A History of Modern Indonesia* (Cambridge: Cambridge University Press, 2005), 17. The phrase "a debt of honor" was derived from the title of an article "Een Eereschuld," written by Dutch liberal politician Conrad Th. van Deventer, which was published in a popular magazine *De Gids* (The Guide) in 1899. See Irene V. Lessmeister, "Between Colonialism and Cold War: The Indonesian War of Independence in World Politics, 1945–1949," PhD diss., Cornell University, 2012, 18.

50. "Electriciteitsvoorziening," 1934.

51. "Landelijke electrificatie een nieuw distributiesysteem," *Alles Electrisch in het Indische Huis en Bedrijf*, no. 10 (April 1938): 7.

52. M. C. Ricklefs, *A History of Modern Indonesia since c. 1200*, 3rd ed. (Basingstoke: Palgrave, 2001), 193.

53. Susie Protschky, "The Empire Illuminated: Electricity, 'Ethical' Colonialism and Enlightened Monarchy in Photographs of Dutch Royal Celebrations, 1898–1948," *Journal of Colonialism and Colonial History* 13, no. 3 (Winter 2012), doi: 10.1353/cch.2012.0040.

54. Protschky, "The Empire Illuminated."

55. Quoted in Rudolf Mrázek, *Engineers of Happy Land: Technology and Nationalism in a Colony* (Princeton, NJ: Princeton University Press, 2002), 95.

56. Quoted in Mrázek, *Engineers of Happy Land*, 95.

57. Sukarno and Adams, *An Autobiography*, 67.

58. Sukarno and Adams, *An Autobiography*, 68.

59. Mrázek, *Engineers of Happy Land*, 81. It was difficult to locate early editions of the magazine. The University of Leiden library only has a partial collection. An online antiques store once sold some of the 1941 issues; see http://patinantique.blogspot.com/2017/08/majalah-ned-indie-alles-electrisch.html.

60. Mrázek, *Engineers of Happy Land*, 81.

61. The number of circulations is noted on the magazine. For example, see *Alles Electrisch in het Indische Huis en Bedrijf*, no. 5 (November 1936): 3 and no. 9 (March 1937): 2.

62. *Alles Electrisch in het Indische Huis en Bedrijf*, nos. 7 (January 1936), 8 (February 1936), 9 (March 1936), 10 (April 1936), 11 (May 1936), and 12 (June 1936).

63. *Alles Electrisch in het Indische Huis en Bedrijf*, no. 5 (November 1936).

64. *Alles Electrisch in het Indische Huis en Bedrijf*, no. 8 (February 1937).

65. Examples can be found on the covers of *Alles Electrisch in het Indische Huis en Bedrijf*, nos. 1 (July 1936), 3 (September 1936), 6 (December 1936), 6 (December 1937), 10 (April 1938), 11 (May 1938), 1 (July 1939), 2 (August 1939), 6 (December 1939), 11 (April 1939), 11 (May 1939), 8 (February 1941), and 12 (June 1941).

66. Covers of *Alles Electrisch in het Indische Huis en Bedrijf*, no. 7 (January 1936) and no. 4 (October 1936).

67. For example, see *Alles Electrisch in het Indische Huis en Bedrijf*, no. 7 (January 1939): 9.

68. *Alles Electrisch in het Indische Huis en Bedrijf*, no. 4 (October 1936): 3.

69. "Kertsdemonstratie," *Alles Electrisch in het Indische Huis en Bedrijf*, no. 8 (February 1937): 13.

70. Maier, "Maelstrom and Electricity," 184.

71. Maier, "Maelstrom and Electricity," 187.

72. Maier, "Maelstrom and Electricity," 188.

73. Mrázek, *Engineers of Happy Land*, 95.

74. Mrázek, *Engineers of Happy Land*, 95.

75. See James Sneddon, *The Indonesian Language Its History and Role in Modern Society* (Sydney: UNSW Press, 2003), 104–5.

76. Maier, "Maelstrom and Electricity," 191.

77. The Youth Pledge of October 28, 1928, declared a commitment to One Motherland Indonesia, recognized One Nation Indonesia, and upheld One Language of Unity Bahasa Indonesia. The language that the Youth Pledge referred to "was Malay, or rather the variety of it that would become the national language of the future Indonesian state." See Sneddon, *The Indonesian Language*, 5.

78. Sugiarta Sriwibawa and Ramadhan K. H., *50 Years of PLN Dedication*, translated by E. Jasjfi (Jakarta: PT PLN [Persero], 1996), 17–18. Djawa Denki Djigjo Kosha later changed its name to Djawa Denki Djigyo Sha.

79. McCawley, "The Indonesian Electric Supply Industry," 35.

80. Darmono et al., *Mineral Dan Energi Kekayaan Bangsa*, 38.

81. Sriwibawa and Ramadhan, *50 Years of PLN Dedication*, English ed. (Jakarta: PT PLN [Persero], 1996), 19.

82. For example, Indonesia's most famous author, Pramoedya Ananta Toer, recalled the Japanese occupation with bitterness. His memory of it was quoted in Vickers, *A History of Modern Indonesia*, 85.

83. Sriwibawa and Ramadhan, *50 Years of PLN Dedication*, 17–18.

84. Sriwibawa and Ramadhan, *50 Years of PLN Dedication*, 18. On electric infrastructure as a military target, see David Milne, "'Our Equivalent of Guerrilla Warfare': Walt Rostow and the Bombing of North Vietnam, 1961–1968," *Journal of Military History* 71, no. 1 (2007): 169–203.

85. Mavis Rose, *Indonesia Free: A Political Biography of Mohammad Hatta* (Ithaca, NY: Southeast Asia Program, 1987), 109.

86. Sukarno and Adams, *An Autobiography*, 157.

87. Sukarno and Adams, *An Autobiography*, 176.

88. Sukarno and Adams, *An Autobiography*, 179.

89. Rose, *Indonesia Free*, 111.

90. Sukarno, "Indonesian Independence and Pancasila," in *Southeast Asian History: Essential Readings*, 2nd ed., edited by D. R. SarDesai (Boulder, CO: Westview Press, 2013), 164–72.

91. Rose, *Indonesia Free*, 115.

92. Hatta, *Memoir*, 437.

93. Rose, *Indonesia Free*, 117.

94. Sukarno and Adams, *An Autobiography*, 211.

95. Sukarno and Adams, *An Autobiography*, 215.

96. Hatta, *Memoir*, 450–51.

97. Sriwibawa and Ramadhan, *50 Years of PLN Dedication*, 24.

98. Sriwibawa and Ramadhan, *50 Years of PLN Dedication*, 25–27.

99. John O. Sutter, *Indonesianisasi Politics in a Changing Economy, 1940–1955* (Ithaca, NY: Southeast Asia Program, Cornell University, 1959), 871.

100. Sutter, *Indonesianisasi*, 886–87.

101. Sutter, *Indonesianisasi*, 888.

102. Sutter, *Indonesianisasi*, 888.

103. Sutter, *Indonesianisasi*, 888–89.

104. Sutter, *Indonesianisasi*, 890.

105. Sutter, *Indonesianisasi*, 890.

106. Sutter, *Indonesianisasi*, 891.

107. Bradley Simpson, *Economists with Guns: Authoritarian Development and U.S.–Indonesia Relations, 1960–1968* (Stanford, CA: Stanford University Press, 2008), 25.

108. McCawley, "The Indonesian Electric Supply Industry," 62–64.

109. McCawley, "The Indonesian Electric Supply Industry," 73.

110. Arsip Nasional Republik Indonesia, *Naskah Sumber Arsip Jejak Demokrasi 1955* (Jakarta: ANRI, 2019), 14.

111. *Naskah Sumber Arsip Jejak Demokrasi 1955*, 149, 154.

112. Sukarno, "Amanat Presiden I: 28-VIII-1959" (Sukarno's spoken speech in front of Depernas on August 28, 1959), in Majelis Permusyawaratan Rakyat Sementara (MPRS), *Lampiran Ketetapan M.P.R.S. No. II/MPRS/1960 Garis-Garis Besar Pola Pembangunan Nasional-Semesta-Berentjana Tahapan Pertama 1961–1969 Djilid I* (Jakarta: MPRS, 1960), 10.

113. Sukarno, "Amanat Presiden," 9–10.

114. Sukarno, "Amanat Presiden," 62.

115. The term is an abbreviation of Manifesto Politik (political manifesto), Undang-Undang Dasar 1945 (the 1945 Constitution), Sosialisme Indonesia (Indonesian socialism), Demokrasi Terpimpin (Guided Democracy), Ekonomi Terpimpin (Guided Economy), and Kepribadian Indonesia (Indonesian identity). See Darmaputera, *Pancasila Identitas*, 113.

116. Jonathan Coopersmith, *The Electrification of Russia, 1880–1926* (Ithaca, NY: Cornell University Press, 1992), 3.

117. Sukarno, "Speech by President Sukarno on the 15th Anniversary of Electricity Day, Kebajoran Baru, 27 October 1960," Pidato Presiden Sukarno no. 227, ANRI, 1.

118. Sukarno, "Speech by President Sukarno on the 15th Anniversary," 2.

119. For example, on mechanized agriculture, see Moon, "Takeoff or Self-Sufficiency?," 187–212.

120. "Pembangunan Kelistrikan," 4–7.

121. McCawley, "The Indonesian Electric Supply Industry," 251.

122. Peter McCawley, "Rural Electrification in Indonesia—Is it Time?," *Bulletin of Indonesian Economic Studies* 14, no. 2 (1978): 51.

123. McCawley, "Rural Electrification in Indonesia," 51.

124. Bambang Purnomo, *Tenaga Listrik Profil dan Anatomi Hasil Pembangunan Dua Puluh Lima Tahun* (Jakarta: Penerbit PT Gramedia Pustaka Utama, 1994), 156–57.

125. Sutami, "Djembatan Daun Semanggi," *Insinjur Indonesia*, no. 2 (February 1961): 12–17.

126. Kitley, *Television, Nation, and Culture*, 22.

127. "Sistem Cakar Ayam Lahir di Ancol," *Teknologi* (January–February 1987): 56–57.

128. "Kebanggaan Nasional Untuk Memperkokoh Persatuan," *Insinjur Indonesia*, no. 8 (August 1962): 1.

129. Azwar Lubis et al., *Meretas Jalan Menggapai Harapan Refleksi Pelayanan PT PLN (Persero) Distribusi Jakarta Raya dan Tangerang* (Jakarta: PT PLN [Persero], 2006), 22.

Chapter 2. The New Order's Patrimonial Technopolitics

1. PLN Distribusi Jawa Barat, "Kertas Kerja: Kebijaksanaan Kelistrikan Desa Di Wilayah PLN Distribusi Jawa Barat" (unpublished manuscript, 1976), 1.

2. For example, see Joshua Barker, "State of Fear: Controlling the Criminal Contagion in Soeharto's New Order," *Indonesia* 66 (October 1998): 6–43.

3. The abbreviation Gestapu was created by the New Order regime to associate it with Gestapo, the Nazi secret police. The link was deliberate to discredit it. Sukarno once objected calling the movement Gestapu and instead proposed to use a different abbreviation, Gestok for Gerakan Satu Oktober, pointing to the day this movement announced itself to the public.

4. Ricklefs, *A History of Modern Indonesia*, 340.

5. Ricklefs, *A History of Modern Indonesia*, 340.

6. This emergency order was treated as a permanent one by Soeharto, argues John Roosa in his book *Pretext for Mass Murder: The September 30th Movement and Suharto's Coup d'État in Indonesia* (Madison: University of Wisconsin Press, 2006), 12.

7. Roosa, *Pretext for Mass Murder*, 201.

8. Hermawan Sulistyo, "Theories behind the Events of 1965–1966," in *Indonesia in the Soeharto Years: Issues, Incidents and Images*, edited by John H McGlynn, Oscar Motuloh, Suzanne Charle, Jeffrey Hadler, Bambang Bujono, Margaret Glade Agusta, and Gedsiri Suhartono (Jakarta, Indonesia: Lontar in association with Ridge Book and KITLV Press, 2005), 6.

9. Sulistyo, "Theories behind the Events," 7.

10. For the fourth theory, see Benedict Anderson and Ruth McVey, *A Preliminary Analysis of the October 1, 1965 Coup in Indonesia* (Ithaca, NY: Cornell University Southeast Asia Program, 1971).

11. Sulistyo, "Theories behind the Events," 8. For the latest scholarship and a new interpretation of the events based on newly discovered evidence, see Roosa, *Pretext for Mass Murder*. Roosa claims that based on his analysis, there was no single mastermind responsible for the movement.

12. See Soeharto's short preface in Ali Moertopo, *Some Basic Thoughts on the Acceleration and Modernization of 25 Years' Development* (Jakarta: Yayasan Proklamasi, Center for Strategic and International Studies, 1973), ix. Soeharto often mentioned this national goal in many of his speeches, including the one he delivered in August 1968, his first annual state-of-the-nation speech. See Soeharto, "Pidato Kenegaraan Presiden Republik Indonesia Djenderal Soeharto Di Depan Sidang DPR-GR 16 Agustus 1968," (Jakarta: Departemen Penerangan R.I., 1968).

13. See Sukarno, "Indonesian Independence and Pancasila."

14. Seung-Won Song, "Back to Basics in Indonesia? Reassessing the Pancasila and Pancasila State and Society, 1945–2007," PhD diss., Ohio University, 2008, 10, original emphasis.

15. "Naskah pidato pada upacara pembukaan penataran calon penatar tingkat Nasional/Manggala BP-7 di Istana Bogor," Pidato Presiden Soeharto 1031,4, Inventaris

Arsip Sekretariat Negara: Seri Pidato Presiden Soeharto 1966–1998 Jilid 2 (No. 761-1389), ANRI. BP-7 is an abbreviation of Badan Pembinaan Pendidikan Pelaksanaan Pedoman Penghayatan dan Pengamalan Pancasila (Education Development Agency for the Implementation of Guidelines for Internalizing and Practicing Pancasila).

16. "P4 Bagi Narapidana," *Kompas*, September 8, 1982, 1, 9.

17. In October 1982, Cipinang Penitentiary inmates took the P4 courses. It was reported in "Pancasila dan UUD 1945 Juga Milik Narapidana," *Kompas*, October 22, 1982.

18. Song, "Back to Basics in Indonesia?," 195.

19. Song, "Back to Basics in Indonesia?," 210. See also Vedi R. Hadiz, *Workers and the State in New Order Indonesia* (London: Routledge, 1997).

20. Song, "Back to Basics in Indonesia?," 257.

21. See Song, "Back to Basics in Indonesia?," 177. For the list of the forty-five codes, see Kementerian Pertahanan Republik Indonesia, "45 butir Pedoman Penghayatan dan Pengamalan Pancasila," *Kemenhan*, November 20, 2014, https://www.kemhan.go.id/renhan/2014/11/20/45-butir-pedoman-penghayatan-dan-pengamalan-pancasila.html.

22. Donald E. Weatherbee, "Indonesia: The Pancasila State," *Southeast Asian Affairs* (1985): 133–51.

23. Song, "Back to Basics in Indonesia?," 11.

24. For a discussion of how *pembangunan*, the Indonesian word for "development," became a key word in the New Order, see Ariel Heryanto, "Pembangunan," in *Language of Development and Development of Language: The Case of Indonesia* (Canberra: Research School of Pacific and Asian Studies, Australian National University, 1995), 8–26.

25. Song, "Back to Basics in Indonesia?," 163.

26. Soeharto, Dwipayana, and Ramadhan, *Soeharto, Pikiran*.

27. These and many other adages are listed at the end of Soeharto's autobiography.

28. Imron Husin's study details the gap between policy formulation and implementation in New Order's rural electrification in East Java. Imron Husin, "Rural Electrification in Indonesia Policy Implementation in Theory and Practice," PhD diss., Australian National University, 1989.

29. For Soeharto's admission on paying a great attention to village development, see Soeharto, Dwipayana, and Ramadhan, *Soeharto, Pikiran*, 400.

30. Moertopo, *Some Basic Thoughts*, 51.

31. Moertopo, *Some Basic Thoughts*, 92.

32. Mohammad Sadli, "Recollections of My Career," *Bulletin of Indonesian Economic Studies* 29, no. 1 (April 1993): 35–51; Emil Salim, "Recollections of My Career," *Bulletin of Indonesian Economic Studies* 33, no. 1 (April 1997): 45–74; Subroto, "Recollections of My Career," *Bulletin of Indonesian Economic Studies* 34, no. 2 (August 1998): 67–92.

33. Since all of them were affiliated with the Faculty of Economics at the University of Indonesia, the faculty became highly influential as well, producing many graduates who have been occupying government positions in the New Order and after.

34. Subroto, "Recollections," 236.

35. The reported total number of Indonesia's villages has changed over time, as new villages were formed and better census techniques produced more accurate data. PLN used the rounded-up figure of 60,000 in its official publications.

36. Sunarto Ndaru Mursito, "Gambaran Umum Tentang Pembangunan Pedesaan di Indonesia," in *Analisa 1981–3 Pembangunan Pedesaan* (Jakarta: Biro Publikasi CSIS, 1981), 207–8.

37. "Cara Menentukan Tahap Perkembangan Desa (Desa Swadaya, Desa Swakarya, Desa Swasembada), Diperbanyak oleh Badan Penelitian dan Pengembangan Pendidikan dan Kebudayaan Departemen Pendidikan dan Kebudayaan" (unpublished manuscript, 1975). Leiden University Library, KITLV3 M m 13431978 mf.

38. Umar Said, the director general of Village Development of the Department of Home Affairs, was quoted by *Bali Post* as saying that he hoped all of Indonesia's villages can be *swasembada* villages by 2000. Made Dibia, "Harapan Di Tahun 2000: Semua Desa Berswasembada," *Bali Post Edisi Pedesaan*, September 16, 1981.

39. Subroto, "Recollections," 235. For studies on the Bimas program, see Irlan Soejono and Wirjadi Prawirohardjo, *Program "Bimas" Sebagai Pendorong Modernisasi Usahatani* (Bogor: Survey Agro Ekonomi Indonesia, 1968); Alexis Rieffel, "The BIMAS Program for Self-Sufficiency in Rice Production," *Indonesia*, no. 8 (October 1969): 103–33; Achmad T. Birowo, *BIMAS: A Package Program for Intensification of Food Crop Production in Indonesia* (New York: Asia Society, SEADAG, 1975).

40. Mursito, "Gambaran Umum," 209.

41. For an elaboration of these paths, see Widjojo Nitisastro, *Pengalaman Pembangunan Indonesia Kumpulan Tulisan dan Uraian Widjojo Nitisastro* (Jakarta: Penerbit Kompas, 2010), 437–46.

42. Kitley, *Television, Nation, and Culture*, 56.

43. Several New Order bureaucrats have used this expression. One of them was the district head of Garut in West Java who uttered these words when he inaugurated a micro-DPP in a village in 1979. See "Pedesaan Adalah Tulang Punggung Pembangunan," *Berita PLN*, May 1979, 35.

44. "Seminar Tarif Listrik Kedua Asia Pasifik Di Denpasar," *Berita PLN*, January 1979, 1–3.

45. The domestic fund allocated to grow Indonesia's electrical infrastructure from April 1, 1969 until March 31, 1984 amounted to Rp 1,556 billion, and the foreign fund the regime received for the same period totaled US$ 5,501 million. See A. S. Moenir et al., *40 Tahun Peranan Pertambangan Dan Energi Indonesia 1945–1985* (Jakarta: Departemen Pertambangan dan Energi, 1986), 387–88. By 1986, PLN had emerged as the second largest state-owned enterprise (after Pertamina) with 50,000 employees, an operational budget of Rp 1.46 trillion (US$1.2 billion), and an investment fund totaling Rp 1.64 trillion (US$1.35 billion) for fiscal year 1986–87. The company at the time was servicing 6.7 million customers, about 2.7 million of whom lived in rural areas. See "Pengambilan Sumpah Jabatan Dan Pelantikan Dewan Pengawas PLN," *Berita PLN*, June 1986, 12–13.

46. Direktorat Djenderal Tenaga dan Listrik, *Hasil-Hasil Workshop Kelistrikan Desa 12 s/D 14 Maret 1970* (Jakarta: Direktorat Djenderal Tenaga dan Listrik, 1970), 1.

47. Prayitno, "Listrik dan Pelayanannya," *Berita PLN*, July 1979, 15.

48. Hecht, *The Radiance of France*, 15.

49. Emmerson, "The Bureaucracy in Political Context," 106–7.

50. Geoffrey C. Gunn, "Ideology and the Concept of Government in the Indonesian New Order," *Asian Survey* 19, no. 8 (August 1979): 760.

51. Hans Antlöv, "Village Government and Rural Development in Indonesia: The New Democratic Framework," *Bulletin of Indonesian Economic Studies* 39, no. 2 (2003): 196.

52. Afan Gaffar, *Javanese Voters: A Case Study of Election under a Hegemonic Party System* (Yogyakarta: Gadjah Mada University Press, 1992).

53. Clifford Geertz introduced these categories to the study of Indonesian religion and society in *The Religion of Java* (Glencoe, IL: Free Press, 1960).

54. Gaffar, *Javanese Voters*, 192.

55. Gaffar, *Javanese Voters*, 192.

56. Soemardjan et al., *Laporan Penelitian Listrik Masuk Desa*, 50.

57. Soemardjan et al., *Laporan Penelitian Listrik Masuk Desa*, 102–4.

58. Soemardjan et al., *Laporan Penelitian Listrik Masuk Desa*, 100.

59. Djiteng Marsudi, interview with the author, February 17, 2012, Jakarta.

60. Marsudi interview.

61. Tim Penyusun, *Development Progress of Provinsi Daerah Istimewa Aceh 40 Tahun Derap Langkah Pembangunan 1959–1998/1999* (Banda Aceh: Pemerintah Provinsi Daerah Istimewa Aceh, 1998). The table is on page 143 and the graph is on page 170.

62. Penyusun, *Development Progress*, 143.

63. Penyusun, *Development Progress*, 170.

64. Ricklefs, *A History of Modern Indonesia*, 388.

65. Liddle, "Indonesia in 1987," 186.

66. Liddle, "Indonesia in 1987," 186.

67. PLN Distribusi Jawa Barat, "Kertas Kerja," 1.

68. PLN Distribusi Jawa Barat, "Kertas Kerja," 4.

69. Ricklefs, *A History of Modern Indonesia*, 373; Patrik Guiness, "Local Society and Culture," in *Indonesia's New Order: The Dynamics of Socio-Economic Transformation*, edited by Hal Hill (Honolulu: University of Hawaii Press, 1994), 272–76.

70. Antlöv, "Village Government and Rural Development," 196.

71. Hans Antlöv, *Exemplary Centre, Administrative Periphery: Rural Leadership and the New Order in Java* (Richmond, UK: Curzon Press, 1995), 59–60.

72. Perusahaan Umum Listrik Negara, "Makalah: Listrik Pedesaan" (unpublished manuscript, December 1980), 31.

73. Perusahaan Umum Listrik Negara, "Makalah: Listrik Pedesaan," 14. In 1980, the average exchange rate was Rp 649 = US$1.

74. "37 Persen Desa Di Bali Sudah Menikmati Listrik," *Bali Post*, March 23, 1982.

75. "Listrik Masuk 25 Desa Di Sumbar," *Kompas*, March 27, 1982.

76. "Listrik Masuk Desa Di Jateng Dan Sulsel," *Kompas*, March 30, 1982.

77. "Listrik Masuk Desa Di Jateng Dan Sulsel," *Kompas*, March 30, 1982.

78. A photo of this can be seen on the cover of *Berita PLN* May 1982 edition. The phrase *Habis Gelap Terbitlah Terang* is the Indonesian translation of *Door Duisternis tot Licht*, a book containing the letters of Raden Ajeng Kartini, Indonesia's revered women's rights advocate, sent to her friends in the Netherlands. It was also translated into English as *Letters of a Javanese Princess*. Her letters contain her visions of a woman's emancipation and educational reforms in the Dutch East Indies.

79. "Kunjungan Kerja Menteri Pertambangan dan Energi ke Jawa Tengah," *Berita PLN*, September–November 1982, 4.

80. "Menteri Kehutanan Resmikan Listrik Masuk Desa di Kalimantan Timur," *Berita PLN*, November 1986, 27.

81. "Peresmian Listrik Masuk Desa: Listrik Masuk Desa Mendorong Perkembangan Industri Kecil Di Pedesaan," *Berita PLN*, October-November-December 1991, 44.

82. "Mensegneg Sudharmono Serahkan DIP Dan Resmikan LMD Di Jawa Tengah," *Kompas*, March 31, 1982.

83. "Menteri Pertambangan Dan Energi: 'Program LMD Bukan Dimaksudkan Untuk Penerangan Saja, Namun Yang Lebih Penting Lagi Untuk Mencerdaskan Masyarakat Banyak,'" *Berita PLN*, March 1982, 5–6.

84. "30,83% Penduduk Jatim," 19–21.

85. "30,83% Penduduk Jatim," 19–21.

86. Johannes J. Rumondor, "Pembangunan Kelistrikan Desa Sebagai Upaya Meningkatkan Taraf Hidup Masyarakat Desa," *Berita PLN*, November 1985, 3–9.

87. Ricklefs, *A History of Modern Indonesia*, 375.

88. "Menteri Sekretaris Negara Sudharmono, SH Resmikan Listrik Masuk Desa Di Jawa Tengah," *Berita PLN*, January 1986, 21, 29; "Peresmian Listrik Masuk Desa Di Jawa Barat," *Berita PLN*, February 1986, 22–24; "Peresmian Listrik Masuk Desa Di 4 Kabupaten Propinsi Sulawesi Selatan," *Berita PLN*, April 1986, 20–21; "Listrik Masuk Desa Di Kabupaten Sleman Propinsi DIY Diresmikan Mensekneg Sudharmono, SH," *Berita PLN*, July, 1986, 29; "Menteri Sekretaris Negara Sudharmono, SH Meresmikan Listrik Masuk Desa Di Kabupaten Lamongan—Jawa Timur," *Berita PLN*, August 1986, 14, 20; "Menteri Sekretaris Negara Sudharmono, SH Meresmikan Listrik Pedesaan Di Desa Maribu, Jayapura," *Berita PLN*, September 1986, 26–27.

89. "Menteri Sekretaris Negara Sudharmono, SH Meresmikan Listrik Pedesaan Di Desa Maribu, Jayapura," 26–27.

90. "188 Desa Lagi Berhasil Dilistriki PLN Di Jawa Timur," *Berita PLN*, March 1986, 3–5.

91. "Walaupun Hujan Lebat," 19–21.

92. "Menteri Pertambangan dan Energi Subroto Resmikan," 25–26; "30,83% Penduduk Jatim."

93. "Kabupaten Lahat Mendapat Listrik."

94. Liddle, "Indonesia in 1987," 184.

95. "Peresmian Listrik Masuk Desa: Mendorong Perkembangan Industri Kecil."

96. "Peresmian Listrik Masuk Desa: Mendorong Perkembangan Industri Kecil," 41.

97. "Peresmian Listrik Masuk Desa: Mendorong Perkembangan Industri Kecil," 74.

98. Komang Sujati (pseudonym), interview with the author, April 2, 2012, Denpasar, Bali.

99. Sujati interview.

100. In the reformation era, many Indonesian politicians have fluid affiliations with the country's political parties, taking advantage of the multiparty system to change party membership or shift allegiances whenever it suits them in the general election.

101. Mahesa Praba (pseudonym), interview with the author, May 25, 2012, Denpasar, Bali.

102. Goenawan Mohamad, interview with the author, July 16, 2012, Denpasar, Bali.

103. Crouch, "Patrimonialism and Military Rule," 571–87.

104. Djiteng Marsudi, "PLN Menghadapi Era Globalisasi," *Berita PLN*, February 1996, 6.

105. "Pemilihan Umum, 29 Mei 1997," *Listrik Indonesia*, May/June 1997, 27.

Chapter 3. The Electric Bureaucracy

1. Law No. 15 of 1985 cemented PLN's status as the single license holder for public electricity provision (*pemegang kuasa usaha ketenagalistrikan*) in Indonesia. It can grant any private businesses a permit to generate electricity (*izin usaha ketenagalistrikan*) but not to distribute it to the public.

2. In *PLN Statistics 1995* (Jakarta: PT PLN [Persero], 1996), iii, it is reported that by the end of that year PLN had built 3,916 generating units with a total installed capacity of 14,987 MW. For comparison, the installed power capacity from private companies in 1994 was 8,240 MW, as reported in Artono Arismunandar, "Overview of Electric Power Development in Indonesia," *Energi & Listrik* 6, no. 2 (June 1996): 5–6.

3. One PLN branch office in the district of Fakfak in West Papua employed two horses and they were called Si Petir (the Lightning) to carry a PLN employee to connect new customers to the grid and read their electric meters. See "'Si Petir' Kuda Beban PLN Cabang Fakfak Siap Meningkatkan Citra PLN," *Berita PLN*, November 1995, 25–27.

4. Indonesia's 1945 Constitution, Article 33, Clause 3, mandates the state to do this. It reads: "The earth and water and the natural resources contained therein are controlled by the state and shall be used for the greatest benefit of the people." Relatedly, Article 33, Clause 2, says: "Branches of production that are vital to the state and which affect people's livelihoods are controlled by the state."

5. Anto Mohsin, "National Electricity Day: From 'Electricity-Minded' Nation to 'My Idea for PLN,'" *Technology's Stories*, December 4, 2017, https://www.technology stories.org/national-electricity-day/.

6. Johannes J. Rumondor, "Program Perusahaan Umum Listrik Negara Untuk Perlistrikan Desa," *Berita PLN*, January 1978, 33.

7. PLN's official website (https://web.pln.co.id/tentang-kami/profil-perusahaan) mentions October 27, 1945, as its founding date. To PLN, one advantage of acknowledging that date is that it aligns with the founding of the republic in 1945, and thus PLN employees can claim that their organization is as old as Indonesia. The October 27 date holds such significance that it is even inscribed in the design of a monument erected in the middle of a pool (twenty-seven concrete pillars and ten water fountains) in the complex of PLN West Kalimantan building. See "Peresmian Gedung Pelayanan PLN Wil. Kalbar: Partisipasi Swasta di Bidang Kelistrikan Perlu Pengaturan," *Berita PLN*, May 1995, 9–10.

8. McCawley, "The Indonesian Electric Supply Industry," 37.

9. "Laporan Khusus," *Fokus*, October 2000, 26.

10. McCawley, "The Indonesian Electric Supply Industry," 38.

11. McCawley, "The Indonesian Electric Supply Industry," 63.

12. McCawley, "The Indonesian Electric Supply Industry," 81–83, 92.

13. McCawley, "The Indonesian Electric Supply Industry," 97–98.

14. McCawley, "The Indonesian Electric Supply Industry," 108.

15. Direktorat Djenderal Tenaga dan Listrik, *Kebidjaksanaan Nasional Dibidang Ketenagaan* (Djakarta: Departemen Pekerdjaan Umum dan Tenaga Listrik, 1969).

16. Artono Arismunandar and Sufrani Atmakusuma, *Laporan Mengikuti International Seminar On Energy Policy and Energy Economy Berlin 9 Oct–2 Nov 1968* (Jakarta: Direktorat Djenderal Tenaga dan Listrik, 1968), 1.

17. Arismunandar and Atmakusuma, *Laporan*, 2–31.

18. Arismunandar and Atmakusuma, *Laporan*, 32–35.

19. For a fuller description of the labor dispute, see "Appendix to Chapter 10: The '77 Employees Problem' in McCawley, "The Indonesian Electric Supply Industry," 325–59.

20. McCawley, "The Indonesian Electric Supply Industry," 330–32.

21. McCawley, "The Indonesian Electric Supply Industry," 334.

22. McCawley, "The Indonesian Electric Supply Industry," 335.

23. McCawley, "The Indonesian Electric Supply Industry," 335.

24. McCawley, "The Indonesian Electric Supply Industry," 352.

25. McCawley, "The Indonesian Electric Supply Industry," 355.

26. Emmerson, "The Bureaucracy in Political Context," 89.

27. Kadir was a former head of PLN Jakarta and Tangerang Distribution (1961–65) and a member of PLN's board of directors in the mid-1960s.

28. Government Regulation No. 18 of 1972, Article 6.

29. Darmono et al., *Mineral Dan Energi Kekayaan Bangsa*, 307.

30. Minister of Public Works and Electric Power Decree No. 013/PRT/1975.

31. For an example of the distribution of military and civilian personnel in the state's ministries in December 1981, see Donald K. Emmerson, "Understanding the New Order: Bureaucratic Pluralism in Indonesia," *Asian Survey* 23, no. 11 (1983): 1226.

32. Emmerson, "Understanding the New Order," 1225.

33. Crouch, "Patrimonialism and Military Rule in Indonesia," 577.

34. Note that one military man had held a high position at PLN. Brigadier General Hartono held a management post for the first half of 1966 in an emergency capacity. See McCawley, "The Indonesian Electric Supply Industry," 112.

35. "In Memoriam Saudara Soepolo Wiradi," *Berita PLN*, November 1977, 50; "Profil Achyar: Tehnisi tiga jaman," *Berita PLN*, November 1983, 12–13.

36. "In Memoriam Saudara Soepolo Wiradi," 50.

37. "Profil Achyar: Tehnisi tiga jaman," 12–13.

38. World Bank, "Staff Appraisal Report Indonesia Rural Electrification Project February 20, 1990," Report No. 8134-IND (1990), 13.

39. "Penutupan Kursus Pendidikan Dasar PLTU di Udiklat Tanjung Priok," *Berita PLN*, September 1978, 48.

40. "PLN Mengirimkan Teknisi-Teknisinya Untuk Mengikuti 'On the Job Training' ke Perancis," *Berita PLN*, May 1979, 44.

41. "Pembukaan Kursus Pendidikan Dasar PLTU Angkatan Ke-V Dan Pendidikan Dasar PLTG Angkatan Ke-III di Udiklat Priuk," *Berita PLN*, March 1979, 46.

42. "Dirut Melantik Pejabat Teras PLN PPE," *Berita PLN*, April 1988, 27.

43. "PLN Cabang Bima Daerah Ujung Timur Sumbawa Yang Perlu Pengembangan," *Berita PLN*, March 1995, 46.

44. His article on the subject, "Apakah Yang Dimaksud Dengan PLTP Kamojang? Panas Bumi Sebagai Sumber Tenaga Listrik," *Berita PLN*, May 1977, 21–25.

45. He proposed the creation of the electric backbone in his inaugural speech to full professorship at the University of Indonesia. Arismunandar's speech, "Energi dan Tenaga Listrik Tegangan Tinggi Sebagai Sarana Peningkatan dan Pemerataan Kesejahteraan Rakyat," was reprinted in *Berita PLN*, January 1978, 23–24. Dr. Arismunandar is the author of several electrical engineering textbooks published in Indonesian. He is also a member of a well-connected family in the New Order. He is the older brother of former Army Special Forces Commandant General Wismoyo Arismunandar and a sibling of former rector of ITB, Dr. Ir. Wiranto Arismunandar, who also served briefly as the minister of Education and Culture in Soeharto's Seventh Development Cabinet (March–May 1998).

46. "Serah Terima Jabatan Kepala Unit Pemimpin PLN Wilayah dan Distribusi," *Berita PLN*, January 1992, 24. The LMK was established in 1965. It was incorporated into PLN in December 1970. See *10 Tahun Penelitian, Pengembangan, dan Jasa Teknik Sektor Tenaga Listrik 1965–1975* (Jakarta: PLN LMK, 1975).

47. Nengah Sudja, "Peranan Sektor Listrik Dalam Pola Pengembangan Wilayah," *Berita PLN*, May 1977, 14.

48. Sudja, "Peranan Sektor Listrik," 14.

49. Johannes J. Rumondor, "Kebijaksanaan PLN dalam program listrik pedesaan," in Direktorat Jenderal Ketenagaan Departemen Pertambangan dan Energi, *Hasil Lokakarya Survai Energi Pedesaan Diselenggarkan di Jakarta Pada Tanggal 1 s/d 11 September 1980 dan 3 s/d Februari 1981* (Jakarta: PT Surya Jaya Utama, 1982), 15–40.

50. By the mid-1970s, PLN had established division and branch offices covering its operations for the entire archipelago.

51. By the mid-1990s, PLN had reduced its regional areas from thirteen to eleven, added a special area of operation for the island of Batam, and transformed PLN regions XII and XIII into PLN Distribution East Java and Central Java, respectively. *PLN Company Profile* (Jakarta: PLN Publication and Documentation Subdivision, 1996), 16.

52. Marsudi interview. Also "Dua Anak Perusahaan PT PLN (Persero) Terbentuk," *Berita PLN*, October 1995, 7–9.

53. The two companies were initially called PT Pembangkitan Jawa Bali I and II. On September 1, 2000, they changed the former to PT Indonesia Power and the latter to PT Pembangkitan Jawa Bali. They are now two of several PLN subsidiaries.

54. "Unit Cabang Merupakan Mata Tombak Terdepan PLN," *Berita PLN*, October–November 1993, 76–79.

55. Zuhal, "Peranan PLN Sebagai Persero Dalam Penyediaan Listrik Nasional," *Berita PLN*, December 1994, 29–32 & 40–41.

56. Marsudi, "PLN Menghadapi Era Globalisasi," 6.

57. During my fieldwork, I found many PLN newsletters and magazines published by a variety of PLN divisions and subsidiaries. They vary in quality and publication frequency. Collectively they made up voluminous archives of PLN's activities reported in many parts of the country. See the Appendix.

58. Ir. Bambang Sulistiono, quoted in "PLN Cabang Biak," *Berita PLN*, December 1994, 44.

59. Sulistiono, quoted in "PLN Cabang Biak," 44.

60. "PLN Cabang Biak," 44.

61. "PLN Cabang Bima," 43–46.

62. "PLN Cabang Bima," 43–46.

63. "49 Anak Yatim Terima Bantuan Biaya Pendidikan," *Media Elektrika*, July 1995, 10, 12.

64. "PLN Cabang Tanjung Karang: Serahkan Bantuan Modal Kepada Pengusaha Kecil dan Koperasi," *Berita PLN*, December 1995, 39–40.

65. "Kopkar 'Gotong Royong' PLN Cabang Fakfak Raih Sertifikat Kopkar Mandiri," *Berita PLN*, December 1995, 48.

66. "Bantuan Pompanisasi PLN Untuk Kelompok Tani Kabupaten Bajo," *Berita PLN*, January–February 1998, 26.

67. Many groups in Indonesia have a march and a hymn, which are common cultural artifacts of Indonesian institutions, to instill pride and loyalty among members.

68. "Pelanggan PLN Menangkan Lomba Mars & Hymne PLN," *Berita PLN*, October-November-December 1997, 14–16.

69. PLN's hymn and march can be heard on the YouTube channel of PLN Tanjung Jati B, "Hymne Dan Mars PLN Dengan Lyric," *YouTube*, December 10, 2016, https://www.youtube.com/watch?v=Jp3rM4dJagE.

70. *Bahan Penataran Pedoman Penghayatan dan Pengamalan Pancasila, Undang-undang Dasar 1945, Garis-Garis Besar Haluan Negara*, Edisi Kedua (Jakarta: Team Pembinaan Penatar dan Bahan Penataran Pegawai Republik Indonesia, 1981).

71. *Bahan Penataran Pedoman Penghayatan dan Pengamalan Pancasila*, xv.

72. "Penataran P4 TYPE A Angkatan XXIX Di Lingkungan Departemen Pertambangan Dan Energi," *Berita PLN*, March 1982, 39.

73. "Pidato Menteri Pertambangan & Energi pada Pembukaan Penataran Tingkat Pusat tipe A, Angkatan ke I PLN tgl. 16-3-79," *Berita PLN*, March 1979, 14.

74. "Penataran P4 Angkatan XXI," *Berita PLN*, October 1985, 27.

75. Jean Gelman Taylor, *Indonesia Peoples and Histories* (New Haven, CT: Yale University Press, 2003), 362.

76. Michael Morfit, "Pancasila: The Indonesian State Ideology According to the New Order Government," *Asian Survey* 21, no. 8 (August 1981): 846.

77. See Soeharto's short preface in Moertopo, *Some Basic Thoughts*, ix.

78. "Rasa Hormat Yang Setinggi-Tingginya," 3–7.

79. Ketut Kontra, "Langkah Kebijaksanaan Dalam Pengelolaan Sektor Tenaga Listrik dan Tantangan Yang Perlu Dihadapi," *Berita PLN*, February 1983, 10.

80. "Pembangunan Kelistrikan Desa Sebagai Upaya Meningkatkan Taraf Hidup Masyarakat Desa," *Berita PLN*, November 1985, 4.

81. Ir. Sardjono, PLN president director between 1980 and 1988, admitted that private electric companies in Indonesia had not accumulated enough knowledge in the electricity industry. See Sardjono, "Prospek Peran Serta Swasta Nasional Dalam Sektor Tenaga Listrik," in *Hasil-Hasil Lokakarya Energi Jakarta* 10–11 Mei 1984, edited by Pramono Djojowikromo and Djatmiko Suwarno (Jakarta: KNI-WEC, 1984), 56–76.

Chapter 4. Java-Centrism and The Two Grid Systems

1. Departemen Pekerdjaan Umum, *Pembinaan Projek/Masalah Prasarana Nota Pendjelasan Projek Tenaga Listrik 1968 (Diperbaharui)* (Djakarta: Studio, 1968).

2. *PLN in 1975/76*.

3. *PLN in 1979/80* (Jakarta: PLN Head Office, 1980).

4. To view the maps, see Sriwibawa and Ramadhan, *50 Years of PLN Dedication*, 356–77.

5. *PLN Statistics 1995*, 17, table 16: Number of Generating Units.

6. *PLN Statistics 1995*, 18, table 17: Installed Capacity (MW).

7. *PLN Statistics 1995*, 18, table 17: Installed Capacity (MW).

8. Most of these DPPs had a small capacity (maximum 10 MW) with a 20 kV distribution system.

9. "Javanese" (*orang Jawa*) usually refer to the East Javanese or the Central Javanese peoples. But in this case, I include the Sundanese and the Bantenese as well, two major sociolinguistic groups who inhabit the western parts of Java. Together they form the largest ethnic group in Indonesia.

10. *PLN in 1976/77* (Jakarta: Dinas Humas dan Protokol PLN Pusat, 1976), 178.

11. The other was the Srivijaya empire, a Buddhist maritime empire based on the island of Sumatra.

12. This Mataram sultanate is not to be confused with the earlier Mataram kingdom of the eighth to eleventh century, which was also located in Central Java. The city of Surakarta is also known as Solo in Indonesian.

13. Sukarno said, "The national state is only Indonesia in its entirety, which was set up in the time of Sriwijaya and Modjopabit [*sic*], and which now we also ought to establish together." See Sukarno, "Indonesian Independence and Pancasila," 168.

14. Benedict R. O'G. Anderson, *Language and Power: Exploring Political Culture in Indonesia* (Jakarta: Equinox Publishing, 2006), 22.

15. Anderson, *Language and Power*, 23.

16. Anderson, *Language and Power*, 23.

17. Anderson, *Language and Power*, 23.

18. Anderson, *Language and Power*, 22.

19. Although power and energy are used interchangeably colloquially, in physics each term has a specific definition, and they are distinguishable from one another. Power is how much energy converted per unit time. Energy is the ability to do work or the rate of power over time.

20. Anderson, *Language and Power*, 27.

21. "Kunjungan Kerja Menteri Pertambangan dan Energi ke Jawa Tengah," 3–6.

22. For a more complete list of World Bank–financed electric power projects in Indonesia, see Purnomo, *Tenaga Listrik*, 370–92. Saguling, Cirata, and Jatiluhur HPPs were constructed along the Citarum River in West Java.

23. Note that PLN defines a large SPP as a one that produces more than 150 MW. See Eddie Widiono, *Electricity for a Better Life* (Jakarta: PT PLN [Persero], 2003), 42. Bakaru HPP had the longest tunnel in Indonesia when it was completed. See "PLTA Bakaru Memiliki Terowongan Terpanjang di Indonesia," *Berita PLN*, July 1989, 3–6.

24. "Kunjungan Kerja Dirut PLN ke Jatim: Kompleks PLTG/U Gresik Terbesar di Dunia," *Berita PLN*, December 1993, 3–13.

25. "Memasuki Era Pembangunan Batubara Secara Besar-Besaran Untuk Pembangkitan Tenaga Listrik," *Berita PLN*, February 1988, 12–13, 21.

26. "Kunjungan Kerja Komisi VI DPR-RI ke Proyek PLTU Suralaya," *Berita PLN* January 1982, 9–12.

27. Denis Riantiza Meilanova, "Proyek Kabel Bawah Laut Sumatra-Jawa Masih Jadi Opsi," *Bisnis.com*, March 23, 2018. https://ekonomi.bisnis.com/read/20180323/44 /753441/proyek-kabel-bawah-laut-sumatra-jawa-masih-jadi-opsi.

28. "Dari Bukit Asam untuk Suralaya," *Teknologi*, November 1986, 16–19.

29. "440.000 ton batubara Australia untuk PLTU Suralaya," *Berita PLN*, March 1985, 14.

30. Hardjoko Seputro, "5 Tahun Tambang Batubara Bukit Asam," *Pertambangan dan Energi*, no. 2 (1986), 9–20.

31. "Presiden Soeharto Resmikan PLTU Suralaya dan Sistem Transmisi Tegangan Ekstra Tinggi," *Berita PLN*, August 1985, 3–7, 29.

32. Vincent Sinaga, "Reaktor, Peranan dan Manfaatnya pada system 500 kV se Jawa," *Berita PLN*, April 1988, 7–11, 24.

33. "Sistem Transmisi Tegangan Ekstra Tinggi Pertama di ASEAN, Kedua di Asia Setelah Jepang," *Berita PLN*, February 1983, 46.

34. "Sistem Transmisi Tegangan," 46.

35. "PBB Gandul Mengendalikan Listrik Se-Jawa," *Teknologi*, March 1987, 18–19. This center was later called Transmission and Load Dispatch Center (Penyaluran dan Pusat Pengatur Beban).

36. "Kabel Laut," *Berita PLN*, June 1987, 3–7; "Menteri Pertambangan Dan Energi Resmikan Kabel Laut Jawa-Bali," *Berita PLN*, August 1989, 3–8.

37. "Lagi, Kabel Laut Terkena Jangkar Gelap di Madura," *Berita PLN*, February 1999, 5.

38. "Perkembangan Kasus Madura," *Berita PLN*, April 1999, 7–8.

39. Mohsin, "Lighting 'Paradise,'" 29.

40. John McBeth, "Bali Struggles to Keep the Lights Lit," *Asia Times*, April 26, 2018, https://asiatimes.com/2018/04/bali-struggles-to-keep-the-lights-lit/.

41. McBeth, "Bali Struggles to Keep the Lights Lit."

42. Ali Mustofa, "Jawa Bali Crossing Batal, PLN Pakai Kabel Laut, Ternyata Karena . . . ," *Radar Bali*, October 25, 2018, https://radarbali.jawapos.com/ekonomi /25/10/2018/jawa-bali-crossing-batal-pln-pakai-kabel-laut-ternyata-karena.

43. Annisa Margrit, "Pemprov Bali Setuju Lanjutkan Proyek Jawa Bali Connection," *Bisnis.com* June 26, 2019, https://ekonomi.bisnis.com/read/20190626/44/938028/pemprov -bali-setuju-lanjutkan-proyek-jawa-bali-connection.

44. See "Earth at Night: Flat Maps," NASA Earth Observatory, NASA, accessed March 1, 2023, https://earthobservatory.nasa.gov/features/NightLights/page3.php.

45. *Statistik PLN 1997* (Jakarta: PT PLN [Persero], 1997), 18. Outside Java, there were four other types of power plants: coal-fired steam, HPP, combined cycle, and natural gas-fired power plants. In Java, you could find a fifth type: GPP.

46. Law No. 1 of 1967 on Foreign Direct Investments (Undang-Undang No. 1 Tahun 1967 Tetang Penanaman Modal Asing). This law was signed by Sukarno on January 10, 1967, while he was still in charge of the government. Soeharto was appointed acting president in March 1967.

47. Daniel Yergin, *The Prize: The Epic Quest for Oil, Money, and Power* (New York: Simon & Schuster, 1991), 652.

48. Bachrawi Sanusi, "Natural Gas Utilization in Indonesia-Past, Present and Future," *Pertambangan dan Energi*, no. 4 (1985), 107.

49. A photo of a woman swimming with a red barrel of oil, pushing it to shore, while being looked on by another woman in a *sampan* can be found on the back cover of a December 1998 issue of *Berita PLN*.

50. Suryono, "Penyediaan Tenaga Listrik Untuk Pedesaan," in Komite National Indonesia World Energy Conference, *Penyediaan Energi Untuk Daerah Pedesaan (Hasil-hasil Lokakarya Energi, 25–26 Mei 1978, Jakarta)* (Jakarta: Percetakan Pertamina, 1978), 89.

51. Arismunandar, "Overview of Electric Power Development in Indonesia," 6.

52. Ali Herman Ibrahim and Akbar Faizal, *General Check-Up Kelistrikan Nasional* (Jakarta: Mediaplus Network, 2008), 75.

53. Tahir Harahap, *Perlistrikan Desa* (Jakarta: Perusahaan Umum Listrik Negara, Pusat Penyelidikan Masalah Kelistrikan, 1977), 3–5.

54. Harahap, *Perlistrikan Desa*, 33.

55. Harahap, *Perlistrikan Desa*, 6.

56. Harahap, *Perlistrikan Desa*, 18.

57. Pedoman dan Petunjuk Pemeliharaan PLTD, 1994, Perpustakaan PLN Pusat Penelitian dan Pengembangan Ketenagalistrikan, 09-30900.

58. Perusahaan Umum Listrik Negara, "SPLN 74: 1987 Standar Listrik Pedessan," July 4, 1987, 10.

59. Rumondor, "Kebijaksanaan PLN dalam program listrik pedesaan" 15.

60. Salim, "Recollections of My Career," 61.

61. Sriwibawa and Ramadhan, *50 Years of PLN Dedication*, 125.

62. Sriwibawa and Ramadhan, *50 Years of PLN Dedication*, 125.

63. Sriwibawa and Ramadhan, *50 Years of PLN Dedication*, 125.

64. Sriwibawa and Ramadhan, *50 Years of PLN Dedication*, 125.

65. Umar Said, the director general of Village Development of the Department of Home Affairs was quoted by *Bali Post* as saying that he hoped all of Indonesia's villages can be *swasembada* villages by 2000. Dibia, "Harapan Di Tahun 2000."

66. World Bank, *Indonesia Rural Electrification Review*, Report no. 6144-IND, East Asia and Pacific Regional Office, 50.

67. Mohsin, "Lighting 'Paradise,'" 11.

68. Marsudi interview.

69. Salim, "Recollections of My Career," 58–59.

70. "Mantan Dirut PLN Ir. Djiteng Marsudi: Kuntoro Minta Maaf Kepada Saya," *Tajuk*, no. 18 (October 26–November 8 2000): 38.

71. Munawar Amarullah, "Pengembangan Wilayah dan Manpower Planning Pelistrikan Desa," *Berita PLN*, March 1978.

72. Piet Haryono, "Peranan Minyak Dalam Pembangunan Nasional," in Komite Nasional Indonesia World Energy Conference, *Penyediaan Energi Untuk Daerah Pedesaan (Hasil-Hasil Lokakarya Energi, 25–26 Mei 1978, Jakarta)* (Jakarta: Percetakan Pertamina, 1978), 18–19.

73. Suryono, "Penyediaan Tenaga Listrik Untuk Pedesaan," 77.

74. Suryono, "Penyediaan Tenaga Listrik Untuk Pedesaan," 85.

75. "PLTM Swadaya Masyarakat Memegang Peranan Penting," *Berita PLN*, February 1985, 28.

76. "Pengembangan PLTM oleh PLN," *Berita PLN*, February 1985, 3.

77. "Pengembangan PLTM oleh PLN," 3–4, 24.

78. The first employee was a PLN West Sumatran worker named Zamrisyaf. His story appears in the article "PLTM Swadaya Masyarakat," 13–14, 28. The second was a PLN employee in the Central Java Hydro Generation Master Project named Soejoedi Soerachmad. He wrote his idea in an article. See Soejoedi Soerachmad, "Desain Adaptasi Sebagai Kunci PLTM Produksi Dalam Negeri," *Berita PLN*, September 1984, 10–13, 25.

79. "PLTM Swadaya Masyarakat," 13–14, 28.

80. "PLTM Swadaya Masyarakat," 13–14, 28.

81. Sardjono, "Usaha-Usaha Diversifikasi Energi Dalam Sektor Tenaga Listrik," in *Diversifikasi Energi Dalam Sektor Tenaga Listrik (Hasil-hasil Lokakarya Energi 17–18 April 1980)*, edited by Sudarsono et al. (Jakarta: Percetakan Pertamina, 1980), 26.

82. In fact, there were popular protests against large dam constructions in Java in the 1980s. See George Aditjondro, "Large Dam Victims and Their Defenders," in *The Politics of Environment in Southeast Asia*, edited by Philip Hirsch and Carol Warren (London: Routledge, 1998); Stanly, *Seputar Kedung Ombo* (Jakarta: Lembaga Studi dan Advokasi Masyarakat, 1994); Agustinus Rumansara, "Indonesia: The Struggle of the People of Kedung Ombo," in *The Struggle for Accountability: The World Bank, NGOs, and Grassroots Movements*, edited by Jonathan Fox and L. David Brown (Cambridge, MA: MIT Press, 1998), 123–49.

83. "Studi Kemungkinan Membangun PLTN di Indonesia Diteruskan," *Surabaya Post*, May 9, 1986.

84. "Studi Kemungkinan Membangun."

85. "Rapinya Pengamanan PLTN Tidak Menutup Kemungkinan Kecelakaan," *Surabaya Post*, May 13, 1986.

86. Charles Perrow similarly argued the same point in his influential book *Normal Accidents: Living with High-Risk Technologies* (New York: Basic Books, 1984).

87. "Belum Ada Keputusan Tentang Rencana Pembangunan PLTN," *Surabaya Post*, May 14, 1986.

88. "Belum Ada Keputusan."

89. "Kerjasama PLN-BATAN," *Berita PLN*, Special Edition, 1990, 32, 49.

90. "Rapat Kerja Komisi VI DPR-RI Dengan Mentamben: PLTN Tetap Alternatif Terakhir," *Berita PLN*, January 1996, 20–23.

91. Sulfikar Amir, "The State and the Reactor: Nuclear Politics in Post-Suharto Indonesia," *Indonesia* 89 (April 2010): 101–47.

Chapter 5. Social Knowledge of Rural Life and Energy Uses

1. M. Pandjaitan, "Maksud dan Tujuan Survai Energi Pedesaan," in Direktorat Jenderal Ketenagaan Departemen Pertambangan dan Energi, *Hasil Lokakarya Survai Energi Pedesaan Diselenggarakan di Jakarta Pada Tanggal 1 s/d 11 September 1980 dan 3 s/d 5 Februari 1981* (Jakarta: PT Surya Jaya Utama, 1982), 75–80.

2. Artono Arismunandar, "Krisis Enersi, Masalah Enersi Dan Kebijaksanaan Enersi Nasional," in Komite Nasional Indonesia World Energy Conference, *Hasil-Hasil Seminar Energi Nasional Jakarta 24–27 Juli 1974* (Jakarta: PT Yudha Gama, 1974).

3. The idea of making society legible to improve their conditions can be found in James C. Scott, *Seeing Like a State: How Certain Schemes to Improve the Human Condition Have Failed* (New Haven, CT: Yale University Press, 1998).

4. Kenneth F. Weaver, "Our Energy Predicament," *National Geographic* (February 1981), 16.

5. Energy Planning for Development in Indonesia, August 1981, USAID Development Experience Clearinghouse, PNAAN338, 9–11.

6. Komite Nasional Indonesia World Energy Conference, *Hasil-Hasil Seminar Energi Nasional, Jakarta, 24–27 Juli 1974*, 456.

7. Komite Nasional Indonesia World Energy Conference, *Hasil-Hasil Seminar Energi Nasional, Jakarta, 24–27 Juli 1974*, 456.

8. Sumitro Djojohadikusumo, "Pola Pengembangan enersi—tinjauan jangka Panjang," in Komite Nasional Indonesia World Energy Conference, *Hasil-Hasil Seminar Energi Nasional, Jakarta, 24–27 Juli 1974*, 39.

9. Sutami, "Pidato Sambutan Menteri Pekerjaan Umum dan Tenaga Listrik Ir. Sutami Pada Seminar Enersi Nasional Di Jakarta Tanggal 24 Juli s/d 27 Juli 1974," in Komite Nasional Indonesia World Energy Conference, *Hasil-Hasil Seminar Energi Nasional Jakarta 24–27 Juli 1974*, 31–33.

10. Abdul Kadir, "Pola Pengembangan Energi di Indonesia Serta Peranan Tenaga Listrik Dalam Pola Tersebut," in Komite Nasional Indonesia World Energy Conference, *Hasil-Hasil Seminar Energi Nasional Jakarta 24–27 Juli 1974*, 109–22.

11. M. T. Zen, "Pola konservasi energi dalam kebijaksanaan energi nasional," in Komite Nasional Indonesia World Energy Conference, *Hasil-Hasil Seminar Energi Nasional Jakarta, 24–27 Juli 1974*, 236.

12. Arismunandar, "Krisis Enersi," 298.

13. Komite Nasional Indonesia World Energy Conference, *Hasil-Hasil Seminar Energi Nasional Jakarta 24–27 Juli 1974*, 13.

14. Subroto, "Pidato Pembukaan Menteri Pertambangan dan Energi Pada Lokakarya Konservasi Energi," in Departemen Pertambangan dan Energi Republik Indonesia, *Konservasi Energi Hasil-hasil Lokakarya Konservasi Energi, 24–25 September 1979, Jakarta* (Jakarta: Spirit International, 1980), 5.

15. Ketetapan Majelis Permusyawaratan Rakyat Republik Indonesia Nomor IV/MPR/1978 Tentang Garis-Garis Besar Haluan Negara.

16. Subroto, "Pidato Pengarahan Menteri Pertambangan dan Energi," in Komite Nasional Indonesia World Energy Conference, *Sumber-Sumber Energi Pengganti Minyak (Hasil-Hasil Lokakarya Energi, 24–25 April 1979, Jakarta)* (Jakarta: Rakan Offset, 1979), 17–21.

17. The proceedings of the symposium, which documented both the papers presented and transcripts of discussions held, run to more than seven hundred pages.

18. Departemen Pertambangan dan Energi Republik Indonesia, *Konservasi Energi Hasil-hasil Lokakarya Konservasi Energi, 24–25 September 1979, Jakarta* (Jakarta: Spirit International, 1980).

19. DME Ministerial Decision No. 734 of 1978 founded the new DGP.

20. Energy Planning for Development in Indonesia, 2.

21. Energy Planning for Development in Indonesia, 7.

22. Pandjaitan, "Maksud dan Tujuan Survai Energi Pedesaan," 75.

23. Energy Planning for Development in Indonesia, vi–ix.

24. Energy Planning for Development in Indonesia, 3.

25. Energy Planning for Development in Indonesia, 3–5.

26. Energy Planning for Development in Indonesia, 5.

27. Energy Planning for Development in Indonesia, 19.

28. Energy Planning for Development in Indonesia, 24.

29. Energy Planning for Development in Indonesia, 21.

30. Energy Planning for Development in Indonesia, 50.

31. Energy Planning for Development in Indonesia, 31.

32. Energy Planning for Development in Indonesia, 32, 428, 429.

33. Energy Planning for Development in Indonesia, 20.

34. "Penyusunan Kwesioner dan Rencana Survai," in Direktorat Jenderal Ketenagaan Departemen Pertambangan dan Energi, *Hasil Lokakarya Survai Energi Pedesaan Diselenggarakan di Jakarta Pada Tanggal 1 s/d 11 September 1980 dan 3 s/d 5 Februari 1981* (Jakarta: PT Surya Jaya Utama, 1982), 81.

35. "Penyusunan Kwesioner dan Rencana Survai," 93–94, 96.

36. Institut Pertanian Bogor, the Forest Products Research Institute, and ITB made up the first panel.

37. Direktorat Jenderal Ketenagaan Departemen Pertambangan dan Energi, *Hasil Lokakarya Survai Energi Pedesaan Diselenggarkan di Jakarta Pada Tanggal 1 s/d 11 September 1980 dan 3 s/d 5 Februari 1981* (Jakarta: PT Surya Jaya Utama, 1982), 249.

38. Gadjah Mada University, Diponegoro University, and Ten November Institute of Technology formed this panel.

39. Direktorat Jenderal Ketenagaan Departemen Pertambangan dan Energi, *Hasil Lokakarya Survai Energi Pedesaan*, 250.

40. The third panel was composed of Hasanuddin University and North Sumatra University.

41. Direktorat Jenderal Ketenagaan Departemen Pertambangan dan Energi, *Hasil Lokakarya Survai Energi Pedesaan*, 250.

42. Energy Planning for Development in Indonesia, 21.

43. Energy Planning for Development in Indonesia, 34.

44. Energy Planning for Development in Indonesia, 34.

45. Energy Planning for Development in Indonesia, 34.

46. Direktorat Jenderal Ketenagaan Departemen Pertambangan dan Energi, *Hasil Lokakarya Survai Energi Pedesaan*, 251.

47. Raymond Atje, "Peranan kayu bakar dalam pemerataan," in Komite Nasional Indonesia World Energy Conference, *Hasil-Hasil Seminar Energi Nasional II, Jakarta, 9–12 Juni 1981* by (Jakarta: Percetakan Rakan Offset, 1981), 161.

48. Energy Planning for Development in Indonesia, 143–45.

49. Energy Planning for Development in Indonesia, 149.

50. Energy Planning for Development in Indonesia, 151.

51. Suryono, "Penyediaan tenaga listrik untuk pedesaan," in Komite Nasional Indonesia World Energy Conference, *Penyediaan Energi Untuk Daerah Pedesaan (Hasil-hasil Lokakarya Energi, 25–26 Mei 1978, Jakarta)* (Jakarta: Cetakan Pertamina, 1978), 85.

52. Rumondor, "Kebijaksanaan PLN dalam program listrik pedesaan," 15–41.

53. The invited branches were PLN Headquarters, PLN Wilayah XIII, PLN Wilayah II, PLN Wilayah VII, PLN Wilayah XI, PLN Distribution West Java, and PLN Transmission West Java.

54. For a more detailed information of the workshop, see M. Machfud, "Beberapa Catatan Dari 'Session on Rural Electrification Feasibility Study Training' yang diadakan oleh PLN atas bantuan USAID/NRECA bertempat di PLN Wil. XIII Semarang tanggal 17 Okt 1977 s/d 22 Okt 1977" (unpublished manuscript, 1977).

55. Perusahaan Umum Listrik Negara, "Pedoman dan Pentunjuk Penyusunan Feasibility Study Listrik Pedesaan" (unpublished manuscript, 1977), 1.

56. Laporan Kronologis Listrik Pedesaan, Lokakarya Kelistrikan Desa, Medan 1978, Perpustakaan PLN Pusat Penelitian dan Pengembangan Ketenagalistrikan, 78-10113, 4.

57. Machfud, "Beberapa Catatan Dari."

58. Laporan Kronologis Listrik Pedesaan, 5.

59. David Devin, "USAID R.E. Program Objectives and Status," in Laporan Session on Rural Electrification Feasibility Study Training III, 23 s/d 28 Januari 1978 PLN-Wilayah VII, Menado, Sulawesi Utara, Perpustakaan PLN Pusat Penelitian dan Pengembangan Ketenagalistrikan, 78-10486.

60. Devin, "USAID R.E. Program Objectives and Status."

61. Laporan Kronologis Listrik Pedesaan.

62. "Hasil Kelompok Seminar Listrik Pedesaan III," in Laporan Session on Rural Electrification Feasibility Study Training III, 23 s/d 28 Januari 1978 PLN-Wilayah VII, Menado, Sulawesi Utara, Perpustakaan PLN Pusat Penelitian dan Pengembangan Ketenagalistrikan, 78-10486.

63. PLN Denpasar Branch Head B. M. Akwan's paper that talked about the PKD was discussed in this workshop and included in the seminar proceedings. See also Mohsin, "Lighting 'Paradise'."

64. Laporan Lokakarya Listrik Pedesaan ke IV Tanggal 28 Juli S/D 3 Agustus 1978 Di PLN Wilayah II Medan, Sumut, 1978, Perpustakaan PLN Pusat Penelitian dan Pengembangan Ketenagalistrikan, 05-26208.

65. Rumondor, "Kebijaksanaan PLN dalam program listrik pedesaan," 17–18.

66. Soemardjan et al., *Laporan Penelitian Listrik Masuk Desa*, 3.

67. Soemardjan et al., *Laporan Penelitian Listrik Masuk Desa*, 3.

68. Soemardjan et al., *Laporan Penelitian Listrik Masuk Desa*, 3.

69. Vedi Hadiz and Daniel Dhakidae, "Introduction," in *Social Science and Power in Indonesia*, edited by Vedi Hadiz and Daniel Dhakidae (Jakarta and Singapore: Equinox Publishing, 2005), 2.

70. The Social Sciences Foundation (Yayasan Ilmu-ilmu Sosial) was founded in 1977 with full support of the Ford Foundation to develop Indonesian social scientists and social sciences.

71. The charter is included in the report prepared by the researchers. They also described signing the agreement.

72. Soemardjan et al., *Laporan Penelitian Listrik Masuk Desa*, 21.

73. Soemardjan et al., *Laporan Penelitian Listrik Masuk Desa*, 22.

74. I must note that they did not produce a complete profile of every village visited. They visited two villages (Bambang Lipuro and Tanjung Bumi) briefly and could not generate much information. When they visited the village of Cokrotulung on July 13, 1979, it was for the sole purpose of observing the MHPP operated by the village cooperative, which they noted was in debilitating condition because the revenue from electricity sales could not cover the maintenance costs of the machine.

75. Soemardjan et al., *Laporan Penelitian Listrik Masuk Desa*, 19, 16.

76. Soemardjan et al., *Laporan Penelitian Listrik Masuk Desa*, 88–133.

77. Soemardjan et al., *Laporan Penelitian Listrik Masuk Desa*, 96.

78. Soemardjan et al., *Laporan Penelitian Listrik Masuk Desa*, 90.

79. Technologies can have these determining effects on society, some more strongly than others. But many STS scholars have pointed out that societies can also influence the adoption and development of technologies, and some societies even resist them. For example, see Ronald Kline and Trevor Pinch, "Users as Agents of Technological Change: The Social Construction of the Automobile in the Rural United States," *Technology and Culture* 37, no. 4 (1996): 763–95; Jameson Wetmore, "Amish Technology Reinforcing Values and Building Community," in *Technology and Society Building Our Sociotechnical Future*, edited by Deborah G. Johnson and Jameson M. Wetmore (Cambridge, MA: MIT Press, 2009), 297–318; Ronald R. Kline, *Consumers in the Country Technology and Social Change in Rural America* (Baltimore, MD: Johns Hopkins University Press, 2000).

80. Hadi Sutrisno and Djoko Santoso, *Pengaruh Kelistrikan Pada Pembangunan Desa* (Fakultas Teknik Elektro Institute Teknologi 10 Nopember Surabaya, Surabaya 1981). The study was carried out by researchers of a well-known technical university and sponsored by the East Java Provincial Government and PLN Twelfth Region. They investigated ten recently lit villages in East Java that received their electricity in 1976/1977 and 1977/1978 fiscal years.

81. Sutrisno and Santoso, *Pengaruh Kelistrikan Pada Pembangunan Desa.*

82. Sukamdi, Heru Nugroho, and Wini Tamtiari, *Listrik, Kemiskinan & Perubahan Sosial* (Yogyakarta: Pusat Penelitian Kependudukan Universitas Gadjah Mada, 1995).

83. Sukamdi, Nugroho, and Tamtiari, *Listrik, Kemiskinan & Perubahan Sosial,* 47, 51.

84. Sugiarto Dakung, Hilderia Sitanggang, Fadjiria Novari Manan, Wahyuningsih, Raf Darnys, and Harry Waluyo, *Dampak Listrik Masuk Desa Di Desa Cisande, Kecamatan Cibadak Kabupaten Sukabumi* (Jakarta: Departemen Pendidikan Dan Kebudayaan Direktorat Jenderal Kebudayaan Direktorat Sejarah Dan Nilai Tradisional Proyek Inventarisasi Dan Pembinaan Nilai-Nilai Budaya, 1990), 40–47.

85. Made Arka, *Pengaruh Listrik Pedesaan Terhadap Kegiatan Ekonomi dan Sosial Masyarakat Di Bali* (Denpasar: Fakultas Ekonomi Universitas Udayana, 1982), 5.

86. Arka, *Pengaruh Listrik Pedesaan,* 5.

87. Dakung et al., *Dampak Listrik Masuk Desa Di Desa Cisande,* 28.

88. Husin, "Rural Electrification in Indonesia," v.

89. Husin, "Rural Electrification in Indonesia," 255–71.

90. Husin, "Rural Electrification in Indonesia," 269–70.

91. When I visited several remote electrified villages during my fieldwork in Indonesia in 2011–12, I needed to travel through unpaved or broken roads leading to these villages. I noticed that while there was a primary school in one remote village in Kintamani, Bali, a secondary school was yet not available there. The closest one is in the subdistrict capital, which could be challenging to reach for many prospective students.

Chapter 6. Rural Electric Cooperatives

1. Rural Electrification for Indonesia; Report of the NRECA Study Team, May 1976, USAID Development Experience Clearinghouse, PNAAK593, 10–11.

2. Rural Electrification for Indonesia, 28. For an account of the Philippines's rural electrification program, see Frank H. Denton, *Lighting up the Countryside: The Story of Electric Cooperatives in the Philippines* (Manila: Academy Press, 1979).

3. Rural Electrification for Indonesia, 28.

4. Rural Electrification for Indonesia, 31.

5. Ibnoe Soedjono, *Perumusan Kumpulan Pendapat Dan Saran Dari Seminar Pembangunan Listrik Pedesaan Secara Koperatif, Jakarta 6–8 Desember 1976* (Jakarta: Direktorat Jenderal Koperasi, Departemen Tenaga Kerja, Transmigrasi dan Koperasi, 1976), 18–19.

6. Quoted in J. B. Djarot Siwijatmo, *Koperasi di Indonesia* (Jakarta: LPFE Universitas Indonesia, 1982), 27.

7. Siwijatmo, *Koperasi di Indonesia*, 27.

8. For a brief history of the transmigration program, see Brian A. Hoey, "Nationalism in Indonesia: Building Imagined and Intentional Communities through Transmigration," *Ethnology* 42, no. 2 (Spring 2003): 109–26.

9. Ima Suwandi, *Perkembangan Koperasi di Indonesia Khususnya KUD* (Jakarta: Penerbit Bhratara Karya Aksara, 1988), 33.

10. Joint Ministerial Decision of 1979. The two ministers who signed it were Dr. Subroto of DME and Dr. Radius Prawiro of the Department of Trade and Cooperative. See Surat Keputusan Bersama No. 755/Kpts/M/Pertamb/1979 dan No. 613/KPB/X/1979 Tentang Pelaksanaan Pengembangan dan Pembinaan Usaha Koperasi Unit Desa di bidang Kelistrikan dan Penyaluran Minyak Tanah.

11. Rural Electrification for Indonesia, 15.

12. Rural Electrification I, June 25, 1980, USAID Development Experience Clearinghouse, PDAAF891A1, 1.

13. Rural Electrification I, 1.

14. Rural Electrification I, 1.

15. The nine electric cooperatives they visited were Moresco, Vresco, Ileco, Capelco, Quezelco, Canoreco, Casureco I, Aleco, and Zamcelco.

16. Johannes J. Rumondor et al., "Report on Conference-Workshop on Initial Steps on Electric Cooperative Development Held in Manila 17 January–26 February 1977," in *Rural Electrification for Indonesia: A Proposal for USAID Assistance* (April 1, 1977), 10.

17. Rumondor et al., "Report on Conference-Workshop," 12.

18. Ima Suwandi et al., "Report on Conference-Workshop on Initial Steps on Electric Cooperative Development Held in Manila 17 January–26 February 1977," in *Rural Electrification for Indonesia: A Proposal for USAID Assistance* (April 1, 1977), 7.

19. For a study of these RE projects, see Janice Donna Brodman, "Technology Change, Equity, and Growth: A Case Study of Rural Electrification in Java," PhD diss., Harvard University, 1983.

20. Project Paper, Proposal and Recommendations For the Review of the Development Loan Committee, Indonesia-Rural Electrification I, AID-DLC/P-2244, August 1977, USAID Development Experience Clearinghouse, PDAAD914B1, 23.

21. Project Paper, 51.

22. Project Paper, 51–52.

23. Project Paper, 8.

24. "Memorandum for the Development Committee in Department of State Agency for International Development," in Project Paper.

25. Department of Cooperatives Final Report: Contract AID/ASIA-C-1357, AID Loan No. 497-T-052 Rural Electrification, December 1984, USAID Development Experience Clearinghouse, PDAAQ724, II-3.

26. Rural Electrification I First Annual Review, USAID Loan 497-T-052, USAID Grant 497-0267, June 1979, USAID Development Experience Clearinghouse, PDAAK 311B1, 4.

27. Rural Electrification I, 4.

28. Department of Cooperatives Final Report, II-2.

29. Rural Electrification I, 5.

30. NRECA Final Report Rural Electrification Projects Department of Cooperatives Contract AID/ASIA-C-1357 AID Loan No. 497-T-052, December 1984, USAID Development Experience Clearinghouse, PDCAM984, 20.

31. Project Assistance Completion Report: AID Project No. 497-0267, AID Loan and Grant No. 497-T-052, AID Project Title: Rural Electrification, 1987, USAID Development Experience Clearinghouse, PDAAV785, 4–5.

32. Project Paper, Annex G-4.

33. Project Paper, 16.

34. Project Paper, Annex G-5.

35. Munawar Amarullah, "Listrik Masuk Desa," *Prisma* 12 (1986): 80.

36. Bustanil Arifin, "Ceramah Menteri Muda Urusan Koperasi, Bustanil Arifin, SH Dalam Lokakarya Dan Latihan Proyek Energy Planning for Development Pada tgl. 2 September 1980 di Jakarta," in Direktorat Jenderal Ketenagaan Departemen Pertambangan dan Energi, *Hasil Lokakarya Survai Energi Pedesaan Diselenggarakan di Jakarta Pada Tanggal 1 s/d 11 September 1980 dan 3 s/d 5 Februari 1981*, 41–45 (Jakarta: PT Surya Jaya Utama, 1982).

37. The seven members were Peter McNeill (team leader), Lyod Lake (sr. RE specialist), Louie Sansing (sr. RE specialist), Sam Adkins (sr. RE specialist, PLN adviser), Paul Swanson (sr. RE specialist), John DeFoor (RE specialist), and Ray Shoff (administrative/finance officer).

38. The NRECA reports ran from March 1981 until December 1984 and detailed various aspects of the REC's development, including a general update, organization and management, training, operations, problem areas, and solutions. I found twenty reports online, the bulk of which were written in 1981 and 1982, when the NRECA produced monthly reports. The main reason for the drop in frequency of reports to the USAID was a 50 percent reduction of the NRECA team members in 1983. Most reports include photos of REC activities, although many photos are unclear because they were scanned in black and white. These reports can be searched and downloaded from https://dec.usaid.gov/dec/home/Default.aspx.

39. The NRECA reports refer to this REC mostly as Luwu REC.

40. For a study of the transmigration program in Luwu, see Hasan Mangunrai, *Evaluation of the Development of Transmigration in South Sulawesi: A Study on the Integration between the Transmigrants and Natives in the Transmigration Area of Luwu, South Sulawesi* (Singapore: Southeast Asia Population Research Awards Program, Institute of Southeast Asian Studies, 1977).

41. When I visited Palopo in July 2018, there was already a flight service from Makassar following the expansion of the Palopo Lagaligo airport in mid-2010.

42. Both Andi Muhammad Nur and Umar Muktamar, two former REC employees whom I interviewed in Luwu on July 27, 2018, recalled these consultants' names well.

43. RE Projects NRECA Team Report PDO Indonesia, May 1981, USAID Development Experience Clearinghouse, PDAAI354.

44. RE Projects NRECA Team Report PDO Indonesia, September 1981, USAID Development Experience Clearinghouse, PDAAL557.

45. RE Projects NRECA Team Report PDO Indonesia, March 1981, USAID Development Experience Clearinghouse, PDAAJ540.

46. RE Projects NRECA Team Report PDO Indonesia, August 1981, USAID Development Experience Clearinghouse, PDAAJ538.

47. RE Projects NRECA Team Report PDO Indonesia, October–December 1982, USAID Development Experience Clearinghouse, PDAAM366.

48. RE Projects NRECA Team Report PDO Indonesia, May–December 1983, USAID Development Experience Clearinghouse, PDAAP140.

49. RE Projects NRECA Team Report PDO Indonesia, June and July 1982, USAID Development Experience Clearinghouse, PDAAL762.

50. NRECA Final Report Rural Electrification Projects Department of Cooperatives Contract AID/ASIA-C-1357 AID Loan No. 497-T-052, December 1984, USAID Development Experience Clearinghouse, PDCAM984.

51. RE Projects NRECA Team Report PDO Indonesia, August and September 1982, USAID Development Experience Clearinghouse, PDAAL743.

52. Umar Muktamar, interview with the author, July 27, 2018, Lagego village, East Luwu.

53. Several Indonesian officials attended the energization ceremony, including the junior minister of Cooperative, Bustanil Arifin; the governor of South Sulawesi, Col. Andi Odang; the Luwu district head, Abdullah Suara; the PDO-RE chief, Sjoufjan Awal; and the chief of DGC-South Sulawesi, Ima Suwandi.

54. RE Projects NRECA Team Report PDO Indonesia, April and May 1982, USAID Development Experience Clearinghouse, PDAAL369.

55. RE Projects NRECA Team Report, May–December 1983.

56. RE Projects NRECA Team Report, May–December 1983.

57. NRECA Final Report.

58. RE Projects NRECA Team Report, May–December 1983.

59. RE Projects NRECA Team Report, May–December 1983.

60. H. Soetendro, S. Soedirman, and N. Sudja, "Rural Electrification in Indonesia," in *Rural Electrification Guidebook for Asia and the Pacific* (Bangkok: Asian Institute of Technology and the Commission of the European Communities, 1992), 374. This number is aligned with a June 5, 1996, *Fajar* article that mentions the cooperative customers were about 16,000 at that time.

61. My interviews with three PLN Palopo employees support the "messy administration" argument of the cooperative. Mustari, Aco, and Muhammad Hairul, interview with the author, July 26, 2018, Palopo, Luwu. Muktamar Umar, a former cooperative employee, told me that part of unsound management practices was the poor

maintenance of the electricity generators. They were not properly serviced at the scheduled times. Muktamar interview.

62. "PT PLN Bersedia Akuisisi Sama Botuna," *Fajar*, May 31, 1996.

63. "Masyarakat Walenrang Tebang Tiang Listrik," *Fajar*, May 25, 1996.

64. "3.033 Tiang Instalasi Listrik Rusak," *Fajar*, June 15, 1996.

65. "Mengeluh Soal Listrik ke Harmoko," *Fajar*, March 25, 1996.

66. "Masyarakat Walenrang Tebang Tiang Listrik."

67. "PT PLN Bersedia Akuisisi Sama Botuna."

68. "Masyarakat Walenrang Tebang Tiang Listrik." The three political parties contesting in the general elections during the New Order had their own colors. Golkar was yellow, the Indonesian Democratic Party red, and the United Development Party green.

69. "PT PLN Bersedia Akuisisi Sama Botuna."

70. "3.033 Tiang Instalasi Listrik Rusak." The twelve subdistricts were Mangkutana, Wotu, Bonebone, Sukamaju, Masamba, Sabbang, Malangke, Lamasi, Walengrang, Tomoni, Burau dan Bae Bunta.

71. "Listrik di Samabotuna Kini Ditangani PT PLN," *Fajar*, June 5, 1996.

72. "Krisis Samabotuna Berakhir Desember 1996," *Fajar*, June 18, 1996.

73. "Ditandatangani Naskah Kesepakatan Bersama Tentang: Perubahan Pola Pengelolaan Kelistrikan Eks KPL [*sic*] Samabotuna Sulawesi Selatan," *Berita PLN*, July 1996, 18, 20.

74. Andi Muhammad Nur took me a tour of the complex and pointed out this house to me.

75. NRECA reports call this cooperative the Lombok REC.

76. RE Projects NRECA Team Report, March 1981.

77. RE Projects NRECA Team Report, May 1981.

78. NRECA Final Report.

79. RE Projects NRECA Team Report PDO Indonesia, April 1981, USAID Development Experience Clearinghouse, PDAAI356.

80. RE Projects NRECA Team Report, April 1981, original emphasis.

81. RE Projects NRECA Team Report, May–December 1983.

82. RE Projects NRECA Team Report, May–December 1983.

83. Soetendro et al., "Rural Electrification in Indonesia," 374. Soetendro et al.'s article incorrectly wrote ninety-seven instead of thirty-seven villages. The latter number is mentioned in Catoer Wibowo's master's thesis (Catoer Wibowo, "Demand-Side Management at KLP Sinar Rinjani, Indonesia," master's thesis, University of Flensburg, 2004) and aligned more with *Lombok Post* articles stating that the cooperative served forty-two villages by mid-2000.

84. Basri Mulyani, "Suara Lonjong Listrik dari Lombok Timur," *Lombok Post*, February 23, 2006; Sapardi, interview with the author, July 18, 2018, Aikmel, East Lombok; Abdul Muttalib, interview with the author July 21, 2018, Aikmel, East Lombok.

85. "Pemda Lotim Tak Tertarik Kelola KLP," *Lombok Post*, November 9, 2005.

86. Muttalib interview.

87. Wibowo, "Demand-Side Managemen," 33.

88. Wibowo, "Demand-Side Management," 3.

89. Wibowo, "Demand-Side Management," 3.

90. "Tuntutan Putus Total Listrik KLP SR Dinilai Berlebihan," *Lombok Post*, December 12, 2005.

91. "KLP SR Dihancurkan Ribuan Massa," *Lombok Post*, January 12, 2006.

92. "Ketika KLP-SR Menghadapi Persoalan Pengelolaan Pasca Amuk Massa (2-Habis)," *Lombok Post*, March 10, 2006.

93. "Tahun Depan PLN Bangun Jaringan di Wilayah Eks KLP," *Lombok Post*, July 27, 2007.

94. The completion of the auction was reported in "Migrasi Eks KLP SR Libatkan Empat Pihak," *Lombok Post*, August 6, 2010. My interview with the chair of the Communities Alliance for Electricity reveals the uncertainties surrounding the funds collected from the auctions. Judan Putrabawa, interview with the author, July 18, 2018, Aikmel, East Lombok.

95. Rury Anjas Andita, "Catatan Lombok Timur Sepanjang 2011 (2) Masyarakat Eks KLPSR Tersenyum, Listrik Kembali Normal," *Lombok Post*, December 27, 2011.

96. Andita, "Catatan Lombok Timur Sepanjang 2011."

97. "Akhirnya Eks KLP-SR Dibubarkan," *Lombok Post*, July 1, 2010.

98. RE Projects NRECA Team Report, March 1981.

99. Lampung REC board of directors had five members, the fewest of all three cooperatives. Lombok had seven and Luwu had nine members.

100. RE Projects NRECA Team Report, May–December 1983.

101. NRECA Final Report.

102. RE Projects NRECA Team Report, April 1981.

103. RE Projects NRECA Team Report PDO Indonesia, July 1981, USAID Development Experience Clearinghouse, PDAAI018.

104. RE Projects NRECA Team Report, May–December 1983.

105. Soetendro et al., "Rural Electrification in Indonesia."

106. Surat Perjanjian Tentang Jual Beli Tenaga Listrik 2.770 kVA Antara Perusahaan Umum Listrik Negara Wilayah IV Dengan Sinar Siwo Mego Tanjung Karang, Nomor Pihak Pertama: 169/Pj/471/W.IV/94, Nomor Pihak Kedua: 011/M/KLP-SSM/V/94.

107. Surat Perjanjian Tentang Jual Beli Tenaga Listrik 2.770 kVA.

108. "Konflik PLN-Koperasi di Lampung Belum Tuntas," *Liputan6.com*, January 29, 2001, https://www.liputan6.com/news/read/7111/konflik-pln-koperasi-di-lampung-belum-tuntas.

109. "PLN Lampung Akan Putuskan Aliran 57 Ribu Pelanggan," *Tempo*, July 28, 2003. https://nasional.tempo.co/read/4886/pln-lampung-akan-putuskan-aliran-57-ribu-pelanggan.

110. "PLN Lampung Akan Putuskan."

111. "Walikota Metro Sampaikan Aspirasi Masyarakat," *Saburai*, March–April 2008.

112. "KLP Sinar Siwo Mego Menolak Pailit."

113. Keputusan Gubernur Lampung Nomor: G/195/B.IV/HK/2009 Tentang Pembentukan Tim Bersama Pengalihan Pelanggan Koperasi Listrik Pedesaan Sinar Siwo Mego (KLP-SSM) Kepada PT PLN (Persero) Tingkat Provinsi Lampung.

114. "Tim Pengalihan Pelanggan KLP SSM ke PLN Diaktifkan," *Lampung Post*, February 6, 2010.

115. "Tim Pengalihan Pelanggan."

116. "Tim Pengalihan Pelanggan."

117. "Alih Listrik KLP SSM Belum Bisa," *Lampung Post*, January 28, 2011.

118. "500 Rumah di Metro Kini Gelap Gulita," *Lampung Post*, January 3, 2011; "Sejak 2006, KLP SM Tak Miliki Stok Trafo," *Lampung Post*, January 5, 2006.

119. "500 Rumah di Metro Kini Gelap Gulita."

120. Hughes calls this phenomenon of how a technology shapes society more than society shaping it as having a "technological momentum." See Thomas P. Hughes, "Technological Momentum," in *Does Technology Drive History? The Dilemma of Technological Determinism*, edited by Leo Marx and Merritt Roe Smith (Cambridge, MA: MIT Press, 1998), 101–113.

121. "IUKU KLP Dicabut Warga Tunggu PLN," *Lampung Post*, March 31, 2011.

122. "Menilik KLP SSM Pascaperalihan ke PLN," *Lampung Post*, May 29, 2011. A photo accompanying the article shows many people queuing up.

123. "Mengharapkan Pelayanan PLN Lebih Baik," *Lampung Post*, May 29, 2011.

124. "Akhir Juni Pasokan Listrik Lampung Bertambah," *Lampung Post*, June 20, 2011; "Pengalihan Listrik Tidak Terhambat," *Lampung Post*, June 11, 2011.

125. "Bernostalgia dengan Pelayanan KLP SSM," *Lampung Post*, September 2013.

126. Sheila Jasanoff, "Future Imperfect: Science, Technology, and the Imaginations of Modernity," in *Dreamscapes of Modernity Sociotechnical Imaginaries and the Fabrication of Power*, edited by Sheila Jasanoff and Sang-Hyun Kim (Cambridge, MA: MIT Press, 2015), 4.

127. Suwandi, *Perkembangan Koperasi di Indonesia*, 38.

128. In 1978, Soeharto separated manpower and transmigration from DMTC and created the Department of Trade and Cooperative and appointed Bustanil Arifin as the junior minister of Cooperative. Five years later, Arifin was promoted to head the newly created Department of Cooperative.

129. Sapardi interview.

130. Haroen, "Usaha Kearah Melistriki Desa di Bali Dengan Pola III" (unpublished manuscript, February 13, 1986).

131. Amarullah, "Listrik Masuk Desa," 81.

132. Haroen, "Listrik Pedesaan dan Permasalahannya" (unpublished manuscript, 1990), 15.

133. Tahir Royaldi, interview with the author, July 21, 2018, Aikmel, East Lombok.

134. "Polisi Periksa Saksi Penjualan Genset KLP," *Lampung Post*, October 4, 2011.

135. "Sekretaris Luwu Utara Didakwa Korupsi Rp 1 Miliar," *Koran Tempo*, May 31, 2013. https://koran.tempo.co/read/makassar/311516/sekretaris-luwu-utara-didakwa-korupsi-rp-1-miliar; "Meski Ditahan, Mujahidin Tetap Jalankan Tugas Sekda," *Koran Tempo*, September 4, 2014. https://koran.tempo.co/read/makassar/350933/meski-ditahan-muja hidin-tetap-jalankan-tugas-sekda both articles were accessed on July 28, 2018.

136. The East Java government officials worked together with ITS faculty members and students and PLN employees to electrify hundreds of villages in the province. The endeavor started in 1976 and on January 31, 1980, the village of Banjarsari was inaugurated as the 1,381st village using this scheme. See Soemardjan et al. *Laporan Penelitian Listrik Masuk Desa*, 40–42.

137. Richard E. Sclove, *Democracy and Technology* (New York: Guilford, 1995).

Conclusion

1. Mrázek, *Engineers of Happy Land*, 95.

2. Division of Commerce, *1930 Handbook*, 273–78.

3. Division of Commerce, *Handbook of the Netherlands East-Indies Edition 1924*, 76–77.

4. Sumanto, Endang Widayanti, et al., *Terang Desaku, Sejahtera Bangsaku* (Jakarta: PT Pola Aneka, 1997), 4.

5. For more comprehensive account of the events, see Kevin O'Rourke, *Reformasi: The Struggle for Power in Post-Soeharto Indonesia* (Crows Nest NSW: Allen & Unwin, 2002).

6. Adam Schwarz, *A Nation in Waiting: Indonesia's Search for Stability*, 2nd ed. (St. Leonards, NSW: Allen & Unwin, 1999), 41.

7. Nurcholish Madjid, *Indonesia Kita* (Jakarta: Gramedia Pustaka Utama, 2004), 96.

8. See Ariel Heryanto, "Pembangunan," 8–26.

9. Xun Wu and Priyambudi Sulistiyanto, "Independent Power Producer (IPP) Debacle in Indonesia and the Philippines: Path Dependence and Spillover Effects," in *De-Regulation and its Discontents: Rewriting the Rules in Asia*, edited by M. Ramesh and Michael Howlett (Cheltenham, UK: Edward Elgar, 2006), 116.

10. "Perjanjian Jual-Beli Tenaga Listrik: Investasi PLTU Paiton Swasta I Terbesar di Dunia di Bidang Tenaga Listrik Swasta," *Berita PLN*, February 1994, 15.

11. Wu and Sulistiyanto, "Independent Power Producer (IPP) Debacle," 109–10.

12. Jay Solomon, "Jakarta and Paiton Reach Interim Payment Accord," *Wall Street Journal*, March 9, 2000, https://www.wsj.com/articles/SB952543856375466688.

13. "Tercapainya Kesepakatan Paiton dan PLN," *Fokus*, January 2002, 17.

14. Fourteen contracts turned into long-term agreements (with renegotiated new prices and conditions), five contracts agreed their projects would be acquired by the Indonesian government, and seven contracts agreed to be closed out. PLN documented the restructuring of the contracts in a brief publication titled *Restrukturisasi 26 Proyek Listrik Swasta* (Jakarta: PT PLN [Persero], 2003).

15. Before the financial crisis, US$1 was about Rp 2,000. After the crisis, US$1 was about Rp 14,000.

16. Kuntoro Mangkusubroto, "Kebijakan Restrukturisasi Sektor Ketenagalistrikan," August 1998, Perpustakaan PLN Pusat Penelitian dan Pengembangan Ketenagalistrikan, 98/22320.

17. Mangkusubroto, "Kebijakan Restrukturisasi," 4, 10.

18. Mangkusubroto, "Kebijakan Restrukturisasi," 10.

19. Batara Lumbanradja, "Tanggapan Terhadap Kebijakan Restrukturisasi Sektor Ketenagalistrikan dan Usulan Kebijakan Reformasi Sebagai Alternatif" (unpublished manuscript, November 1998).

20. Lumbanradja, "Tanggapan Terhadap Kebijakan Restrukturisasi," I-8.

21. Lumbanradja, "Tanggapan Terhadap Kebijakan Restrukturisasi," I-8, original emphasis.

22. "'Byar Pet' Akhirnya Mampet," *Fokus*, August 2010, 7–8.

23. Ibrahim and Faizal, *General Check-Up*, 49.

24. Puspasari Setyaningrum, "PLTS Likupang, Pemanen Energi Matahari Terbesar di Indonesia," *Kompas*, February 13, 2022, https://regional.kompas.com/read/2022/02/13

/185831678/plts-likupang-pemanen-energi-matahari-terbesar-di-indonesia; Reny Sri Ayu, "PLTB Sidrap Menyongsong Energi Hijau," *Kompas*, October 25, 2021, https://www.kompas.id/baca/nusantara/2021/10/25/pltb-sidrap-menyongsong-energi-hijau.

25. PLN, "Subholding dan Anak Perusahaan," https://web.pln.co.id/tentang-kami/anak-perusahaan (accessed on November 29, 2020).

26. *PLN Company Profile*. Jakarta: PLN, 2016.

27. Yayasan Lembaga Konsumen Indonesia and Koalisi Masyarakat Sipil Untuk Perbaikan Pelayanan Listrik, *Masalah Ketenagalistrikan di Indonesia (Kumpulan Artikel)* (Jakarta: Sentralisme Production, 2004).

28. Eduardus Dosi, "Konstruksi Realitas Berita Kampanye Pilpres 2014 di Koran Pos Kupang dan Timor Espres," *Prosiding Konferensi Nasional Komunikasi* 2, no. 1 (2018): 221.

29. Monica Wareza and Samuel Pablo, "Janji 100 Hari Pertama Prabowo: Tarif Listrik Turun!," *CNBC Indonesia*, April 7, 2019, https://www.cnbcindonesia.com/news/20190407090541-4-65057/janji-100-hari-pertama-prabowo-tarif-listrik-turun.

30. Melissa Brown, *Perusahaan Listrik Negara (PLN): A Power Company Out of Step with Global Trends* (Lakewood, OH: Institute for Energy Economics and Financial Analysis, 2018).

31. *The Economist*, "Indonesia's Leader, Jokowi, Is Splurging on Infrastructure," *The Economist*, May 5, 2018, 51, https://www.economist.com/asia/2018/05/05/indonesias-leader-jokowi-is-splurging-on-infrastructure.

32. Palce Amalo, "Terang Benderang hingga ke Batas Negeri," *Media Indonesia*, September 14, 2019, https://mediaindonesia.com/read/detail/259406-terang-benderang-hingga-ke-batas-negeri.

33. Mohsin, "National Electricity Day."

Bibliography

Archives

Arsip Nasional Republik Indonesia (ANRI), Jakarta, Indonesia
  Naskah Sumber Arsip Jejak Demokrasi 1955 (2019).
  Naskah pidato pada upacara pembukaan penataran calon penatar tingkat Nasional/
  Manggala BP-7 di Istana Bogor. Pidato Presiden Soeharto 1031,4, Inventaris Arsip
  Sekretariat Negara: Seri Pidato Presiden Soeharto 1966–1998 Jilid 2 (No. 761-1389).
  Speech by President Sukarno on the 15th Anniversary of Electricity Day, Kebajoran
  Baru, 27 October 1960. Pidato Presiden Sukarno no. 227.
Nationaal Archief Ministerie van Onderwijss, Cultuur en Weternschap
  Inventaris van het archief van de NV Handelsvennootschap voorheen Maintz & Co.
  te Amsterdam, 1874–1970.
USAID Development Experience Clearinghouse
  Rural Electrification Preliminary Engineering and Feasibility Study Report North
  Central Klaten, Central Java, Indonesia. August 1977. PNAAF716.
  NRECA Final Report Rural Electrification Projects Department of Cooperatives
  Contract AID/ASIA-C-1357 AID LOAN No. 497-T-052. December 1984. PDCAM
  984.
  RE Projects NRECA Team Report PDO Indonesia. March 1981. PDAAJ540.
  RE Projects NRECA Team Report PDO Indonesia. April 1981. PDAAI356.
  RE Projects NRECA Team Report PDO Indonesia. May 1981. PDAAI354.
  RE Projects NRECA Team Report PDO Indonesia. July 1981. PDAAI018.
  RE Projects NRECA Team Report PDO Indonesia. August 1981. PDAAJ538.
  RE Projects NRECA Team Report PDO Indonesia. September 1981. PDAAL557.
  RE Projects NRECA Team Report PDO Indonesia. April and May 1982. PDAAL369.
  RE Projects NRECA Team Report PDO Indonesia. June and July 1982. PDAAL762.
  RE Projects NRECA Team Report PDO Indonesia. August and September 1982.
  PDAAL743.
  RE Projects NRECA Team Report PDO Indonesia, October–December 1982.
  PDAAM366.
  RE Projects NRECA Team Report PDO Indonesia. May–December 1983. PDAAP140.

Rural Electrification for Indonesia; Report of the NRECA Study Team. May 1976. PNAAK593.

Department of Cooperatives Final Report: Contract AID/ASIA-C-1357, AID Loan No. 497-T-052 Rural Electrification. December 1984. PDAAQ724.

Report No. 47: Rural Electrification Project—Indonesia, USAID, Loan No. 497-T-052 Project Report for Second Quarter. 1984. PDAAQ217.

Energy Planning for Development in Indonesia. August 1981. PNAAN338.

Project Assistance Completion Report: AID Project No. 497-0267, AID Loan and Grant No. 497-T-052, AID Project Title: Rural Electrification. 1987. PDAAV785.

Rural Electrification I. June 25, 1980. PDAAF891A1.

Project Paper, Proposal and Recommendations For the Review of the Development Loan Committee, Indonesia-Rural Electrification I, AID-DLC/P-2244. August 1977. PDAAD914B1.

Rural Electrification I First Annual Review, USAID Loan 497-T-052, USAID Grant 497-0267. June 1979. PDAAK311B1.

Perpustakaan PLN Pusat Penelitian dan Pengembangan Ketenagalistrikan (PLN Center for Electric Power Research and Development Library)

Laporan Kronologis Listrik Pedesaan. Lokakarya Kelistrikan Desa, Medan 1978. 78-10113.

Laporan Lokakarya Listrik Pedesaan ke IV tanggal 28 Juli s/d 3 Agustus 1978 Di PLN Wilayah II, Medan, Sumut. 05-26208.

Laporan Session on Rural Electrification Feasibility Study Training III, 23 s/d 28 Januari 1978 PLN-Wilayah VII, Menado, Sulawesi Utara. 78-10486.

Mangkusubroto, Kuntoro. "Kebijakan Restrukturisasi Sektor Ketenagalistrikan." August 1998. 98/22320.

Pedoman dan Petunjuk Pemeliharaan PLTD. 1994. 09-30900.

Interviews

Mustari, Aco, and Muhammad Hairul. July 26, 2018. Palopo, Luwu.

Djiteng Marsudi. February 17, 2012. Jakarta.

Goenawan Mohamad. July 16, 2012. Denpasar, Bali.

Andi Muhammad Nur. July 27, 2018. Lagego village, East Luwu.

Umar Muktamar. July 27, 2018. Lagego village, East Luwu.

Abdul Muttalib. July 21, 2018. Aikmel, East Lombok.

Mahesa Praba (pseudonym). May 25, 2012. Denpasar, Bali.

Judan Putrabawa. July 18, 2018. Aikmel, East Lombok.

Tahir Royaldi. July 21, 2018. Aikmel, East Lombok.

Sapardi. July 18, 2018. East Lombok.

Komang Sujati (pseudonym). April 2, 2012. Denpasar, Bali.

Primary and Secondary Sources

10 Tahun Penelitian, Pengembangan dan Jasa Teknik Sektor Tenaga Listrik 1965–1975. Jakarta: PLN LMK, 1975.

"188 Desa Lagi Berhasil Dilistriki PLN Di Jawa Timur." *Berita PLN*, March 1986.

"3.033 Tiang Instalasi Listrik Rusak." *Fajar*, June 15, 1996.

"30,83% Penduduk Jatim Sudah Menikmati Listrik." *Berita PLN*, February 1987.

"37 Persen Desa Di Bali Sudah Menikmati Listrik." *Bali Post*, March 23, 1982.

"440.000 ton batubara Australia untuk PLTU Suralaya." *Berita PLN*, March 1985.

"49 Anak Yatim Terima Bantuan Biaya Pendidikan." *Media Elektrika*, July 2015.

"500 Rumah di Metro Kini Gelap Gulita." *Lampung Post*, January 3, 2011.

Abraham, Itty. *The Making of the Indian Atomic Bomb: Science, Secrecy and the Postcolonial State*. New York: Zed Books, 1998.

Adas, Michael. *Dominance by Design: Technological Imperatives and America's Civilizing Mission*. Cambridge, MA: Belknap Press of Harvard University Press, 1998.

Aditjondro, George. "Large Dam Victims and Their Defenders." In *The Politics of Environment in Southeast Asia*, edited by Philip Hirsch and Carol Warren, 44–69. New York: Routledge, 1998.

"Akhir Juni Pasokan Listrik Lampung Bertambah." *Lampung Post*, June 20, 2011.

"Akhirnya Eks KLP-SR Dibubarkan." *Lombok Post*, July 1, 2010.

"Alih Listrik KLP SSM Belum Bisa." *Lampung Post*, January 28, 2011.

Allen, G. C., and Audrey G. Donnithorne. *Western Enterprise in Indonesia and Malaya: A Study in Economic Development*. Norwich: Jarrold and Sons, 1957.

Amalo, Palce. "Terang Benderang hingga ke Batas Negeri." *Media Indonesia*, September 14, 2019. https://mediaindonesia.com/read/detail/259406-terang-benderang-hingga-ke-batas-negeri.

Amarullah, Munawar. "Listrik Masuk Desa." *Prisma* 12 (1986): 73–85.

Amarullah, Munawar. "Pengembangan Wilayah dan Manpower Planning Pelistrikan Desa." *Berita PLN*, March 1978.

Amir, Sulfikar. "The State and the Reactor: Nuclear Politics in Post-Suharto Indonesia." *Indonesia* 89 (April 2010): 101–47.

Amir, Sulfikar. *The Technological State in Indonesia: The Co-Constitution of High Technology and Authoritarian Politics*. London: Routledge, 2012.

Anderson, Benedict. *Imagined Communities Reflections on the Origin and Spread of Nationalism*, rev. ed. New York: Verso, 2006.

Anderson, Benedict R. O'G. *Language and Power Exploring Political Culture in Indonesia*. Jakarta: Equinox Publishing, 2006.

Anderson, Benedict R. O'G. "Old State, New Society: Indonesia's New Order in Comparative Historical Perspective." *Journal of Asian Studies* 42, no. 3 (1983): 477–96.

Anderson, Benedict, and Ruth McVey. *A Preliminary Analysis of the October 1, 1965 Coup in Indonesia*. Ithaca, NY: Cornell University Southeast Asia Program, 1971.

Anderson, Warwick. "Re-Orienting STS: Emergent Studies of Science, Technology, and Medicine in Southeast Asia." *East Asian Science, Technology and Society: An International Journal* 3, nos. 2–3 (2009): 163–71.

Andita, Rury Anjas. "Catatan Lombok Timur Sepanjang 2011 (2) Masyarakat Eks KLPSR Tersenyum, Listrik Kembali Normal." *Lombok Post*, December 27, 2011.

Antlöv, Hans. *Exemplary Centre, Administrative Periphery: Rural Leadership and the New Order in Java*. Richmond, UK: Curzon Press, 1995.

Antlöv, Hans. "Village Government and Rural Development in Indonesia: The New Democratic Framework." *Bulletin of Indonesian Economic Studies* 39, no. 2 (2003): 193–214.

Arifin, Bustanil. "Ceramah Menteri Muda Urusan Koperasi, SH Dalam Lokakarya Dan Latihan Proyek Energy Planning for Development Pada tgl. 2 September 1980 di Jakarta." In Direktorat Jenderal Ketenagaan Departemen Pertambangan dan Energi, *Hasil Lokakarya Survai Energi Pedesaan Diselenggarkan di Jakarta Pada Tanggal 1 s/d 11 September 1980 dan 3 s/d Februari 1981*, 41–45. Jakarta: PT Surya Jaya Utama, 1982.

Arismunandar, Artono. "Energi dan Tenaga Listrik Tegangan Tinggi Sebagai Sarana Peningkatan dan Pemerataan Kesejahteraan Rakyat." *Berita PLN*, January 1978.

Arismunandar, Artono. "Krisis Enersi, Masalah Enersi Dan Kebijaksanaan Enersi Nasional." In Komite Nasional Indonesia World Energy Conference, *Hasil-Hasil Seminar Energi Nasional Jakarta 24–27 Juli 1974*, 289–313. Jakarta: PT Yudha Gama, 1974.

Arismunandar, Artono. "Overview of Electric Power Development in Indonesia." *Energi & Listrik* 6, no. 2 (June 1996): 1–8.

Arismunandar, Artono, and Sufrani Atmakusuma. *Laporan Mengikuti International Seminar on Energy Policy and Energy Economy Berlin 9 Oct–2 Nov 1968*. Jakarta: Direktorat Djenderal Tenaga dan Listrik, 1968.

Arka, Made. *Pengaruh Listrik Pedesaan Terhadap Kegiatan Ekonomi dan Sosial Masyarakat Di Bali*. Denpasar: Fakulas Ekonomi Universitas Udayana, 1982.

Atje, Raymond. "Peranan kayu bakar dalam pemerataan." In Komite Nasional Indonesia World Energy Conference, *Hasil-Hasil Seminar Energi Nasional II, Jakarta, 9–12 Juni 1981*, 147–64. Jakarta: Percetakan Rakan Offset, 1981

Ayu, Reny Sri. "PLTB Sidrap Menyongsong Energi Hijau." *Kompas*, October 25, 2021. https://www.kompas.id/baca/nusantara/2021/10/25/pltb-sidrap-menyongsong-energi -hijau.

Bahan Penataran Pedoman Penghayatan dan Pengamalan Pancasila, Undang-Undang Dasar 1945, Garis-Garis Besar Haluan Negara. Edisi Kedua. Jakarta: Team Pembinaan Penatar dan Bahan Penataran Pegawai Republik Indonesia, 1981.

"Bantuan Pompanisasi PLN Untuk Kelompok Tani Kabupaten Bajo." *Berita PLN*, January–February 1998.

Barker, Joshua. "Engineers and Political Dreams: Indonesia in the Satellite Age." *Current Anthropology* 46, no. 5 (2005): 703–27.

Barker, Joshua. "State of Fear: Controlling the Criminal Contagion in Soeharto's New Order." *Indonesia* 66 (October 1998): 6–43.

"Belum Ada Keputusan Tentang Rencana Pembangunan PLTN." *Surabaya Post*, May 14, 1986.

"Bernostalgia dengan Pelayanan KLP SSM." *Lampung Post*, September 2013.

Bijker, Wiebe, and John Law, eds. *Shaping Technology/Building Society*. Cambridge, MA: MIT Press, 1994.

Birowo, Achmad T. *BIMAS: A Package Program for Intensification of Food Crop Production in Indonesia*. New York: Asia Society, SEADAG, 1975.

Brodman, Janice Donna. "Technology Change, Equity, and Growth: A Case Study of Rural Electrification in Java." PhD diss., Harvard University, 1983.

Brown, Melissa. *Perusahaan Listrik Negara (PLN): A Power Company Out of Step with Global Trends*. Lakewood, OH: Institute for Energy Economics and Financial Analysis 2018.

Brown, Shannon R. "The Ewo Filature: A Study in the Transfer of Technology to China in the 19th Century." *Technology and Culture* 20, no. 3 (1979): 550–68.

"Byar Pet' Akhirnya Mampet." *Fokus*, August 2010.

"Cara Menentukan Tahap Perkembangan Desa (Desa Swadaya, Desa Swakarya, Desa Swasembada), Diperbanyak oleh Badan Penelitian dan Pengembangan Pendidikan dan Kebudayaan Departemen Pendidikan dan Kebudayaan (unpublished manuscript, 1975). Leiden University Library, KITLV3 M m 13431978 mf.

Carney, Judith. "Landscapes of Technology Transfer: Rice Cultivation and African Continuities." *Technology and Culture* 37, no. 1 (1996): 5–35.

Choi, Hyungsub. "The Social Construction of Imported Technologies: Reflections on the Social History of Technology in Modern Korea." *Technology and Culture* 58, no 4. (2017): 905–20.

Clancey, Gregory. "Dangerous, Disruptive, or Irrelevant? History (of Technology) as an Acquired Taste in Asia." *East Asian Science, Technology and Society: An International Journal* 6, no. 2 (2012): 243–47.

Coleman, Leo. *A Moral Technology Electrification as Political Ritual in New Delhi.* Ithaca, NY: Cornell University Press, 2017.

Coopersmith, Jonathan. *The Electrification of Russia, 1880–1926.* Ithaca, NY: Cornell University Press, 1992.

Crouch, Harold. "Patrimonialism and Military Rule in Indonesia." *World Politics* 31, no. 4 (1979): 571–87.

Dakung, Sugiarto, Hilderia Sitanggang, Fadjiria Novari Manan, Wahyuningsih, Raf Darnys, and Harry Waluyo. *Dampak Listrik Masuk Desa Di Desa Cisande, Kecamatan Cibadak Kabupaten Sukabumi.* Jakarta: Departemen Pendidikan Dan Kebudayaan Direktorat Jenderal Kebudayaan Direktorat Sejarah Dan Nilai Tradisional Proyek Inventarisasi Dan Pembinaan Nilai-Nilai Budaya, 1990.

"Dari Bukit Asam untuk Suralaya." *Teknologi*, November 1986.

Darmaputera, Eka. *Pancasila Identitas Dan Modernitas Tinjauan Etis Dan Budaya.* Jakarta: BPK Gunung Mulia, 1987.

Darmono, Djoko et al. *Mineral Dan Energi Kekayaan Bangsa Sejarah Pertambangan dan Energi Indonesia.* Jakarta: Departemen Energi dan Sumber Daya Mineral, 2009.

Denton, Frank H. *Lighting Up the Countryside: The Story of Electric Cooperatives in the Philippines.* Manila: Academy Press, 1979.

Departemen Pekerdjaan Umum. *Pembinaan Projek/Masalah Prasarana Nota Pendjelasan Projek Tenaga Listrik 1968 (Diperbaharui).* Djakarta: Studio, 1968.

Departemen Pertambangan dan Energi Republik Indonesia. *Konservasi Energi (Hasil-Hasil Lokakarya Konservasi Energi 24–25 September 1979, Jakarta).* Jakarta: Spirit International, 1980.

Dibia, Made. "Harapan Di Tahun 2000: Semua Desa Berswasembada." *Bali Post Edisi Pedesaan*, September 16, 1981.

Dick, H. W. *Surabaya, City of Work: A Socioeconomic History 1900–2000.* Athens: Ohio University Press, 2002.

Direktorat Djenderal Tenaga dan Listrik. *Kebidjaksanaan Nasional Dibidang Ketenagaan.* Djakarta: Departemen Pekerdjaan Umum dan Tenaga Listrik Direktorat Djenderal Tenaga dan Listrik, 1969.

Direktorat Jenderal Ketenagaan Departemen Pertambangan dan Energi. *Hasil Loka-karya Pengembangan Energi Non Konvensional Jakarta 28–29 Januari 1980.* Jakarta: Departemen Pertambangan dan Energi Republik Indonesia, 1980.

Direktorat Jenderal Ketenagaan Departemen Pertambangan dan Energi. *Hasil Loka-karya Survai Energi Pedesaan Diselenggarkan di Jakarta Pada Tanggal 1 s/d 11 September 1980 dan 3 s/d Februari 1981.* Jakarta: PT Surya Jaya Utama, 1982.

Direktorat Djenderal Tenaga and Listrik. *Hasil-Hasil Workshop Kelistrikan Desa 12 S/D 14 Maret.* Jakarta: Direktorat Djenderal Tenaga dan Listrik, 1970.

"Dirut Melantik Pejabat Teras PLN PPE." *Berita PLN,* April 1988.

"Ditandatangani Naskah Kesepakatan Bersama Tentang: Perubahan Pola Pengelolaan Kelistrikan Eks KPL [*sic*] Samabotuna Sulawesi Selatan." *Berita PLN,* July 1996.

Division of Commerce of the Deparment of Agriculture, Industry, and Commerce. *1930 Handbook of the Netherlands East-Indies.* Batavia: G. Kolff, 1930.

Division of Commerce of the Department of Agriculture, Industry, and Commerce. *Handbook of the Netherlands East-Indies Edition 1924.* Buitenzorg, Java: G. Kolff, 1924.

Djojohadikusumo, Sumitro. "Pola Pengembangan enersi—tinjauan jangka Panjang." In Komite Nasional Indonesia World Energy Conference, *Hasil-Hasil Seminar Energi Nasional, Jakarta 24–27 Juli,* 37–53. Jakarta: PT Yudha Gama, 1974.

Dosi, Eduardus. "Konstruksi Realitas Berita Kampanye Pilpres 2014 di Koran Pos Kupang dan Timor Espres." *Prosiding Konferensi Nasional Komunikasi* 2, no. 1 (2018): 218–28.

"Dua Anak Perusahaan PT PLN (Persero) Terbentuk." *Berita PLN,* October 1995.

Edgerton, David. *The Shock of the Old: Technology and Global History since 1900.* New York: Oxford University Press, 2007.

Edwards, Paul N. "Infrastructure and Modernity: Force, Time, and Social Organization in the History of Sociotechnical Systems." In *Modernity and Technology,* edited by Thomas J. Misa, Philip Brey, and Andrew Feenberg, 185–225. Cambrige, MA: MIT Press, 2003.

Emmerson, Donald K. "The Bureaucracy in Political Context: Weakness in Strength." In *Political Power and Communications in Indonesia,* edited by Karl D. Jackson and Lucian W. Pye, 82–136. Berkeley: University of California Press, 1978.

Emmerson, Donald K. "Understanding the New Order: Bureaucratic Pluralism in Indonesia." *Asian Survey* 23, no. 11 (1983): 1220–41.

Escobar, Arturo. *Encountering Development: The Making and Unmaking of Third World.* Princeton, NJ: Princeton University Press, 1995.

Ferguson, James. *The Anti-Politics Machine Development, Depoliticization, and Bureaucratic Power in Lesotho.* Minneapolis: University of Minnesota Press, 1994.

Fitzgerald, Deborah. "Exporting American Agriculture: The Rockefeller Foundation in Mexico, 1943–53." *Social Studies of Science* 16, no. 3 (1986): 457–83.

Gaffar, Afan. *Javanese Voters: A Case Study of Election under a Hegemonic Party System.* Yogyakarta: Gadjah Mada University Press, 1992.

Geertz, Clifford. *The Religion of Java.* Chicago: University of Chicago Press, 1976.

Gore, Christopher D. *Electricity in Africa The Politics of Transformation in Uganda.* Melton, UK: James Currey, 2017.

Guiness, Patrik. "Local Society and Culture." In *Indonesia's New Order: The Dynamics of Socio-Economic Transformation,* edited by Hal Hill, 272–76. Honolulu: University of Hawaii Press, 1994.

Gunn, Geoffrey C. "Ideology and the Concept of Government in the Indonesian New Order." *Asian Survey* 19, no. 8 (1979): 751–69.

Hadiz, Vedi R. *Workers and the State in New Order Indonesia.* London: Routledge, 1997.

Hadiz, Vedi, and Daniel Dhakidae, eds. *Social Science and Power in Indonesia.* Jakarta: Equinox Publishing (Asia), 2005.

Harahap, Tahir. *Perlistrikan Desa.* Jakarta: Perusahaan Umum Listrik Negara, Pusat Penyelidikan Masalah Kelistrikan, 1977.

Haroen. "Listrik Pedesaan dan Permasalahannya." Unpublished manuscript, 1990.

Haroen. "Usaha Kearah Melistriki Desa di Bali Dengan Pola III." Unpublished manuscript, February 13, 1986.

Haryono, Piet. "Peranan Minyak Dalam Pembangunan Nasional." In Komite Nasional Indonesia World Energy Conference, *Penyediaan Energi Untuk Daerah Pedesaan (Hasil-Hasil Lokakarya Energi, 25–26 Mei 1978, Jakarta),* 17–23. Jakarta: Percetakan Pertamina, 1978.

"Hasil Kelompok Seminar Listrik Pedesaan III." In Laporan Session on Rural Electrification Feasibility Study Training III, 23 s/d 28 Januari 1978 PLN-Wilayah VII, Menado, Sulawesi Utara, Perpustakaan PLN Pusat Penelitian dan Pengembangan Ketenagalistrikan, 78-10486.

Hatta, Mohammad. *Memoir.* Jakarta: Tintamas Indonesia, 1979.

Hecht, Gabrielle. "Introduction." In *Entangled Geographies Empire and Technopolitics in the Global Cold War,* edited by Gabriel Hecht, 1–12. Cambridge, MA: MIT Press.

Hecht, Gabrielle. *The Radiance of France: Nuclear Power and National Identity after World War II.* Cambridge, MA: MIT Press, 1998.

Heryanto, Ariel. *Language of Development and Development of Language: The Case of Indonesia.* Canberra: Research School of Pacific and Asian Studies, Australian National University, 1995.

Hoey, Brian A. "Nationalism in Indonesia: Building Imagined and Intentional Communities through Transmigration." *Ethnology* 42, no. 2 (2003): 109–26.

Hughes, Thomas P. "Technological Momentum." In *Does Technology Drive History? The Dilemma of Technological Determinism,* edited by Leo Marx and Merritt Roe Smith, 101–113. Cambridge, MA: MIT Press, 1998.

Hughes, Thomas P. *Networks of Power: Electrification in Western Society, 1880–1930.* Baltimore, MD: Johns Hopkins University Press, 1983.

Husin, Imron. "Rural Electrification in Indonesia Policy Implementation in Theory and Practice." PhD diss., Australian National University, 1989.

Ibrahim, Ali Herman, and Akbar Faizal. *General Check-Up Kelistrikan Nasional.* Jakarta: Mediaplus Network, 2008.

"In Memoriam Saudara Soepolo Wiradi." *Berita PLN,* November 1977.

Itagaki, Yoichi. "Criticism of Rostow's Stage Approach: The Concepts of Stage, System and Type." *The Developing Economies* 1, no. 1 (March 1963): 1–17.

"IUKU KLP Dicabut Warga Tunggu PLN." *Lampung Post,* March 31, 2011.

Jackson, Karl D. "Bureaucratic Polity: A Theoretical Framework for the Analysis of Power and Communications in Indonesia." In *Political Power and Communications in Indonesia,* edited by Karl D. Jackson and Lucian W. Pye, 3–22. Berkeley: University of California Press, 1978.

Jasanoff, Sheila. "Future Imperfect: Science, Technology, and the Imaginations of Modernity." In *Dreamscapes of Modernity Sociotechnical Imaginaries and the Fabrication of Power*, edited by Sheila Jasanoff and Sang-Hyung Kim, 1–33. Cambridge, MA: MIT Press, 2015.

Jasanoff, Sheila, ed. *States of Knowledge The Co-production of Science and Social Order.* London and New York: Routledge, 2004.

Jasanoff, Sheila. "Technology as a Site and Object of Politics." In *The Oxford Handbook of Contextual Political Analysis*, edited by Robert E. Goodin and Charles Tilly, 745–63. Oxford: Oxford University Press, 2006.

"Kabel Laut." *Berita PLN*, June 1987.

"Kabupaten Lahat Mendapat Listrik." *Berita PLN*, April 1987.

Kadir, Abdul. "Pola Pengembangan Energi di Indonesia Serta Peranan Tenaga Listrik Dalam Pola Tersebut." In Komite Nasional Indonesia World Energy Conference, *Hasil-Hasil Seminar Energi Nasional Jakarta 24–27 Juli 1974*, 109–22. Jakarta: PT Yudha Gama Corporation, 1974.

Kale, Sunila. *Electrifying India: Regional Political Economies of Development.* Stanford, CA: Stanford University Press, 2014.

"Kebanggaan Nasional Untuk Memperkokoh Persatuan." *Insinjur Indonesia*, August 1962, 1.

Kementerian Pertahanan Republik Indonesia. "45 butir Pedoman Penghayatan dan Pengamalan Pancasila." *Kemenhan*, November 20, 2014. https://www.kemhan.go.id /renhan/2014/11/20/45-butir-pedoman-penghayatan-dan-pengamalan-pancasila.html.

Keputusan Gubernur Lampung Nomor: G/195/B.IV/HK/2009 Tentang Pembentukan Tim Bersama Pengalihan Pelanggan Koperasi Listrik Pedesaan Sinar Siwo Mego (KLP-SSM) Kepada PT PLN (Persero) Tingkat Provinsi Lampung.

"Kerjasama PLN-BATAN." *Berita PLN*, Special Edition, 1990.

"Kertsdemonstratie." *Alles Electrisch in het Indische Huis en Bedrijf*, February 1937.

Ketetapan Majelis Permusyawaratan Rakyat Republik Indonesia Nomor IV/MPR/1978 Tentang Garis-Garis Besar Haluan Negara.

"Ketika KLP-SR Menghadapi Persoalan Pengelolaan Pasca Amuk Massa (2-Habis)." *Lombok Post*, March 10, 2006.

Kitley, Philip. *Television, Nation, and Culture in Indonesia.* Athens: Ohio University Center for International Studies, 2000.

Kline, Ronald R. *Consumers in the Country Technology and Social Change in Rural America.* Baltimore, MD: Johns Hopkins University Press, 2000.

Kline, Ronald R. "Resisting Development, Reinventing Modernity: Rural Electrification in the United States before World War II." *Environmental Values* 11 (2002): 327–44.

Kline, Ronald, and Trevor Pinch. "Users as Agents of Technological Change: The Social Construction of the Automobile in the Rural United States." *Technology and Culture* 37 no. 4 (1996): 763–95.

"KLP Sinar Siwo Mego Menolak Pailit." *Lombok Post*, March 10, 2010.

"KLP SR Dihancurkan Ribuan Massa." *Lombok Post*, January 12, 2006.

Komite Nasional Indonesia World Energy Conference. *Hasil-Hasil Seminar Energi Nasional 24–27 Juli 1974.* Jakarta: PT Yudha Gama, 1974.

Komite Nasional Indonesia World Energy Conference. *Hasil-Hasil Seminar Energi Nasional II, Jakarta, 9–12 Juni 1981.* Jakarta: Percetakan Rakan Offset, 1981.

Komite Nasional Indonesia World Energy Conference. *Hasil-Hasil Seminar Energi Nasional III Jakarta, 21–24 Juli 1987.* Jakarta: PT Melton Putra, 1988.

Komite Nasional Indonesia World Energy Conference. *Penyediaan Energi Untuk Daerah Pedesaan (Hasil-Hasil Lokakarya Energi, 25–26 Mei 1978, Jakarta).* Jakarta: Percetakan Pertamina, 1978.

Komite Nasional Indonesia World Energy Conference. *Perkiraan Kebutuhan Energi Indonesia 1975–2000 (Hasil-Hasil Lokakarya Energi, 12–13 Mei 1977, Jakarta).* Jakarta: Spirit International, 1977.

Komite Nasional Indonesia World Energy Conference. *Sumber-Sumber Energi Pengganti Minyak (Hasil-Hasil Lokakarya Energi, 24–25 April 1979, Jakarta).* Jakarta: Rakan Offset, 1979.

"Konflik PLN-Koperasi di Lampung Belum Tuntas." *Liputan6.com*, January 29, 2001.

Kontra, Ketut. "Langkah Kebijaksanaan Dalam Pengelolaan Sektor Tenaga Listrik dan Tantangan Yang Perlu Dihadapi." *Berita PLN*, 1983.

"Kopkar 'Gotong Royong' PLN Cabang Fakfak Raih Sertifikat Kopkar Mandiri." *Berita PLN*, December 1995.

Krige, John, and Jessica Wang. "Nation, Knowledge, and Imagined Futures: Science, Technology, and Nation-Building, Post-1945." *History and Technology* 31, no. 3 (2015): 171–79.

"Krisis Samabotuna Berakhir Desember 1996." *Fajar*, June 18, 1996.

"Kunjungan Kerja Dirut PLN ke Jatim, Kompleks PLTG/U Gresik Terbesar di Dunia." *Berita PLN*, December 1993.

"Kunjungan Kerja Komisi VI DPR-RI ke Proyek PLTU Suralaya." *Berita PLN*, January 1982.

"Kunjungan Kerja Menteri Pertambangan dan Energi." *Pertambangan dan* Energi, no. 3 (1987).

"Kunjungan Kerja Menteri Pertambangan dan Energi ke Jawa Tengah." *Berita PLN*, September–November 1982.

"Kunjungan Kerja Menteri Pertambangan dan Energi Ke Propinsi Nusa Tenggara Barat Pemerintah ORDE BARU tidak jemu jemu menyediakan Tenaga Listrik BAGI RAKYAT KITA." *Berita PLN*, January 1987.

"Kunjungan Kerja Menteri Pertambangan dan Energi Ke Propinsi Nusa Tenggara Timur 'Bagi Rakyat Yang Belum Mendapatkan Listrik Agar Bersabar.'" *Berita PLN*, February 1987.

Kusno, Abidin. *Behind the Postcolonial Architecture, Urban Space and Political Cultures in Indonesia.* London: Routledge, 2000.

"Lagi, Kabel Laut Terkena Jangkar Gelap di Madura." *Berita PLN*, February 1999.

"Landelijke electrificatie een nieuw distributiesysteem." *Alles Electrisch in het Indische Huis en Bedrijf*, April 1938.

"Laporan Khusus." *Fokus*, October 2000.

Larkin, Brian. "The Politics and Poetics of Infrastructure." *Annual Review of Anthropology* 42 (2013): 327–43.

Lessmeister, Irene V. "Between Colonialism and Cold War: The Indonesian War of Independence in World Politics, 1945–1949." PhD diss., Cornell University, 2012.

Liddle, R. William. "Indonesia in 1987: The New Order at the Height of its Power." *Asian Survey* 28, no. 2 (1988): 180–91.

Liddle, R. William. "Soeharto's Indonesia: Personal Rule and Political Institutions." *Pacific Affairs* 58, no. 1 (1985): 68–90.

Lim, Merlyna. "Dis/Connection: The Co-Evolution of Sociocultural and Material Infrastructures of the Internet in Indonesia." *Indonesia* 105 (2018): 155–72.

Lindsay, Christina. "From the Shadows: Users as Designers, Producers, Marketers, Distributors, and Technical Support." In *How Users Matter*, edited by Nelly Oudshoorn and Trevor Pinch, 29–50. Cambridge, MA: MIT Press, 2003.

"Listrik di Samabotuna Kini Ditangani PT PLN." *Fajar*, June 5, 1996.

"Listrik Masuk 25 Desa Di Sumbar." *Kompas*, March 27, 1982.

"Listrik Masuk Desa Di Jateng Dan Sulsel." *Kompas*, March 30, 1982.

"Listrik Masuk Desa Di Kabupaten Sleman Propinsi DIY Diresmikan Mensekneg Sudharmono, SH." *Berita PLN*, July 1986.

Lubis, Azwar et al., eds. *Meretas Jalan Menggapai Harapan Refleksi Pelayanan PT PLN (Persero) Distribusi Jakarta Raya dan Tangerang*. Jakarta: PT PLN (Persero), 2006.

Lumbanradja, Batara. "Tanggapan Terhadap Kebijakan Restrukturisasi Sektor Ketenagalistrikan dan Usulan Kebijakan Reformasi Sebagai Alternatif." Unpublished manuscript, November 1998.

Mackie, Jamie. "Patrimonialism: The New Order and Beyond." In *Soeharto's New Order and its Legacy*, edited by Edward Aspinall and Greg Fealy, 81–96. Canberra: ANU E Press, 2010.

Mackie, Jamie, and Andrew MacIntyre. "Politics." In *Indonesia's New Order: The Dynamics of Socio-Economic Transformation*, edited by Hal Hill, 1–53. Honolulu: University of Hawaii Press, 1994.

Machfud, M. "Beberapa Catatan Dari 'Session on Rural Electrification Feasibility Study Training' yang diadakan oleh PLN atas bantuan USAID/NRECA bertempat di PLN Wil. XIII Semarang tanggal 17 Okt 1977 s/d 22 Okt 1977." Unpublished manuscript, 1977.

Madjid, Nurcholish. *Indonesia Kita*. Jakarta: Gramedia Pustaka Utama, 2004.

Maier, H. M. J. "Maelstrom and Electricity: Modernity in the Indies." In *Outward Appearances Dressing State and Society in Indonesia*, edited by Henk Schulte Nordholt, 181–97. Leiden: KITLV Press, 1997.

Mangunrai, Hasan. *Evaluation of the Development of Transmigration in South Sulawesi: A Study on the Integration between the Transmigrants and Natives in the Transmigration Area of Luwu, South Sulawesi*. Singapore: Institute of Southeast Asian Studies, 1977.

"Mantan Dirut PLN Ir. Djiteng Marsudi: Kuntoro Minta Maaf Kepada Saya." *Tajuk*, no. 18 (October 26–November 8, 2000).

Margrit, Annisa. "Pemprov Bali Setuju Lanjutkan Proyek Jawa Bali Connection." *Bisnis.com*, June 26, 2019. https://ekonomi.bisnis.com/read/20190626/44/938028/pemprov-bali-setuju-lanjutkan-proyek-jawa-bali-connection.

Marsudi, Djiteng. "PLN Menghadapi Era Globalisasi." *Berita PLN*, February 1996.

"Masyarakat Walenrang Tebang Tiang Listrik." *Fajar*, May 25, 1996.

McBeth, John. "Bali Struggles to Keep the Lights Lit." *Asia Times*, April 26, 2018. https://asiatimes.com/2018/04/bali-struggles-to-keep-the-lights-lit/.

McCawley, Peter. "The Indonesian Electric Supply Industry." PhD diss., Australian National University, 1971.

McCawley, Peter. "Rural Electrification in Indonesia—Is It Time?" *Bulletin of Indonesian Economic Studies* 14, no. 2 (1978): 34–69.

Meilanova, Denis Riantiza. "Proyek Kabel Bawah Laut Sumatra-Jawa Masih Jadi Opsi." *Bisnis.com*, March 23, 2018. https://ekonomi.bisnis.com/read/20180323/44/753441/proyek-kabel-bawah-laut-sumatra-jawa-masih-jadi-opsi.

"Memasuki Era Pembangunan Batubara Secara Besar-Besaran Untuk Pembangkitan Tenaga Listrik." *Berita PLN*, February 1988.

"Mengeluh Soal Listrik ke Harmoko." *Fajar*, March 25, 1995.

"Mengharapkan Pelayanan PLN Lebih Baik." *Lampung Post*, May 29, 2011.

"Menilik KLP SSM Pascaperalihan ke PLN." *Lampung Post*, May 29, 2011.

"Mensegneg Sudharmono Serahkan DIP Dan Resmikan LMD Di Jawa Tengah." *Kompas*, March 31, 1982.

"Menteri Kehutanan Resmikan Listrik Masuk Desa di Kalimantan Timur." *Berita PLN*, November 1986.

"Menteri Pertambangan dan Energi Meresmikan Listrik Masuk Desa di Jawa Timur." *Berita PLN*, May 1987.

"Menteri Pertambangan Dan Energi Resmikan Kabel Laut Jawa-Bali." *Berita PLN*, August 1989, 3–8.

"Menteri Pertambangan dan Energi Subroto Meresmikan Listrik Masuk Desa & Kabel Laut Jawa-Madura di Jatim." *Berita PLN*, April 1987, 12–13, 20.

"Menteri Pertambangan dan Energi Subroto Resmikan PLTD Dan Listrik Desa di Tim-Tim." *Berita PLN*, February 1987.

"Menteri Pertambangan Dan Energi, 'Program LMD Bukan Dimaksudkan Untuk Penerangan Saja, Namun Yang Lebih Penting Lagi Untuk Mencerdaskan Masyarakat Banyak.'" *Berita PLN*, March 1982.

"Menteri Sekretaris Negara Sudharmono, SH Meresmikan Listrik Masuk Desa Di Kabupaten Lamongan—Jawa Timur." *Berita PLN*, August 1986.

"Menteri Sekretaris Negara Sudharmono, SH Meresmikan Listrik Pedesaan Di Desa Maribu, Jayapura." *Berita PLN*, September 1986.

"Menteri Sekretaris Negara Sudharmono, SH Resmikan Listrik Masuk Desa Di Jawa Tengah." *Berita PLN*, January 1986.

"Meski Ditahan, Mujahidin Tetap Jalankan Tugas Sekda." *Koran Tempo*, September 4, 2014. https://koran.tempo.co/read/makassar/350933/meski-ditahan-mujahidin-tetap-jalankan-tugas-sekda.

Miescher, Stephan F. *A Dam for Africa Akosombo Stories from Ghana*. Bloomington: Indiana University Press, 2022.

"Migrasi Eks KLP SR Libatkan Empat Pihak." *Lombok Post*, August 6, 2010.

Milne, David. "'Our Equivalent of Guerrilla Warfare': Walt Rostow and the Bombing of North Vietnam, 1961–1968." *Journal of Military History* 71, no. 1 (January 2007): 169–203.

Mitchell, Timothy. *Rule of Experts: Egypt, Techno-Politics, Modernity*. Berkeley: University of California Press, 2002.

Moenir, A. S. et al., eds. *40 Tahun Peranan Pertambangan Dan Energi Indonesia 1945–1985*. Jakarta: Departemen Pertambangan dan Energi, 1986.

Moertopo, Ali. *Some Basic Thoughts on the Acceleration and Modernization of 25 Years' Development.* Jakarta: Yayasan Proklamasi, Center For Strategic and International Studies, 1973.

Mohsin, Anto. "Lighting 'Paradise': A Sociopolitical History of Electrification in Bali." *East Asian Science, Technology and Society: An International Journal* 29, no. 1 (2017): 9–34.

Mohsin, Anto. "National Electricity Day: From 'Electricity-Minded' Nation to 'My Idea for PLN.'" *Technology's Stories,* December 4, 2017. https://www.technology stories.org/national-electricity-day/.

Mohsin, Anto. "Wiring the New Order: Indonesian Village Electrification and Patrimonial Technopolitics (1966–1998)." *Sojourn: Journal of Social Issues in Southeast Asia* 29, no. 1 (2014): 63–95.

Moon, Suzanne. "Justice, Geography, and Steel: Technology and National Identity in Indonesian Industrialization." *Osiris* 24 (2009): 253–77.

Moon, Suzanne. "Takeoff or Self-Sufficiency? Ideologies of Development in Indonesia, 1957–1961." *Technology and Culture* 39, no. 2 (1998), 187–212.

Morfit, Michael. "Pancasila: The Indonesian State Ideology According to the New Order Government." *Asian Survey* 21, no. 8 (1981): 838–51.

Mrázek, Rudolf. *Engineers of Happy Land Technology and Nationalism in a Colony.* Princeton, NJ: Princeton University Press, 2002.

Mulyani, Basri. "Suara Lonjong Listrik dari Lombok Timur." *Lombok Post,* February 23, 2006.

Mursito, Sunarto Ndaru. "Gambaran Umum Tentang Pembangunan Pedesaan di Indonesia." In *Analisa 1981–3 Pembangunan Pedesaan,* 205–19. Jakarta: Biro Publikasi CSIS, 1981.

Mustofa, Ali. "Jawa Bali Crossing Batal, PLN Pakai Kabel Laut, Ternyata Karena . . ." *Radar Bali,* October 25, 2018. https://radarbali.jawapos.com/ekonomi/25/10/2018 /jawa-bali-crossing-batal-pln-pakai-kabel-laut-ternyata-karena.

Nederlandsch-Indische Gas-Maatschappij. *Gedenkboek Nederlandsch-Indische Gas-Maatschappij, 1863–1913.* Rotterdam: M. Wyt & Zonen, 1913.

Nitisastro, Widjojo. *Pengalaman Pembangunan Indonesia Kumpulan Tulisan dan Uraian Widjojo Nitisastro.* Jakarta: Penerbit Kompas, 2010.

"Op Bezoek bij de Goodyear—Fabrieken." *Alles Electrisch in het Indische Huis en Bedrijf,* January 1937.

O'Rourke, Kevin. *Reformasi: The Struggle for Power in Post-Soeharto Indonesia.* Crows Nest NSW: Allen & Unwin, 2002.

"P4 Bagi Narapidana." *Kompas,* September 8, 1982.

"Pancasila dan UUD 1945 Juga Milik Narapidana." *Kompas,* October 22, 1982.

Pandjaitan, M. "Maksud dan Tujuan Survai Energi Pedesaan." In Direktorat Jenderal Ketenagaan Departemen Pertambangan dan Energi, *Hasil Lokakarya Survai Energi Pedesaan Diselenggarkan di Jakarta Pada Tanggal 1 s/d 11 September 1980 dan 3 s/d Februari 1981,* 75–80. Jakarta: PT Surya Jaya Utama, 1982.

"PBB Gandul Mengendalikan Listrik Se-Jawa." *Teknologi,* March 1987.

"Pedesaan Adalah Tulang Punggung Pembangunan." *Berita PLN,* May 1979.

"Pelanggan PLN Menangkan Lomba Mars & Hymne PLN." *Berita PLN,* October-November-December 1997.

"Pembangunan Kelistrikan Desa Sebagai Upaya Meningkatkan Taraf Hidup Masyar-akat Desa." *Berita PLN*, November 1985, 4.

"Pembangunan Kelistrikan oleh P.L.N. Dinas Perentjanaan dan Pembangunan." *Insin-jur Indonesia* (August 1960): 4–7.

"Pembukaan Kursus Pendidikan Dasar PLTU Angkatan Ke-V Dan Pendidikan Dasar PLTG Angkatan Ke-III di Udiklat Priuk." *Berita PLN*, March 1979.

"Pemda Lotim Tak Tertarik Kelola KLP." *Lombok Post*, November 9, 2005.

"Pemilihan Umum, 29 Mei 1997." *Listrik Indonesia*, May/June, 1997.

"Penataran P4 Angkatan XXI." *Berita PLN*, October 1985.

"Penataran P4 TYPE A Angkatan XXIX Di Lingkungan Departemen Pertambangan Dan Energi." *Berita PLN*, March 1982, 39.

"Pengalihan Listrik Tidak Terhambat." *Lampung Post*, June 11, 2011.

"Pengambilan Sumpah Jabatan Dan Pelantikan Dewan Pengawas PLN." *Berita PLN*, June 1986.

"Pengembangan PLTM oleh PLN." *Berita PLN*, February 1985, 3–5.

"Penutupan Kursus Pendidikan Dasar PLTU di Udiklat Tanjung Priok." *Berita PLN*, September 1978.

"Penyusunan Kwesioner dan Rencana Survai." In Direktorat Jenderal Ketenagaan Departemen Pertambangan dan Energi, *Hasil Lokakarya Survai Energi Pedesaan Diselenggarakan di Jakarta Pada Tanggal 1 s/d 11 September 1980 dan 3 s/d 5 Februari 1981*, 81–85. Jakarta: PT Surya Jaya Utama, 1982.

Penyusun, Tim. *Development Progress of Provinsi Daerah Istimewa Aceh 40 Tahun Derap Langkah Pembangunan 1959–1998/1999*. Banda, Aceh: Pemerintah Provinsi Daerah Istimewa Aceh, 1998.

"Peresmian Gedung Pelayanan PLN Wil. Kalbar: Partisipasi Swasta di Bidang Kelist-rikan Perlu Pengaturan." *Berita PLN*, May 1995.

"Peresmian Listrik Masuk Desa Di 4 Kabupaten Propinsi Sulawesi Selatan." *Berita PLN*, April 1986.

"Peresmian Listrik Masuk Desa Di Jawa Barat." *Berita PLN*, February 1986.

"Peresmian Listrik Masuk Desa: Listrik Masuk Desa Mendorong Perkembangan Indus-tri Kecil Di Pedesaan." *Berita PLN*, October-November-December 1991.

"Perjanjian Jual-Beli Tenaga Listrik, Investasi PLTU Paiton Swasta I Terbesar di Dunia di Bidang Tenaga Listrik Swasta." *Berita PLN*, February 1994.

"Perkembangan Kasus Madura." *Berita PLN*, April 1999.

Perrow, Charles. *Normal Accidents: Living with High-Risk Technologies*. New York: Basic Books, 1984.

Perusahaan Umum Listrik Negara "Pedoman dan Pentunjuk Penyusunan Feasibility Study Listrik Pedesaan." Unpublished manuscript, 1977.

Perusahaan Umum Listrik Negara. "Makalah: Listrik Pedesaan." Unpublished manu-script, December 1980.

Perusahaan Umum Listrik Negara. "Program Pelaksanaan Pembangunan REPELITA V Sistem Kelistrikan Jawa-Bali Dalam Rangka Peningkatan Pemasaran, Efisiensi, Mutu & Keadilan dan Pelayanan." Unpublished manuscript, 1989.

Perusahaan Umum Listrik Negara. "SPLN 74: 1987 Standar Listrik Pedessan." July 4, 1987, 10.

Pfaffenberger, Bryan. "The Harsh Facts of Hydraulics: Technology and Society in Sri Lanka's Colonization Schemes." *Technology and Culture* 31, no. 3 (1990): 361–97.

"Pidato Menteri Pertambangan & Energi pada Pembukaan Penataran Tingkat Pusat tipe A, Angkatan ke I PLN tgl. 16-3-79." *Berita PLN*, March 1979.

PLN. *Restrukturisasi 26 Proyek Listrik Swasta*. Jakarta: PT PLN (Persero), 2003.

"PLN Cabang Biak." *Berita PLN*, December 1994, 44.

"PLN Cabang Bima Daerah Ujung Timur Sumbawa Yang Perlu Pengembangan." *Berita PLN*, March 1995.

"PLN Cabang Tanjung Karang, Serahkan Bantuan Modal Kepada Pengusaha Kecil dan Koperasi." *Berita PLN*, December 1995.

PLN Company Profile. Jakarta: PLN Publication and Documentation Subdivision, 1996.

PLN Company Profile. Jakarta: PLN, 2016.

PLN Distribusi Jawa Barat. "Kertas Kerja: Kebijaksanaan Kelistrikan Desa Di Wilayah PLN Distribusi Jawa Barat." Unpublished manuscript, 1976.

PLN in 1975/76. Jakarta: Dinas Humas dan Protokol PLN Pusat, 1976.

PLN in 1976/77. Jakarta: Dinas Humas dan Protokol PLN Pusat, 1977.

PLN in 1979/80. Jakarta: Dinas Humas dan Protokol PLN Pusat, 1980.

"PLN Lampung Akan Putuskan Aliran 57 Ribu Pelanggan." *Tempo*, July 28, 2003. https://nasional.tempo.co/read/4886/pln-lampung-akan-putuskan-aliran-57-ribu -pelanggan.

"PLN Mengirimkan Teknisi-Teknisinya Untuk Mengikuti 'On the Job Training' ke Perancis." *Berita PLN*, May 1979.

PLN Statistics 1995. Jakarta: PT PLN (Persero), 1996.

"PLTA Bakaru Memiliki Terowongan Terpanjang di Indonesia." *Berita PLN*, July 1989.

"PLTM Swadaya Masyarakat Memegang Peranan Penting." *Berita PLN*, February 1985.

"Polisi Periksa Saksi Penjualan Genset KLP." *Lampung Post*, October 4, 2011.

Prayitno, "Listrik dan Pelayanannya." *Berita PLN*, July 1979,

"President Soeharto Resmikan PLTU Suralaya dan Sistem Transmisi Tegangan Ekstra Tinggi." *Berita PLN*, August 1985, 3–7, 29.

"Profil Achyar, Tehnisi tiga jaman." *Berita PLN*, November 1983.

Protschky, Susie. "The Empire Illuminated: Electricity, 'Ethical' Colonialism and Enlightened Monarchy in Photographs of Dutch Royal Celebrations, 1898–1948." *Journal of Colonialism and Colonial History* 13, no. 3 (2012). doi: 10.1353/cch.2012.0040.

"PT PLN Bersedia Akuisisi Sama Botuna." *Fajar*, May 31, 1996.

Purnomo, Bambang. *Tenaga Listrik Profil dan Anatomi Hasil Pembangunan Dua Puluh Lima Tahun*. Jakarta: Penerbit PT Gramedia Pustaka Utama, 1994.

Radja, Vincent T. "Apakah Yang Dimaksud Dengan PLTP Kamojang? Panas Bumi Sebagai Sumber Tenaga Listrik." *Berita PLN*, May 1977.

"Rapat Kerja Komisi VI DPR-RI Dengan Mentamben, PLTN Tetap Alternatif Terakhir." *Berita PLN*, January 1996.

"Rapinya Pengamanan PLTN Tidak Menutup Kemungkinan Kecelakaan." *Surabaya Post*, May 13, 1986.

"Rasa Hormat Yang Setinggi-Tingginya Atas Kesadaran Dan Kesediaan Penduduk Untuk Meninggalkan Daerah Ini Demi Pembangunan PLTA Cirata." *Berita PLN*, May 1986.

Revesteijn, Wim, and Marie-Louise ten Horn-van Nispen. "Engineering an Empire The Creation of Infrastructural Systems in the Netherlands East Indies 1800–1950." *Indonesia and the Malay World* 35, no. 103 (November 2007): 273–92.

Ricklefs, M. C. *A History of Modern Indonesia since c. 1200.* 3rd ed. Basingstoke, UK: Palgrave, 2001.

Rieffel, Alexis. "The BIMAS Program for Self-Sufficiency in Rice Production." *Indonesia*, no. 8 (October 1969): 103–33.

Roosa, John. *Pretext for Mass Murder: The September 30th Movement and Suharto's Coup d'État in Indonesia.* Madison: University of Wisconsin Press, 2006.

Rose, Mavis. *Indonesia Free: A Political Biography of Mohammad Hatta.* Ithaca, NY: CMIP Monograph Series, Southeast Asia Program, 1987.

Rostow, W. W. *The Stages of Economic Growth: A Non-Communist Manifesto.* Cambridge: Cambridge University Press, 1960.

Roth, Gunther. "Personal Rulership, Patrimonialism, and Empire-building in the New States." *World Politics* 20, no. 2 (January 1968): 194–206.

Rumansara, Agustinus. "Indonesia: The Struggle of the People of Kedung Ombo." In *The Struggle for Accountability: The World Bank, NGOs, and Grassroots Movements*, edited by Jonathan Fox and David L. Brown, 123–49. Cambridge, MA: MIT Press, 1998.

Rumondor, Johannes J. "Kebijaksanaan PLN dalam program listrik pedesaan." In Direktorat Jenderal Ketenagaan Departemen Pertambangan dan Energi, *Hasil Lokakarya Survai Energi Pedesaan Diselenggarkan di Jakarta Pada Tanggal 1 s/d 11 September 1980 dan 3 s/d Februari 1981*, 15–40. Jakarta: PT Surya Jaya Utama, 1982.

Rumondor, Johannes J. "Pembangunan Kelistrikan Desa Sebagai Upaya Meningkatkan Taraf Hidup Masyarakat Desa." *Berita PLN*, November 1985, 3–9.

Rumondor, Johannes J. "Program Perusahaan Umum Listrik Negara Untuk Perlistrikan Desa." *Berita PLN*, January 1978.

Rumondor, Johannes J., et al. "Report on Conference-Workshop on Initial Steps on Electric Cooperative Development Held in Manila 17 January–26 February 1977." In *Rural Electrification for Indonesia: A Proposal for USAID Assistance*, April 1, 1977.

"Rute Gasoline Druklicht." *Matahari Borneo*, December 19, 1929.

Sadli, Mohammad. "Recollections of My Career." *Bulletin of Indonesian Economic Studies* 29 no. 1 (1993): 35–51.

Salim, Emil. "Recollections of My Career." *Bulletin of Indonesian Economic Studies* 33 no. 1, (1997): 45–74.

Sanusi, Bachrawi. "Natural Gas Utilization in Indonesia-Past, Present and Future." *Pertambangan dan Energi*, no. 4 (1985): 107–14.

Sardjono. "Prospek Peran Serta Swasta Nasional Dalam Sektor Tenaga Listrik." In Pramono Djojowikromo and Djatmiko Suwarno, *Hasil-Hasil Lokakarya Energi Jakarta, 10–11 Mei 1984*, 56–76. Jakarta: KNI-WEC, 1984.

Sardjono. "Usaha-Usaha Diversifikasi Energi Dalam Sektor Tenaga Listrik." In *Diversifikasi Energi Dalam Sektor Tenaga Listrik (Hasil-hasil Lokakarya Energi 17–18 April 1980)*, edited by Sudarsono et al., 47–77. Jakarta: Percetakan Pertamina, 1980.

Schivelbusch, Wolfgang. *Disenchanted Night: The Industralization of Light in the Nineteenth Century.* Berkeley: University of California Press, 1995.

Schwarz, Adam. *A Nation in Waiting: Indonesia's Search for Stability.* 2nd ed. St. Leonards: Allen & Unwin, 1999.

Sclove, Richard E. *Democracy and Technology*. New York: Guilford, 1995.

Scott, James C. *Seeing Like a State: How Certain Schemes to Improve the Human Condition Have Failed*. New Haven, CT: Yale University Press, 1998.

"Sejak 2006, KLP SM Tak Miliki Stok Trafo." *Lampung Post*, January 5, 2006.

"Sekretaris Luwu Utara Didakwa Korupsi Rp 1 Miliar." *Koran Tempo*. May 31, 2013. https://koran.tempo.co/read/makassar/311516/sekretaris-luwu-utara-didakwa-korupsi-rp-1-miliar.

"Seminar Tarif Listrik Kedua Asia Pasifik Di Denpasar." *Berita PLN*, January 1979.

Seputro, Hardjoko. "5 Tahun Tambang Batubara Bukit Asam." *Pertambangan dan Energi*, no. 2 (1986): 9–20.

"Serah Terima Jabatan Kepala Unit Pemimpin PLN Wilayah dan Distribusi." *Berita PLN*, January 1992.

Setyaningrum, Puspasari. "PLTS Likupang, Pemanen Energi Matahari Terbesar di Indonesia." *Kompas*, February 13, 2022. https://regional.kompas.com/read/2022/02/13/185831678/plts-likupang-pemanen-energi-matahari-terbesar-di-indonesia.

"Si Petir' Kuda Beban PLN Cabang Fakfak Siap Meningkatkan Citral PLN." *Berita PLN*, November 1995.

Simpson, Bradley. *Economists with Guns: Authoritarian Development and U.S.-Indonesia Relations, 1960–1968*. Stanford, CA: Stanford University Press, 2008.

Sinaga, Vincent. "Reaktor, Peranan dan Manfaatnya pada system 500 kV se Jawa." *Berita PLN*, April 1988.

"Sistem Cakar Ayam Lahir di Ancol." *Teknologi*, January–February 1987, 56–57.

"Sistem Transmisi Tegangan Ekstra Tinggi Pertama di ASEAN, Kedua di Asia Setelah Jepang." *Berita PLN*, February 1983.

Siwijatmo, J. B. Djarot. *Koperasi di Indonesia*. Jakarta: LPFE Universitas Indonesia, 1982.

Smit, C. "Review of the History of the Overseas Gas and Electricity Company Limited." In *A Century of Light and Power*. The Hague: Dijkman, 1963.

Sneddon, James. *The Indonesian Language: Its History and Role in Modern Society*. Sydney: UNSW Press, 2003.

Soedjono, Ibnoe. *Perumusan Kumpulan Pendapat Dan Saran Dari Seminar Pembangunan Listrik Pedesaan Secara Koperatif, Jakarta 6–8 Desember 1976*. Jakarta: Direktorat Jenderal Koperasi, Departemen Tenaga Kerja, 1976.

Soeharto. "Pidato Kenegaraan Presiden Republik Indonesia Djenderal Soeharto Di Depan Sidang DPR-GR 16 Agustus 1968." Jakarta: Departemen Penerangan R.I., 1968.

Soeharto, G. Dwipayana, and Ramadhan K. H. *Soeharto Pikiran Ucapan Dan Tindakan Saya Otobiografi*. Jakarta: Citra Lamtoro Gung Persada, 1989.

Soejono, Irlan, and Wirjadi Prawirohardjo. *Program "Bimas" Sebagai Pendorong Modernisasi Usahatani*. Bogor: Survey Agro Ekonomi Indonesia, 1968.

Soemardjan, Selo, Mohammad Sadli, Soedjatmoko, and Saparinah Sadli. *Laporan Penelitian Listrik Masuk Desa*. Jakarta: Direktorat Pembinaan Penelitian dan Pengabdian pada Masyarakat, Direktorat Jenderal Pendidikan Tinggi, Departemen Pendidikan dan Kebudayaan, 1980.

Soerachmad, Soejoedi. "Desain Adaptasi Sebagai Kunci PLTM Produksi Dalam Negeri." *Berita PLN*, September 1984.

Soetendro, Haryo. "Mengenal Sumber Energi Alternatip Untuk Kelistrikan Desa Daerah Terpencil." *Berita PLN*, September, 1989.

Soetendro, Haryo, S. Soedirman, and N. Sudja. "Rural Electrification in Indonesia." In *Rural Electrification Guidebook for Asia and the Pacific*, 363–79. Bangkok: Asian Institute of Technology and the Commission of the European Communities, 1992.

Solomon, Jay. "Jakarta and Paiton Reach Interim Payment Accord." *Wall Street Journal*, March 9, 2000.

Song, Seung-Won. "Back to Basics in Indonesia? Reassessing the Pancasila and Pancasila State and Society, 1945–2007." PhD diss., Ohio University, 2008.

Sriwibawa, Sugiarta and Ramadhan K. H. *50 Years of PLN Dedication*. Translated by E. Jasjfi. Jakarta: PT PLN (Persero), 1996.

Stanly. *Seputar Kedung Ombo*. Jakarta: Lembaga Studi dan Advokasi Masyarakat, 1994.

Star, Susan Leigh. "The Ethnography of Infrastructure." *American Behavioral Scientist* 43, no. 3 (1999): 377–91.

Statistik PLN 1997. Jakarta: PT PLN (Persero), 1997.

Stibbe, D. G., and F. J.W.H. Sandbergen, eds. *Encyclopedia van Nederlandsch-Indie Aanvullingen En Wijzingen*. 'S-Gravenhage: Martinus Nijhoff, 1939.

"Studi Kemungkinan Membangun PLTN di Indonesia Diteruskan." *Surabaya Post*, May 9, 1986.

Subroto. "Recollections of My Career." *Bulletin of Indonesian Economic Studies* 34, no. 2 (1998): 67–92.

Subroto. "Pidato Pembukaan Menteri Pertambangan dan Energi Pada Lokakarya Konservasi Energi." In Departemen Pertambangan dan Energi Republik Indonesia, *Konservasi Energi (Hasil-Hasil Lokakarya Konservasi Energi 24–25 September 1979, Jakarta)*. Jakarta: Spirit International, 1980.

Sudja, Nengah. "Peranan Sektor Listrik Dalam Pola Pengembangan Wilayah." *Berita PLN*, May 1977.

Sukamdi, Heru Nugroho, and Wini Tamtiari. *Listrik, Kemiskinan & Perubahan Sosial*. Yogyakarta: Pusat Penelitian Kependudukan Universitas Gadjah Mada, 1995.

Sukarno. "Amanat Presiden I; 28-VIII-1959." In Majelis Permusyawaratan Rakyat Sementara (MPRS), *Lampiran Ketetapan M.P.R.S. No.: II/MPRS/1960 Garis-Garis Besar Pola Pembangunan Nasional-Semesta-Berentjana Tahapan Pertama 1961–1969 Djilid I*. Jakarta: MPRS, 1960.

Sukarno. "Indonesian Independence and Pancasila." In *Southeast Asian History: Essential Readings*, 2nd ed., edited by D. R. SarDesai, 164–72. Boulder, CO: Westview Press, 2013.

Sukarno, and Cindy Adams. *Sukarno an Autobiography as Told to Cindy Adams*. Hong Kong: Gunung Agung, 1966.

Sulistyo, Hermawan. "Theories behind the Events of 1965–1966." In *Indonesia in the Soeharto Years: Issues, Incidents and Images*, edited by John H. McGlynn, Oscar Motuloh, Suzanne Charle, Jeffrey Hadler, Bambang Bujono, Margaret Glade Agusta, and Gedsiri Suhartono, 6–8. Jakarta: Lontar in association with Ridge Book and KITLV Press, 2005.

Sumanto, Endang Widayanti, et al. *Terang Desaku Sejahtera Bangsaku*. Jakarta: PT Pola Aneka, 1997.

Surat Keputusan Bersama No. 755/Kpts/M/Pertamb/1979 dan No. 613/KPB/X/1979 Tentang Pelaksanaan Pengembangan dan Pembinaan Usaha Koperasi Unit Desa di bidang Kelistrikan dan Penyaluran Minyak Tanah.

Surat Perjanjian Tentang Jual Beli Tenaga Listrik 2.770 kVA Antara Perusahaan Umum Listrik Negara Wilayah IV Dengan Sinar Siwo Mego Tanjung Karang, Nomor Pihak Pertama: 169/Pj/471/W.IV/94, Nomor Pihak Kedua: 011/M/KLP-SSM/V/94.

Suryono. "Penyediaan Tenaga Listrik Untuk Pedesaan." In Komite Nasional Indonesia World Energy Conference, *Penyediaan Energi Untuk Daerah Pedesaan Hasil-hasil Lokakarya Energi, 25–26 Mei 1978, Jakarta*, 73–83. Jakarta: Percetakan Pertamina, 1978.

Sutami. "Djembatan Daun Semanggi." *Insinjur Indonesia*, no. 2 (February 1961): 12–17.

Sutami. "Pidato Sambutan Menteri Pekerjaan Umum dan Tenaga Listrik Ir. Sutami Pada Seminar Enersi Nasional Di Jakarta Tanggal 24 Juli s/d 27 Juli 1974." In Komite Nasional Indonesia World Energy Conference, *Hasil-Hasil Seminar Energi Nasional Jakarta 24–27 Juli 1974*, 31–33. Jakarta: PT Yudha Gama Corporation, 1974).

Sutrisno, Hadi, and Djoko Santoso. *Pengaruh Kelistrikan Pada Pembangunan Desa*. Surabaya: Fakultas Teknik Elektro Institute Teknologi 10 Nopember, 1981.

Sutter, John O. *Indonesianisasi Politics in a Changing Economy, 1940–1955*. Ithaca, NY: Southeast Asia Program, Cornell University, 1959.

Suwandi, Ima. *Perkembangan Koperasi di Indonesia Khususnya KUD*. Jakarta: Penerbit Bhratara Karya Aksara, 1988.

Suwandi, Ima, et al. "Report on Conference-Workshop on Initial Steps on Electric Cooperative Development Held in Manila 17 January–26 February 1977." In *Rural Electrification for Indonesia: A Proposal for USAID Assistance*, April 1, 1977.

"Tahun Depan PLN Bangun Jaringan di Wilayah Eks KLP." *Lombok Post*, July 27, 2007.

"Tambahan penerangan listrik untuk 112 desa di propinsi Maluku." *Berita PLN*, June 1987.

Tan, Ying Jia. *Recharging China in War and Revolution, 1882–1995*. Ithaca, NY: Cornell University Press, 2021.

Taylor, Jean Gelman. *Indonesia Peoples and Histories*. New Haven, CT: Yale University Press, 2003.

"Tercapainya Kesepakatan Paiton dan PLN." *Fokus*, January 2002.

The Economist. "Indonesia's Leader, Jokowi, Is Splurging on Infrastructure." *The Economist*, May 5, 2018. https://www.economist.com/asia/2018/05/05/indonesias-leader -jokowi-is-splurging-on-infrastructure.

Theobald, Robin. "Patrimonialism." *World Politics* 34, no. 4 (July 1982): 549.

"Tim Pengalihan Pelanggan KLP SSM ke PLN Diaktifkan." *Lampung Post*, February 6, 2010.

"Tuntutan Putus Total Listrik KLP SR Dinilai Berlebihan." *Lombok Post*, December 12, 2005.

"Unit Cabang Merupakan Mata Tombak Terdepan PLN." *Berita PLN*, October–November 1993.

Vickers, Adrian. *A History of Modern Indonesia*. Cambridge: Cambridge University Press, 2005.

"Walaupun Hujan Lebat Masyarakat Tetap Menghadiri Peresmian Listrik Masuk Desa." *Berita PLN*, January 1987.

"Walikota Metro Sampaikan Aspirasi Masyarakat." *Saburai*, March–April 2008.

Wareza, Monica, and Samuel Pablo. "Janji 100 Hari Pertama Prabowo: Tarif Listrik Turun!" *CNBC Indonesia*, April 7, 2019. https://www.cnbcindonesia.com/news/2019 0407090541–4-65057/janji-100-hari-pertama-prabowo-tarif-listrik-turun.

Weatherbee, Donald E. "Indonesia: The Pancasila State." *Southeast Asian Affairs* (1985): 133–51.

Weaver, Kenneth F. "Our Energy Predicament." *National Geographic*, February 1981.

Weber, Max. *Economy and Society: An Outline of Interpretive Sociology.* New York: Bedminster Press, 1968.

Wetmore, Jameson. "Amish Technology Reinforcing Values and Building Community." In *Technology and Society Building Our Sociotechnical Future*, edited by Deborah G. Johnson and Jameson M. Wetmore, 297–318. Cambridge, MA: MIT Press, 2009.

Wibowo, Catoer. "Demand-Side Management at KLP Sinar Rinjani, Indonesia." Master's thesis, University of Flensburg, 2004.

Widiono, Eddie. *Electricity for a Better Life.* Jakarta: PT PLN (Persero), 2003.

Winner, Langdon. "Do Artifacts Have Politics?" *Daedalus* 109, no. 1 (Winter 1980): 121–36.

Winther, Tanja. *The Impact of Electricity: Development, Desire, Dilemmas.* New York: Berghahn Books, 2008.

World Bank. *Indonesia Rural Electrification Review.* Report No. 6144-IND. East Asia and Pacific Regional Office. Washington, DC: World Bank, 1986.

World Bank. *Staff Appraisal Report.* Report No. 8134-IND. Indonesia Rural Electrification Project. Washington, DC: World Bank, 1990.

World Bank. *Rural Electrification: A World Bank Paper.* Washington, DC: World Bank, 1975.

Wu, Xun, and Priyambudi Sulistiyanto. "Independent Power Producer (IPP) Debacle in Indonesia and the Philippines: Path Dependence and Spillover Effects." In *Deregulation and its Discontents: Rewriting the Rules in Asia*, edited by M. Ramesh and Michael Howlett, 109–23. Cheltenham, UK: Edward Elgar, 2006.

Yayasan Lembaga Konsumen Indonesia and Koalisi Masyarakat Sipil Untuk Perbaikan Pelayanan Listrik. *Masalah Ketenagalistrikan di Indonesia (Kumpulan Artikel).* Jakarta: Sentralisme Production, 2004.

Yergin, Daniel. *The Prize: The Epic Quest for Oil, Money, and Power.* New York: Simon & Schuster, 1991.

Zen, M. T. "Pola konservasi energi dalam kebijaksanaan energi nasional." In Komite Nasional Indonesia World Energy Conference, *Hasil-Hasil Seminar Energi Nasional Jakarta, 24–27 Juli 1974*, 231–48. Jakarta: PT Yudha Gama, 1974.

Zuhal, "Peranan PLN Sebagai Persero Dalam Penyediaan Listrik Nasional." *Berita PLN*, December 1994.

Index

Page numbers in italic indicate figures or tables.

New Perspectives in Southeast Asian Studies